The Real
Hank Aaron

The Real Hank Aaron

AN INTIMATE LOOK AT THE LIFE AND LEGACY OF THE HOME RUN KING

Terence Moore

TRIUMPH
BOOKS

Library of Congress Cataloging-in-Publication Data

Names: Moore, Terence (Sports journalist), author.

Title: The real Hank Aaron: an intimate look at the life and legacy of the home run king / Terence Moore.

Description: Chicago, Illinois: Triumph Books, [2022] | Summary: "This book gives an up close and look at legendary baseball player Hank Aaron"—Provided by publisher.

Identifiers: LCCN 2021056912 | ISBN 9781629379883 (hardcover)

Subjects: LCSH: Aaron, Hank, 1934-2021. | Baseball players—United States—Biography. | African American baseball player—Biography.

Classification: LCC GV865.A25 M655 2022 | DDC 796.357092 B 23/eng/20211223—dcundefined

LC record available at https://lccn.loc.gov/2021056912

This book is available in quantity at special discounts for your group or organization. For further information, contact:

Triumph Books LLC
814 North Franklin Street
Chicago, Illinois 60610
(312) 337-0747
www.triumphbooks.com

Printed in U.S.A.

ISBN: 978-1-62937-988-3

Design by Sue Knopf

To Samuel and Annie Moore,
the perfect parents and my personal Jackie Robinsons,
and to my brothers, Dennis and Darrell,
who occasionally listened to their big brother

CONTENTS

FOREWORD

I've often thought about this: Hank Aaron was more special than what the average person saw on television or read about in newspaper and magazine articles or even in books. He was a man. I mean, he was a strong, proud, and fearless Black man. He was a dedicated father to his children. He was a social leader back in the days helping Andrew Young, Ralph Abernathy, Martin Luther King Jr., Jesse Jackson, Herman Russell, Maynard Jackson, and then governor Jimmy Carter. He was wise. He was extremely generous, and his help extended to so many people, especially to young African Americans.

He helped me.

Next to my dad, Hank Aaron was the most influential man in my life, and my dad meant everything to me.

So did my mom. When I graduated from Del Campo High School in Sacramento, California, as a four-sports standout in baseball, basketball, football, and track, my parents wanted me to go to college. I wasn't against the idea. I thought about playing basketball at one of the Division I schools offering me a scholarship, but my parents got divorced at the same time I was drafted by the Atlanta Braves. They picked me in the 1967 Major League Draft while offering me a contract and a signing bonus, which was perfect timing for our household back then. I figured I could help the family financially by taking what the Braves were offering.

Those were big factors, but what pushed me toward joining the Braves was Hank getting involved. By then, he already was the all-time best player for the franchise and he was among the best ever in major league history. He spent the previous year in 1966 with a National League-high 44 home runs and he led baseball overall with 127 RBIs. He was going into his 14th season and he had never missed an All-Star Game after his rookie year.

So, that was the same Hank Aaron who promised my mom in 1967 that he would take care of me. As a young man in his late teens, I could be a little wild. I liked to have a good time, but I wasn't what you would call a bad kid. I was close to trouble and I needed some guidance because if you're close to trouble, it could lead to something worse.

Hank sensed all of that. He told my mom he would look after me—both on and off the field—like I was his own son. That was amazing, and to hear it coming from Hank Aaron, it was impossible to turn down. I agreed to take the Braves' offer, and after that Hank did something more impressive than giving those promises to my mom. He kept them. He kept every one of them during the eight years we were together in the Braves organization. He made sure I got enough sleep. He made sure I ate right. He made sure I kept my spiritual life together by going to church.

I used Hank Aaron as a reference point for achieving success throughout my baseball career and actually throughout my life.

One of the biggest examples came off the field. I'm a California guy and I thought I knew about racism after we moved from Riverside, where I was born and raised in the southern part of the state, to Sacramento in the northern part of California. I spent my junior and senior years attending a Sacramento high school that was all White except for me and my brother. My parents bought a house in Sacramento in an all-White neighborhood.

Those situations still didn't prepare me for my first five years in professional baseball with the Braves franchise when I played for a bunch of minor league teams in the Deep South in Austin, Texas; Greenwood, South Carolina; West Palm Beach, Florida; Shreveport, Louisiana; and Richmond, Virginia. Compared to Sacramento, the racism in those cities was at a completely different level during the late 1960s and early 1970s. I couldn't stay in the same apartment complexes as my White teammates, and more than a few restaurants or bars were off-limits to Black people.

Since Hank dealt with much worse as a guy who played in the Negro Leagues and who operated in the minor leagues of the Milwaukee Braves during the early 1950s in Jim Crow places like Jacksonville, Florida, he helped me put things into perspective. I mean, it was rough for me as a Black man playing in the Land of Dixie, but it wasn't Hank Aaron rough. He told me his stories and—just like me—Hank loved Jackie Robinson. Hank idolized Jackie Robinson and Hank knew Jackie personally. I enjoyed those many times Hank gave me an insider's version of the racism and adversity Jackie encountered after Jackie broke baseball's color barrier on April 15, 1947, with the Brooklyn Dodgers.

I saw Hank become Jackie. In fact, I was an eyewitness to the Jackie-like hell Hank Aaron encountered along his way to breaking Babe Ruth's career home run record of 714 on April 8, 1974. First, I was promoted as an outfielder to start with the Braves before the 1972 season and before long I was around when Hank received death threats and hate mail while chasing Ruth. The whole situation was awful, but during that time, Hank tried to keep things as normal as possible for me and my roommate on road trips with the Braves. My roommate was Ralph Garr, another African American, and we signed with the franchise on the same day.

We both were Hank's unofficial sons.

Wherever Hank went, we were right there. But as close as we were, more than once, I saw Hank's threatening letters buried in his locker or on the floor. The future Baseball Hall of Famer that we admired so much wanted to protect us from most of the terrible things he suffered through. That's why it meant so much for me to be right there on April 8, 1974, when Hank broke Ruth's record at Atlanta-Fulton County Stadium against the Los Angeles Dodgers.

I was in the on-deck circle in the bottom of the fourth inning, and before Hank walked to the plate—with cameras flashing everywhere and the whole world watching—he said, "Dusty, I'm going to get this over with right now." He swung, and the pitch he hit from Al

Downing headed toward the bullpen behind the left-center-field fence. I could have been the first person to greet him after he made history, but I stayed put. The way I looked at it: that was Hank's moment, and I didn't want to do anything to disrupt it.

At Hank's request, he was traded to the Milwaukee Brewers after that 1974 season. He wanted to finish his major league playing career in the city where it started, and that was in Milwaukee before the Braves moved to Atlanta in 1966 and before the Brewers came into existence four years later. I stayed with the Braves for the 1975 season and I spent the next eight years with the Dodgers before I ended my playing career following the 1986 season after stops with the San Francisco Giants and Oakland A's.

Then I coached with the Giants for five seasons, but I spent nearly the last three decades of Hank's life managing five different major league teams, and he was so proud—especially since he devoted his post-playing career as a Braves executive to advocating for more Black coaches, managers, scouts, executives, umpires, and even players in the game. I wish he could have lived to see me managing the Houston Astros in the 2021 World Series against the Braves.

There was rarely a time I came to Atlanta as a player, a manager, or just in general when I didn't try to contact Hank. He always had something to make you laugh, something inspirational to say, or something memorable from the past, or he was just The Hammer. He was always The Hammer. I miss him.

—*Dusty Baker played for the Atlanta Braves, Los Angeles Dodgers, San Francisco Giants, and Oakland A's during a Major League Baseball career spanning 1968–1986. As the current manager of the Houston Astros, he took his team to the World Series in 2021 before losing to the Braves. He previously managed the Giants, Chicago Cubs, Cincinnati Reds, and Washington Nationals.*

INTRODUCTION

As news, weather, and sports continued to flash on the television screen across the way, Henry Louis Aaron went to sleep in an easy chair in the bedroom of his Atlanta home on the night of Thursday, January 21, 2021. He drifted into eternal peace by early the next morning. Later that evening his wife-turned-widow, Billye, asked me a question that felt like a Hammerin' Hank line drive slamming against the logical part of my mind.

Who…me? That's what I thought. Then again, Billye's question made sense. "Will you be one of Hank's honorary pallbearers?" she said over the phone with the reality of Hank's death still fresh and shocking.

Of course, I said yes.

No sports journalist understood the essence of Hank Aaron better than I, and as our years of conversations turned into one, two, and before long four decades of riveting dialogue for the ages, we grew close enough as friends for me to hang up later from Billye to rejoice more than grieve. I kept focusing on how "the Good Lord," as Hank often used to say, gave all of us several extra innings with the greatest baseball player in history.

After all, Henry Louis Aaron almost died seven years before he did, but hardly anybody knew as much. I knew.

From the time I first spoke to Hank over the phone during the spring of 1982, when I did research at the *San Francisco Examiner* on a groundbreaking series called "Blacks in Baseball," through his final

Courtesy: Aric Thompson/Dream Multimedia Group Inc.

days on Earth, no reporter chatted with Hank more than I. He was famously private. Even so, he was totally open whenever we huddled either in person or on the phone. We were kindred souls, and here's why: Jackie Robinson.

We both understood Jack Roosevelt Robinson, the idol of Henry Louis Aaron and among my all-time favorite sports personalities. Since Hank and Jackie remained men of conviction despite everything—and since Hank saw the same traits in me while he provided guidance through much of my 25 years of racial turmoil inside and outside *The Atlanta Journal-Constitution* as a lightning rod of a Black sports columnist in the Deep South—he understood the truth.

The truth was that I got it.

I really got it regarding all things Henry Louis Aaron, the most genuine, the most courageous, and the most outspoken of the wise men who ever played games for a living at the highest level. Every once in a while, Hank would utter something like this: "For you to keep standing your ground despite all the crap you have to take with people trying to intimidate you into changing who you are as a writer or just trying to make you quit, I admire what you're doing, Terence."

I always would get chills. Then, I would quickly say, "Well, sir, I admire what you're doing, too."

We both would chuckle.

During my stay at *The AJC* through April 2009—and later when I became a national columnist for various Internet sites as well as a frequent commentator on national television—Hank contacted me to deliver his inner thoughts regarding just about everything, especially when he wished to communicate to the rest of the world.

Hank told me rare stories about his playing days for the Braves of Milwaukee and Atlanta and later for the Milwaukee Brewers during the final two of his 23 major league seasons in 1975 and 1976. He explained his admiration for Jackie Robinson and his fearlessness as an outspoken proponent for social justice. He ripped baseball officials regarding their treatment of African Americans both on and off the field and he hadn't a problem challenging the attitudes of those reflecting negatively on humanity. The bottom line: Hank spoke here and there to reporters, but he saved his deepest thoughts for me on everything. Even on Barry Bonds.

Otherwise, Hank vanished from the end of the 2006 Major League Baseball season through most of the next one, when Barry raced toward breaking Hank's record for career home runs at 755. Hank spoke to me, though, because, well, I got it. Before Barry edged close to Hank's record, Hank bore his soul to me in unprecedented ways on his turmoil as a Black man dealing with death threats and hate mail during the 1970s. He was assaulted for racing toward passing the home run mark of 714 established by Babe Ruth, America's most celebrated Great White Hope. Hank told me that commenting on the Barry chase to people other than myself would remind him of what he wanted to forget, which were the horrors surrounding his Ruth chase.

Beyond the Barry Bonds ordeal stirring emotions for Hank, you had his anger over those imploding numbers involving African Americans on the field, at major league headquarters, and for various teams. You had his love affair with giving, helping, and inspiring, especially youth. You had his sweet-and-sour relationship within the Braves organization as a team executive. You had his dealings with the rich and famous beyond the game. You had the side of his personality that contained levels of richness in body, mind, and soul that he rarely allowed the average person to see.

You had Hank's affection for Jack Roosevelt Robinson, which only grew after Jackie died in October 1972.

I heard it all from Hank.

I knew it all.

So in September 2020, I thought about something I pondered often for a couple of decades, but this time the whole thing screamed inside of my head. Despite the slew of Hank Aaron books written in history and the documentaries produced, none had what I had. None had anything close.

I called Hank to see if he would do a book with me to fill in the considerable gaps that remained about his life and his philosophies, and he agreed without hesitation. Then he called back the next day, saying, "Okay, before we do anything, Terence, I need to check with my lawyer. I can't remember for sure what the situation is, but there might be a conflict."

The next week, I asked Hank for an update. "My lawyer is out of the country, but I'll tell you what. Let's go ahead and do the book and you just tell me what I need to do on my end," Hank said before he laughed his contagious laugh, recalling how the conversation began with me telling him I had returned from a cycling trip of 35 miles on a bike trail. He thought about his nearly 87-year-old legs that once were swift enough to steal 240 bases to complement his other fancy numbers (2,297 RBIs, 6,856 total bases, and those 755 home runs). Then he said, laughing some more, "I'm proud of you for doing that because I can't even get on a bike. I've got a lot of things aching and

I can't get around like I used to really. So, for this book I wouldn't be able to fly anywhere or go anywhere to promote it."

No worries, I told Hank, and the Triumph Books editors agreed. Then came mid-October 2020, when Hank's lawyer, Allan Tanenbaum, apologized while saying he had to nix my book idea—at least that one. He said he joined Hank in making a gentleman's agreement during the previous year and he said it involved presidential historian Douglas Brinkley, who Tanenbaum said wanted to do Hank's autobiography to coincide with the 50th anniversary of Hank's Ruth-passing 715th home run and 90th birthday. Both would come in 2024. "But," Tanenbaum said, after he praised my relationship with and coverage of Hank through the years, "even though Douglas Brinkley would have exclusive rights to talk to Hank and to his family, that doesn't mean you couldn't write a book about Hank on your own."

I could do that for several reasons:

- Throughout the decades I saved the overwhelming majority of my recorded interviews with Hank. I used a lot of what I had at the time, but there was so much that remained (I mean, so, so, so much).

- There were stories Hank told me he never shared with any other reporter, and they ranged between captivating and incredible. I have them throughout this book.

- Nothing topped this: Hank was connected to Jackie Robinson, and in a slew of ways, I was connected to both of them. You'll see in the coming chapters that I was the Jackie Robinson of sports reporting in mainstream media—complete with hate and threats hurled my way—especially during my 25 years of racial strife at *The Atlanta Journal-Constitution*. What helped me survive were Jackie's teachings through his writings and Hank's inspiration through our conversations.

I had enough material to make the real Hank Aaron shine more than whatever came before or whatever would come in the future, and the decision makers at Triumph Books agreed.

Several weeks later, Hank died just before the spring of 2021, and I'm not sure what that did to the Brinkley project. For mine, it did nothing. I had four decades of those Hank conversations—many of them recorded—and of my other exclusive dealings with Henry Louis Aaron.

For instance: seven years before Hank left us to join Jackie Up There, I saw up close and personal how Henry Louis Aaron was given at least a second life by "the Good Lord." I wrote in this book about his near-death experience in detail with Hank's insight in between regarding a bunch of Hank things.

You'll see his wisdom.

You'll see his foresight.

You'll see his humor.

You'll see his anger.

You'll see his humanity.

You'll see Henry Louis Aaron as you've never seen him before and you'll see how his presence—combined with that of Jackie Robinson—transformed me into the definitive person to tell this story.

I spoke with Hank several times during his final couple of months, but I did my last official interview with him in early October 2020. It was for the quarterly magazine of the Baseball Hall of Fame. The following contributes to my credentials as the Jackie Robinson among journalists in mainstream media: I'm a member of the Baseball Writers Association of America and I've voted for Baseball Hall of Famers as a member of the organization longer than any African American in history.

As had happened in the past, I got a call from those who run the magazine to do a piece on Hank for their edition in early 2021. The theme involved home runs and social justice. I dialed Hank, and our conversation was so typical, so brilliant, so Henry Louis Aaron, talking to me as if he were only talking to me. No matter how many times we discussed old topics—particularly the ones involving the combination of Hank, baseball, and society—he rarely failed to reveal something new to me and to the world.

Such was the case during the fall of 2020 when Hank pontificated on the events leading up to April 8, 1974, to an extent that he hadn't before. I used the least explosive parts for my Baseball Hall of Fame magazine story. What follows is mostly that full Hank interview, and it was his final one with me as the perfect lead into the rest of *The Real Hank Aaron: An Intimate Look at the Life and Legacy of the Home Run King.*

For the Baseball Hall of Fame magazine piece, I called 86-year-old Henry Louis Aaron at his home in southwest Atlanta on October 2, 2020, and the conversation became more than just my last official interview with Hank. This was the final time he discussed his raw emotions regarding the racial hatred he endured for a couple of years leading to Monday, April 8, 1974, at Atlanta-Fulton County Stadium, where he broke Ruth's career home run record of 714.

Hank remained eternally scarred by the Chase.

He despised talking about it.

Even so, he never gave more personal details than he did on this afternoon about operating as a highly principled Black man with considerable brain, brawn, and guts, pursuing the Great White Hope. I listened in awe. During this interview the depth, in which he expressed his thoughts about those horrifying days, was unprecedented.

The Baseball Hall of Fame magazine piece was meant to be more upbeat than what Hank eventually provided. As a result, I only used a small portion of our conversation for the Cooperstown folks. I saved the rest for this book. Except for the irrelevant chitchat between Hank and me that I deleted, here's the whole interview:

"I got a call from the Baseball Hall of Fame," I told Hank. "And, of course, I'm a Baseball Hall of Fame voter and I do different things for them from time to time, and they're doing a special program on home runs. They want me to do something on you and home runs, and I want to ask you some questions about that. Do you have time right now?"

"Sure. Go ahead," he said.

"One of the things they want me to ask is [Baseball Hall of Fame officials] say you have saved all of the letters from the time you were chasing Babe Ruth in '73 and '74 and they want to kind of display the letters with the story I write. And I was curious. Have you saved any of those letters yourself?"

"Um, quite a few of them. I don't know if I could go and put my hands on them right now, but I do have a few of them saved up."

"That's fine. [Baseball Hall of Fame officials] don't want the letters. I was just kind of curious if you still saved them."

"Yeah."

"And the ones you saved, I guess you had to make a decision: the ones you would save and the ones you would throw away. Of the ones you saved, what was it that made you want to save them?"

"Oh, boy, whew, that should be an easy question. It really should be…the ones that I saved, well, I think one reason is that, if you look at life, and you say, 'Are things any different than they were before?' I don't know if I'm making myself clear or what…I think that I kind of look back [at the death threats and the hate mail I received while chasing Ruth's record] and say, 'You know, things are the same really,' and I kind of look back at some of the things that are happening today, and they're just about the same as they were 10 years ago in some respect—only they just color it a little bit different. But I think things are the same, and I thought at that time out of all the things I was doing I was only playing a little game of baseball, trying to have it so people could enjoy it. Then I was looking around, and people were getting so irritated and aggravated because of the fact it was a Black man that was chasing a White man's record that he held for a long time. And yet, that White man, and I hate to say this—Babe Ruth, please forgive me—but he played with and against some guys who didn't have the ability to play Major League Baseball. And that was the thing that bothered me more than anything: was the fact that Ty Cobb and all the rest of these people ended up with so many stolen bases, base hits, and all of these other things yet they didn't play against real, genuine baseball players."

"And I understand exactly what you're saying because I've written this before. My thing is everything before April 15, 1947, [when Jackie Robinson broke baseball's color barrier with the Brooklyn Dodgers] should have an asterisk behind it," I said before we both laughed.

"Yeah, well, well, that's true. That's why they tried to get me on several occasions to try to do things to make fun, well, not make fun, but to do things on [Barry Bonds]. And I wasn't going to get involved with that. I don't know what [Bonds] had [done involving steroids]. He came from a Black family, and anything might have happened [regarding the motivations of racist folks who disliked Bonds when he was chasing and passing Hank's career homer record of 755 in August 2007], anything could have happened."

"That's exactly right...and you know one of the things to me that was very interesting about you, going back to that home run thing in '73 and '74, for being a Black baseball fan like I was, I mean, I could realize how huge that was. To me, it was more of a civil rights thing as much as it was a baseball thing. Did you look at yourself as being more than a baseball player during that time period or did you just think strictly that I'm trying to be the best baseball player I can be?"

"No, I talked to, I talked to a number of civil rights icons. Andy [Young, the former Atlanta mayor, U.N. ambassador, and U.S. Congressman] being the main one. And they kept saying, 'Hey, you keep doing what you're doing and you're doing as much as we are doing.' They kept saying, 'You keep hitting home runs and making things what they are now, and we are doing the things that we need to be doing by marching and doing the other things.'"

"When you and I did that CNN television show [in the spring of 2014 to commemorate the 40th anniversary of Hank's record-breaking 715th homer to surpass Ruth] the ratings were high for that thing, by the way. The CNN folks really enjoyed that," I said before we both laughed. "I asked you this for CNN, but I'm going to ask you this for this story here. So, when you were going through that day [on

April 8, 1974], the day that you actually broke the record, what was the thought process when you were running around the bases?"

"I thought it was over with, done with. I don't have to worry about [the safety] of my teammates in the dugout. I no longer have to worry about going out to lunch with any of my teammates. And I had two players that I was particularly fond of: Dusty Baker and Ralph Garr, and they were both just young kids and they really didn't know what was happening. Any chance they got, they were right under me. You've got some underhanded people in this world really, and some people that are dirty."

"So [Baker and Garr] were sort of protecting you during that time period?"

"They weren't protecting me. They didn't know [how to do it without getting in trouble]. Dusty didn't know. Dusty had gotten into two or three arguments in West Palm Beach with some White guys down there, and I got him out of a mess down there. Ralph had a little bit more intelligence [on how to handle this type of racism] because Ralph was born in the South and knew a little bit more of what was going on."

"What about you during that time period? Did you, when you went to a southern city, like St. Louis or Cincinnati, which is kind of like a southern city, and you're going out in Cincinnati to have something to eat or what have you during that time period...did you have anybody come up to you and swear at you and call you a racial slur? How did that go?"

"Oh, all the time. I had one guy come up to me and say, 'Oh, yeah. You dirty SOB,' and you're this and that. And [then the guy] said, 'Yeah, I know. My wife told me about [what you said about Babe Ruth] last night. How do you know [what you're talking about?]' And I said, 'Well, you have to remember. Your wife probably told me last night when I was with her,'" he said before we both laughed. "And the last that I saw of him, he had a tail stuck between his legs, going up the stairs and out of the ballpark. Those are the kinds of things you don't want to bring up and you don't want to say, but they make you say them."

"And I guess the obvious question would be: during that time how many times or how often did you actually fear for your life, when you thought somebody might take a shot at you or something?"

"Oh, many times, many times. I thought, Terence, I thought, I swear, I thought the safest spot was—the safest place for me rather—would be on a baseball field. Anywhere else, I thought I didn't have a chance. I thought I was doomed."

"Boy, and that makes it even more amazing that you were able to do what you were able to do. So when you got up there in the batter's box, was there anything you thought about, anything but baseball in the batter's box?"

"Never thought about anything but baseball. The Good Lord carried me in that regard really, and I say, if it hadn't been for Him, I don't know what I would have done. But the only thing I thought about at that time was baseball."

"When you think back to that time you were chasing Babe Ruth, do you still get angry with that? Or do you look back with joy that you broke the record? What's your feelings now that you look back at what happened back then?"

"I don't think I get either way, Terence. I get disgusted, yes, because I think this [didn't happen] to anybody else. I think about Pete Rose when he was going through his chase of Ty Cobb's [career hits] record, and he was just having the time of his life, the time of his life. Nobody said anything; nobody did anything. He did what he wanted to do, and I couldn't do one damn thing. I was not blessed to even go out to have lunch or dinner. If it hadn't been for teammates of mine bringing me lunch or dinner…If we played a night game, they would bring a sandwich up to my room. [If it weren't for my teammates,] I would have starved to death…That's the kind of stuff that people don't really understand…No. No, they don't understand. And see: that's the thing about it. They don't understand because they never been through it and they don't want to understand it because they'll say right quick, 'Oh, that never happened.'"

"Uh huh. And I guess the other obvious thing is: outside of a Ralph Garr and a Dusty Baker, did any of the White players understand what you were going through during that time period?"

"Quite a few of them did. You know, they kept to themselves mostly. The only hard thing, sad thing about it was the fact that every afternoon or every day before the game started, I, and when I say I, I'm talking about myself, had a press conference in the clubhouse and after the game was over with. And we didn't have the New York Yankees [kind of talent] at that time. We had a bunch of guys who were just trying to win some games. We had a rough time."

"Yeah, everything about [what you're saying] is fascinating, and I'm telling you: some of this is good for the Baseball Hall of Fame magazine piece. But for the book, this will be even better. You've got a lot of deep knowledge here, to say the least."

"Okay, Terence. Thank you. Thank you very much."

"Oh, no. Thank you."

That was my last interview with him. He would pass away three months later.

The Real
Hank Aaron

THE NURSING HOME

Suddenly, there I was, standing before Henry Louis Aaron as he sat on the edge of his bed inside the hospital-like room of a bright, yet depressing building dominated by the weak, the old, and the dying. At best, this was a nursing home disguised as a rehabilitation center, and Hank was among the patients.

I wanted to cry.

Only a few of us knew during the late winter of 2014 that Major League Baseball's legitimate home run king had become the tired and aching man. On this gloomy afternoon in March, he prepared for one of his few trips in weeks away from the friendly confines of his pillow. He had lived in southwest Atlanta since 1966, when his playing days of nine years with the Atlanta Braves began after the franchise relocated from Milwaukee, where he spent his first dozen years in the major leagues. He was in his 38th year as a Braves executive and he ranked among the sports icons for the ages.

As I studied the tired and aching man, I envisioned Hank Aaron moving gracefully toward flyballs in outfields around the major leagues but only when he wasn't ripping pitches through gaps between defenders or over the farthest of barriers with his 35-inch bat of 33 ounces. I envisioned Hank Aaron gliding around bases faster than your eyes realized—until he was safe again. I envisioned Hank Aaron showcasing those and other parts of his Baseball Hall of Fame arsenal with the greatest of ease during his 25 trips to All-Star Games.

What I envisioned seemed fantasy against this reality. Here I was helping the tired and aching man into his pullover shirt that barely cooperated despite a bunch of my tugs. When a nurse dropped by to help me finish making the tired and aching man look casually sharp in several of the clothes I brought in a bag ("I have nothing to wear," he told me that morning over the phone before I headed his way in a driving rainstorm), the nurse grabbed the tired and aching man by one arm, and I latched onto the other as he settled into a wheelchair.

I was preparing the tired and aching man for a 10-minute trip across this facility, and we were slated to climb into a waiting car provided by CNN as the rain still raged. *Good luck with that*, I thought, after the first of my many interactions on this day. After we reached our CNN ride, the plan was to make a brief trip to a golf club, where we would record an interview I was scheduled to conduct with Henry Louis Aaron (as opposed to the tired and aching man) on national television for the cable network. The producers. The camera crew. The makeup folks. They would be in place, ready to roll upon our arrival at the makeshift studio in a ballroom of the golf club.

Every so often, I heard a ring or a beep from my cell phone, which was working harder than it ever had before. It was them again: "So, what's your ETA?"

Sometimes, the CNN callers were more direct by uttering (no, pleading) with the likes of: "We're hoping to get started within the next 30 minutes or whenever we can, just waiting for you and Mr. Aaron."

What they were saying was: *GET HERE NOW!*

I understood the reason for their urgency, but given the state of the tired and aching man, I kept recalling the words of famed college basketball coach John Wooden, who once told me during an interview that he used to tell his UCLA players when they needed to rally down the stretch: "Be quick but don't hurry."

For those CNN producers, "hurry" was the operative word for this situation followed closely by "panic." They knew I was dealing with the tired and aching man in a complicated situation, but they also knew the same members of the camera crew scheduled to shoot my Hank interview were fretting over the next thing on their schedule. After they finished at the golf club, they needed to hop in a vehicle, rush to the Atlanta airport through the storm that wouldn't quit, and fly to Afghanistan for another assignment.

There was that ringing again, or was it buzzing? Maybe it was thunder.

As I studied the tired and aching man, sitting in the wheelchair, I kept saying to myself, *This won't happen.*

Nevertheless, we headed for the door with me maneuvering the tired and aching man into the hallway. The nurse wished us well, but she failed to hide the fear bursting through the smile on her face. Then it struck me. *I'm getting ready to push the greatest baseball player of all time down the hallway of a nursing home in a wheelchair!*

Several weeks earlier, the final blast of winter pounded Hank's neighborhood during a February day in 2014. Those living nearby included civil rights heroes John Lewis, C.T. Vivian, Andrew Young, and Joseph Lowery—all fellow marchers with Dr. Martin Luther King Jr., an Atlanta native. Others among the city's Black rich and famous also resided in that southwest area of town, but neither they nor anybody else could help Henry Louis Aaron on this day.

Despite Hank's always careful steps during his senior years, he couldn't survive an ice patch, which was nastier than anything hurled his way by Sandy Koufax or Bob Gibson. This frozen version of a knockdown pitch sent Hank crashing to the ground of his driveway, and he lacked a batting helmet to cover his head or a bunch of ballpark dirt to replace his concrete landing spot. While he laid there waiting for help, he forgot about the haircut he was off to receive. He cared more about everything aching throughout his body that had turned 80 years old the previous week on February 5.

What a contrast.

During the days before Hank's fall, he was the vibrant birthday boy, whose gifts were as splendid as his life. He grew up with a struggling yet supportive family in the Jim Crow South of Mobile, Alabama. He eventually became a dominating baseball player and a businessman, philanthropist, and civil rights advocate. Through it all, he functioned as a quiet man who hadn't a problem sharing his principles with boldness.

So, Henry Louis Aaron was toasted for functioning as Henry Louis Aaron at a banquet during his 80th birthday week in Washington, D.C., by fellow Hall of Famers such as Ozzie Smith, Rickey Henderson, and Jim Rice. Later, with Hank still around the nation's capital, he received what he told me was one of his all-time greatest thrills. Famed artist Ross Rossin did a portrait of Hank so lifelike it made you think the image on the canvas would ease into one of Hank's laughs that always made you do the same. Rossin's work went that week to the National Portrait Gallery during an event featuring the man himself, his family, and a slew of guests for the unveiling at the Smithsonian American Art Museum. With face beaming, Hank spoke to the crowd.

Days later, courtesy of Hank's slip in a flash on that ice patch along his driveway in southwest Atlanta, there was no crowd. There was nobody. There was only Henry Louis Aaron, and he was hurting just about more physically than he had at any point of his life.

The majority of the pain visited Hank's left hip, and that was the one he used to lead his swing of beauty as a right-handed hitter through 23 major league seasons of accomplishments beyond 755—among the magic numbers in sports history. He also was the guy with four home run championships and four RBI titles in the National League. He complemented those honors with three Gold Gloves, two NL batting titles, an NL Most Valuable Player Award, a World Series ring, and his record 25 trips to the All-Star Game for first-ballot entry into the Baseball Hall of Fame.

I didn't see Hank's fall, but my broken heart was there in spirit, especially after I heard the news lead on a local television report that evening. Before long I centered on one word: hip.

Just like that, I was a nine-year-old boy again in my hometown of South Bend, Indiana, where Sarah Wilkerson, my great-grandmother, went from fairly vibrant to a nicely lined coffin. She became the first of several elderly people I would know through the years to break their hip and die. She was just three years older than Hank.

The difference: while Great-Grandma Sarah wasn't beyond guzzling shots of whiskey, Hank spent his baseball career—along with his nearly 40 years (at the time of his accident) of post-playing retirement as an Atlanta Braves senior vice president, king of business, charity worker, and spokesperson on social issues—turning exercising into one of his best friends.

That ice patch couldn't care less.

After Hank's family members rushed him to the emergency room, doctors performed a procedure that led to a partial left hip replacement before he departed the hospital. (I kept thinking, *Wow. Great-Grandma Sarah never made it that far.*) This was huge news involving one of the most famous living persons on the planet. Somebody needed to update the public on Hank's condition whenever it was deemed necessary, and the Braves assumed that role since he remained active with the team as a front-office executive. Prior to that, he spent all but the final two of his major league seasons playing for the Milwaukee-turned-Atlanta franchise.

The reports from the Braves on Hank's condition were few and brief. To paraphrase the only one of note, which the team released soon after his accident in February of 2014: Dr. Scott Gillogly expects Hank "to have a full recovery and return to his routine activities within six to eight weeks." The Braves also suggested Hank would become whole enough to join the franchise and Major League Baseball at the team's home ballpark of Turner Field to celebrate the 40th anniversary of April 8, 1974.

That date was the night Hank became baseball's all-time home run champion against Los Angeles Dodgers pitcher Al Downing at Atlanta-Fulton County Stadium. He ended two-plus seasons of chasing Babe Ruth's ghost, but from the start of that pursuit to the end of his life, Hank suffered more mental turmoil involving those days than he ever told most folks in public or private.

Hank told me. I was The Hank Aaron Whisperer.

Bit by bit over years, Hank shared his Sultan of Swat demons during our conversations, and those demons were considerable. They remained with Hank even after he spent that rainy night in Georgia ripping a Downing pitch over the left-center-field fence. Just like that, Henry Louis Aaron, the Black slugger who jumped from the shadows for the first time in his career, was better than George Herman Ruth, the flashy Great White Hope of those racists hurling death threats, hate mail, and vicious phone messages Hank's way during his years, weeks, and then seconds moving toward his destiny.

Well, the Ruth chase was part of his destiny. Hank was so much more than 715, his final home run total of 755, or anything else involving what he liked to call "the game of baseball." Even so, his grace under pressure while catching and passing The Great Bambino showed the essence of Henry Louis Aaron to everybody as much as anything else. But consider this: except for a select group of people that included his Whisperer, he spent the bulk of his lifetime holding back much of The Real Hank, especially when it came to April 8, 1974.

No matter how much Hank tried to place the glory of becoming baseball's home run king above that other stuff, that other stuff always won. The bad stuff. Those Sultan of Swat demons.

"I know I've said this many times before, Hank," I told him during a phone interview in 2013, "but I can't even possibly begin to imagine how bad it was for you dealing with all of those rednecks and other hateful folks while you were chasing the record. That had to be beyond stressful."

"Oh, it was," he said. "Whew. Terence, I don't try to pretend to be different than any other ballplayer. I guess you have to speak to them. But after all of that, I was ready to retire. That's No. 1."

"Yeah, I'm sure. I know you asked the Braves to let you spend your last two seasons back in Milwaukee [with the Brewers, the American League team that replaced the Braves in 1970, five years after the Braves left town]. What was going through your mind in 1976 during your last season in the major leagues?"

"The year I said I wanted to retire, everything was drained out of me at that time. Everything. I mean, I had been through literally hell during the last two years, actually the last two-and-a-half years of my career. The newspaper articles, everybody saying this and saying that, and other people doing this and doing that—Terence, I was just absolutely worn out. The *greatest* thing that ever happened to me, the greatest thing—and I've never mentioned this before to anybody—when I was traded to the Brewers, I was able to go to Sun City, Arizona, for spring training. Sun City, Arizona, is a retirement area for people 75 and older, where the Brewers train. I got me an apartment there and I swear I didn't come out. The only thing I did was train and come back to the apartment. That was the greatest sense of just doing nothing that I ever had, and it was exactly what I needed. I didn't even want to deal with the thought of [the Ruth chase] anymore."

That's why, when officials of the Braves and Major League Baseball began discussing their plans in early 2014 for the 40th celebration of No. 715, Hank didn't mind the idea, but he didn't embrace it.

Hank eventually had bigger concerns in February. He just wanted to walk again.

During those updates by the Braves on Hank's condition after his accident and his surgery leading to a hip replacement, this wasn't mentioned: the franchise's invincible right fielder of yore—who once told me he never even missed exhibition games during his career— was headed to a rehabilitation center that resembled more of a facility for Uncle Frank and Aunt Lillie before they headed to hospice or worse.

Hardly anybody knew. I knew. Of course, I knew. I was The Hank Aaron Whisperer.

"How many U.S. presidents have you met?" I asked him during a chat at Turner Field during the summer of 2011.

"I've met, ohhhhhhhhh, let's see. I've met a whole bunch of them through the years. I've met Kennedy. I've met Johnson, Carter, Clinton, both of the Bushes…Ronald Reagan…Barack Obama."

"What about Richard Nixon?"

"Sure have. I've met Richard Nixon. Yep, I've met quite a few of them and I've been able to talk to quite a few of them. I've also been honored by a lot of them."

"What about Eisenhower? I know he was the president when you were starting in 1954 with the Milwaukee Braves."

"Nah, I didn't meet him, but let me tell you this," he said, laughing. "Did I ever tell you my George [W.] Bush story back when I got my Presidential Medal of Honor from him?"

"I don't think you ever told me that one."

"Who was the guy? The comedian was up there with me. Oh, Bill Cosby, and he was nearby because after you got your Medal of Honor, you stood in this receiving line to shake hands with guests. So. President Bush is standing between me and Bill, and President Bush leans over and whispers in my ear, 'Hank. How's your brother Tommie?'

"I said, 'Mr. President, he's been dead for 18 years.'"

Hank and I laughed.

"He said, 'Oh, I'm sorry.' And I told him, 'Yeah, he's been gone awhile,' but I just said to myself, 'Uh, uh, uh, oh, my goodness.'"

GREATEST EVER

The nursing home disguised as a rehabilitation center.
The tired and aching man.
The dressing of the tired and aching man.
The nurse trying to hide her sad face.
The wheelchair with me pushing.

I'd never seen anything close to this Henry Louis Aaron during our nearly 40-year relationship. It shocked my senses, but in the strangest of ways, the whole thing slowly became bearable.

As I pushed the tired and aching man farther down the hallway with activity up ahead, he appeared slightly less lethargic than before. I also began remembering things. We had those decades of discussions in person sprinkled between a slew of phone calls. There were always the phone calls—those wonderful phone calls when Hank became Hank—which was a blessing each time he spoke on the other end. He had that baritone voice with his distinctive cadence dominated by Hank words and phrases.

"Have you received all of the honors you believe you could have received?" I asked Hank during a phone conversation in November 2008.

"I think I understand what you're saying. You know, I, the one thing that I think I have always been blessed with is: I have always been blessed by my own peers. Now that may not have held true in the case of many years in New York. There were many times even now I look back on my record, and I say to myself, 'Henry, you had this great career, this great career for 23 years, and yet, you only won the Most Valuable Player award once.' And I came very close winning it two or three times, but somebody else would win it, and those are the kinds of things I look back and say, 'If I had been a White player or if I had played in New York City, I would have probably won it two or three times.' Those are things I wish, and the other thing I wish was my own doing, and this is that I thought that out of all the things that I have accomplished in baseball, the one thing that escaped me that I probably could have done better with was winning the Triple Crown. I think I could have, well, you never know. I do know I can't do it now," he said, causing both of us to laugh. "But those are the type of things you think about, but, Terence, there aren't too many other things that I think about [along the lines of regrets in the game]. You know me better than just about anybody and you know I played the game for 23 years, and I gave it every little thing, everything I had, and that was all I could do, whether I was playing with the Braves, the Brewers. Wherever I was playing, I gave my very best."

On this July afternoon, when Major League Baseball's all-time greatest player waved me into a side room at Turner Field in Atlanta, I could see it all over his face. He couldn't take it anymore. The closer that other guy moved to the home run record, the angrier Henry Louis Aaron became.

Oh, I'm sorry, this wasn't about Barry Bonds. It was about Mark McGwire.

Actually, Hank wasn't as much upset with McGwire during that summer and fall of 1998 as he was with the media coverage of the St. Louis Cardinals slugger. McGwire was on the verge of slamming a 62nd homer for the season (while on his way to 70) to surpass the old mark of 61 set by Roger Maris in 1961.

"They keep changing what they say, and I'm confused. Which is it? That's what I want to know. Which is it?" Hank said, growing more irritated by the moment. So I decided to sit there, using my ears instead of my mouth as I nodded as Major League Baseball's all-time greatest player continued to vent. "All I'm hearing on television and from the newspaper is: if Mark McGwire hits more home runs than Roger Maris, he'll be the home run king. How does that make him the home run king when I have 755 home runs?"

How, indeed? Hank was the Home Run King. Actually, Hank is the Home Run King, and I know about August 7, 2007, when Barry Bonds slid past Hank's career total before Bonds ended with an all-time major league high of 762.

Bonds had help, though, and I know. Bonds said he mistakenly used steroids provided by his trainer, but that still classifies as help—lots of help—so much help that it was the antithesis of Hank's career.

Henry Louis Aaron only terrorized opponents with adrenaline, which means Dr. Harry Edwards had it about right near the end of 2007. That's when I asked the accomplished sports sociologist from northern California how history should sort out Aaron, Bonds, performance-enhancing drugs, and the home run crown, and Edwards gave an answer for the ages: "Barry may have the record, but Hank always will be the standard bearer."

If nothing else, Hank has the statues.

Greatness often is measured in statues, and nobody outside of maybe dictators from the old Soviet Union have inspired the building of more statues in their likeness than Henry Louis Aaron.

There are two Hank statues in Atlanta. The first is around the spot of Atlanta-Fulton County Stadium, where he ripped No. 715 to topple Babe Ruth's career home run record. The other sits near Truist Park, the Braves' home after the 2016 season. There is a Hank statue at the Milwaukee Brewers' home ballpark called American Family Field, and another one in Eau Claire, Wisconsin, where he began his professional career as a shortstop. By the end of 2022, he also is slated to have a statue in Mobile, Alabama, his hometown. City officials plan to place five statues along their riverfront inside what they'll call Hall of Fame Courtyard, which is scheduled to feature eight-foot images in bronze of Willie McCovey, Satchel Paige, Billy Williams, Ozzie Smith, and

Aaron. They're all Mobile natives and they're all inducted into the Baseball Hall of Fame. Hank's statue is the first under construction. In the meantime, the Double A Mobile BayBears play in Hank Aaron Stadium. His boyhood home was moved during the summer of 2008 from its original spot to next to the ballpark. And Hank Aaron Stadium does have a bust of Hank.

Twenty-three seasons. That's how long Henry Louis Aaron played in the major leagues, featuring 21 years with the Braves of Milwaukee and Atlanta before he finished his Baseball Hall of Fame career in 1976 after two seasons in Wisconsin with the Brewers. Even beyond 755, Hank's lifetime numbers are ridiculous. According to the folks at Elias Sports Bureau, they haven't created a method to determine for sure if Hank Aaron holds the record for most offensive records in Major League Baseball history, but it feels that way. Despite 45 years between his last at-bat and his final breath, he still owned more RBIs (2,297), total bases (6,856), and extra bases (1,477) than anybody. He had 25 trips to All-Star Games, four National League titles for both home runs and RBIs, two NL batting championships, three Gold Gloves in right field to show he also sparkled beyond the plate, an NL MVP award, and a world championship ring.

If you take away Hank's career home run total, he still would have more than 3,000 hits, because he collected 3,771 of them.

That's for starters. All of Hank's shots over fences were nice—along with his only inside-the-park homer that happened on May 10, 1967, against the Phillies in Philadelphia—but what thrilled Hank nearly as much as those homers was never striking out 100 times or more in a season.

Hank also was faster than you think. He attempted 311 steals and he was successful 77 percent of the time, which was the same as Willie Mays, who was supposedly more gifted than Hank on the basepaths. Hank versus Willie is often a thing: Willie had nine more Gold Gloves than Hank, but Hank was a right fielder during the era of Roberto

Clemente, the Pittsburgh Pirates glove master who essentially invented defense in right field. As for Willie, a bunch of Gold Gloves happen when you're playing the already glamorous center field with drama and flair and when you spend the start of your career in New York, where Hank was only a visitor.

With apologies to Willie (Hank had better numbers for homers, hits, RBIs, batting average, runs scored, total bases, strikeouts, etc.) and to Babe Ruth (Hank had 41 more home runs and faced stiffer competition since baseball was segregated back then) and to Barry Bonds (performing-enhancing drugs) and to the figment of Joe DiMaggio's imagination (he insisted on that introduction as the greatest living baseball player), Henry Louis Aaron was the best ever, dead or alive, and there were so many reasons that happened.

Several of those reasons got overlooked like this one: this man with God-given skills as a baseball player was also a workaholic. Hank rarely left the Braves' lineup during the preseason, regular season, or postseason because he made sure he was physically and mentally strong from the start of spring training through whenever his team stopped playing that September or October. "I worked very hard, Terence, very hard when I went to spring training every year," Hank told me, beaming with the memories during the mid-1990s in the home clubhouse at Atlanta Fulton-County Stadium, where he relaxed as a team executive at an empty locker. He thought about his February and March days, when the Milwaukee Braves called Bradenton, Florida, their spring home before they moved to West Palm Beach in 1963. The Braves stayed there when they relocated to Atlanta after the 1965 season and they didn't leave for another spring-training site in Florida until they went to Orlando, 22 years after Hank retired as the African American version of *The Natural*.

"Staying in shape, doing even more, that was one of the things I always took pride in. When I got to spring training. I worked extra hard," Hank said, nodding. "Of course, they don't do it anymore, the way we used to do it with somebody standing up in front of you and throwing the ball from side to side. Things like that and running laps, and on my own, I ran an awful lot. I got my legs in very good shape and I was ready for the season. I never was overweight, never was overweight. I guess for the first 15 or 16 years, my weight didn't vary more than a pound and a half or two pounds, never was overweight. I weighed 178 pounds for a long time, a loooong time."

Hank eased into one of his glorious laughs that gave you no choice but to join him and then he said, "I was very, very little really. Very small. In fact, when I first got to the big leagues, if you would notice something, I could show you. I was looking at some pants when I first got to the big leagues and I didn't have pants to fit me. It wasn't like it is today. These players get it cut where they've got some tailor-made pants on. Back then, you had to take what they gave you, wrap them around, and I had them all bagged up and everything. Terence, I was just glad to have a pair of pants in the major leagues."

Designer threads or not, history is more intrigued by what Hank did inside of whatever pants he wore during and after his major league debut with the Milwaukee Braves on April 13, 1954. History often starts with his hands, specifically his wrists, labeled as "quick." History suggests that given the ability of somebody who Hank himself described as "very, very little really" while ripping homers at a higher rate than the thicker likes of Harmon Killebrew, Frank Howard, the two Willies (McCovey and Stargell), and other such sluggers of his day, Henry Louis Aaron triggered his offensive sprint toward Cooperstown with those "quick" hands and wrists leading the way.

History isn't wrong along those lines. History is just incomplete.

To hear Hank tell it, his work ethic enhanced his natural attributes, and his work ethic contributed the most to his durability. Only Pete Rose (3,562) and Carl Yastrzemski (3,308) played more games during their major league careers than Hank's 3,298, but he wasn't invincible. His rookie season with the Milwaukee Braves ended September 5,

1954, after he broke his ankle sliding into third base, and then there was his fairly unknown surgery for bone spurs on his ankle during the spring of 1965. Other than that, Hank said, "I never had a hamstring problem. Never did or anything like that, so I was very fortunate, but I worked at it."

Hank had other aches and pains throughout his 23 seasons beyond that broken ankle and those bone spurs. He just chose to keep playing despite them with much help from his mental toughness. Take those bone spurs, which came down the stretch of the 1964 season. With 12 games left, the Phillies were blowing a six-and-a-half-game lead in the National League before divisions existed. The St. Louis Cardinals (the eventual winners) and the Cincinnati Reds were charging from behind, but the Braves weren't in contention.

Even so, Hank contributed to the Phillies' choke that late September, when he ignored his physical woes to stay in the lineup along the way to a four-game sweep for the Braves in Philadelphia. "I had a cracked ankle. Well, it was a spur in my ankle, and right after that, I needed the operation, but I played the three games because I felt it was my obligation. They had to put [a competitive] lineup out there," Aaron told me. "I just went out there to do the best I could. I played through a lot of scrapes and tears through the years. I sat out maybe one or two games, but I was in for the duration. The one thing that bothered me a lot: I had my ankles. I sprained my ankles an awful lot. But other than that, I played through a lot of things really. There were times I went to the ballpark and I didn't feel like playing, but I knew I had to and I just went out there and played. I don't know. I see guys now sit out when they have headaches, things like that. No, I never did. I played every single game. I played a lot of baseball games."

I took a quick look around the Braves' clubhouse during our conversation, hours before a game to make sure nobody was around. I wanted to ask Hank something about old-school players compared to modern-day ones, and since the coast was clear, I did. "So, why are these guys injured way more now than they were in your day?" I asked. "I think of Ken Griffey Jr., spending many of his post-Seattle Mariners years sitting more than playing for the Reds, and that's ending what was once his serious chase of your home run record. Are these guys, including Griffey, just softer than you and your peers, or is it something they're doing or not doing with conditioning?"

"Well, I think, you know, in baseball you have to strengthen certain parts of your body," Hank said. "You don't have to strengthen everything. Just like football players don't have to have strong hands necessarily when compared to baseball or some other sport. They need to have strong legs. If you're a baseball player and if you're working with weights and all of that other stuff and if you don't work with them right, it will cause you major damage more than anything else. So, you have to be very careful. I think as strong as some of these guys are, I think some of them get injured from being that strong. If you look at your pitchers, the good ones who have been successful down through the years, they all are built like your Greg Madduxes and your Tom Glavines and your John Smoltzes. They're not bulky and all of that stuff, and your real, good ballplayers, they're built the same way. In baseball you have to have strong hands, strong arms, good eyes. That's it. You don't need to go into the weight room and lift in order for you to go out there and pick up somebody who weighs 300 pounds," he said, laughing. "I think a lot of these ballplayers are working on the wrong things really."

Baseball's all-time greatest player worked on the right things, and then he did them every time he took the field. Or so it seemed.

Whether you're watching Henry Louis Aaron in black and white as he slammed a curveball over the fence in center field at Milwaukee County Stadium on September 23, 1957 to walk off with the National League pennant for the Braves, or as he circled the bases 17 years later on April 8 at Atlanta-Fulton County Stadium in living color after he became better than Babe Ruth in home runs, or as he performed any of his other mind-boggling feats in between, the following thoughts about Henry Louis Aaron jumped from the screen into your consciousness: he never missed a cutoff man. He never got thrown out on base. He never managed less than a line drive at the plate. He never missed a sign. He never struck out (well, maybe he did, but only on a called third strike when an umpire blew it.) He never failed with runners in scoring position. I mean, did Hank ever make an error, and are you sure he didn't reach base just about every time he swung a bat? Regarding the baseball career of Henry Louis Aaron, it resembled those of his legendary peers in this regard: mythology was mixed with reality, and it was often difficult to separate the two. The difference? For Hank, mythology and reality mostly were one.

Then came the 21st century baseball chauvinists who studied everything beyond incredible on Hank's resume and screamed: "Yeah, he did all of that, but those were different times." *But were they?* During the summer of 2016, I asked Hank about this current time in baseball, and we went back to the future.

"I was just wondering," I asked Hank. "What do you think—if you were in your prime right now in Major League Baseball—how well do you think you would be able to do under these circumstances? For instance, if you were in your prime right now, playing for the Atlanta Braves and playing at Turner Field, say, as opposed to Atlanta-Fulton County Stadium, do you think you would be able to do as well as you did throughout your career, better, or about the same?"

"I think, Terence, I think I would be able to figure it out, whatever it was for me to do. I've thought about that for a long time. I said, 'What would I do if I was playing today?' Then I started thinking about the different situations that we had to handle when I played. Lower the mound. Raise it high and make the mound flatter. I had to contend with the slider that was coming down from guys like Gibson. So, I sort of figured that out, and when I first got to the big leagues, my first year coming from Class A ball and then immediately getting into the big leagues, I didn't have that great of a year, but I did end up hitting 13 home runs and I think it was 69 runs batted in. Then I broke my ankle, but I had figured it out from coming from A ball to the big leagues. So to answer your question, I think that, I don't see, I wouldn't see any problem other than probably the way the game is structured today [regarding pitching strategy of teams]. You've got to be ready in all situations because today the pitcher doesn't go no more than five innings, and then they bring somebody in for two, and then they bring somebody in for one or two more. So you gotta be ready for all of those particular situations, and I think if I see other guys figuring it out, I think my talent could do the same thing."

"You mention the pitching thing, and that to me seems to be one of the biggest differences. Like back when you were coming up in the '50s and the '60s, you didn't have all of these late-inning relief pitchers and what have you now, and I don't know if that's an advantage for the hitter or disadvantage. But, like you say, I know you would kind of figure it out. But do you think you would somehow have an advantage having to face all of these pitchers, as opposed to back in the '50s and '60s?"

"Well, I don't think that particular thing would bother me as far as facing different pitchers. But the thing that would bother me most would be pitchers [coming and going] through interleague trading—pitchers coming from the National to the American League and going back and forth. You would have to learn how those pitchers' fastballs would move and other things. So, yes, it would be a learning experience, but by the same token, I would be able to figure it out. The other thing, too, is the traveling. It would seem to me—correct me if I'm wrong—it would be easier to travel now than it was back in the '50s, I guess, with planes as opposed to trains. [Flying] would help you more.

"Oh, no question about it. I mean, we didn't have, in fact, I was just talking about this the other day. I said, 'When I first got to the big leagues, there was no such thing as a bus coming to pick you up at the airport or train station or whatever it was. They would pull that cart on the side, the boxcar you were sleeping in, and you would get up any time you would want to get up, and you would see ballplayers at 9:00, 10:00, 11:00, 12:00, pushing those big, old trunks down the highway, trying to get them a ride"...Yeah, and you had to eat whatever they wanted you to eat. You didn't have meal money. There wasn't such thing as meal money, and your travel would be on trains. So, yes, yes, [traveling today,] that would be of some help to you.

"Anyway, you look at all the things in the big leagues now, and I think the only thing that probably would be of a disadvantage for me would be trying to figure out different pitchers [from the other league]. I don't think that stuff wise, you can say anybody now has better stuff than guys like Gibson and Koufax and Drysdale and those guys. No question, they had as good of stuff or better stuff, and then the thing that was so bad about it—there was no protection for a hitter. They would throw inside and knock you down, and the umpire would just say, 'Ball one, ball two,' and you would just have to get up," he said causing us both to laugh. "Nowadays, you come close to a guy, and the first thing you know you've got two teams out there fighting with each other."

"That's true definitely. A couple of other things I was thinking of regarding the differences. Back in your day, you just had newspaper guys you had to deal with. Now, you've got anything that anybody does good or bad, it's on ESPN, FOX. It's on the Internet. It's on these blogs. How would you have been able to handle all of that sort of 24-hour media?"

"You know, Terence, that would give me more problems than somebody's fastball because I've never been one to look for publicity or to try to look for anything in particular. I just felt like for all of the news media, the way that they do it today would be a serious problem with me. Even now, when I go to the Braves' camp, I try not to go down there with the idea of trying to create any kind of problems other than just going down there, watching the game, and going home."

"Oh, no doubt."

"So, I don't know how I would handle it. That would be a serious problem for me really."

"And I tell you, Hank, just from me being in media, I was telling this to somebody the other day: I've been covering major sports for four decades, but to be honest with you, if I were a player right now, I don't know how much I would talk to the media."

"Yeah, it's kind of tough."

"Yeah, and here's another thing I was thinking about. If you were in your prime today, there are way fewer Black players than there were when you were playing."

"No question about it. No matter whether you played the Pittsburgh Pirates or the St. Louis Cardinals, most or all the clubs had at least one or two [Black players]. But nowadays, none of them for the most part have a Black player at all on their club. They don't care about Black players, and the whole thing is sickening."

"Sad situation. So, if you're in the lineup of the Braves today, and if it just involves playing baseball and nothing else, how well do you do?"

"Oh, I think I would do well. I don't know of anybody who would be in somebody's lineup that I would think could do better than what I could do. Nobody. I'd bat, well, it would depend on where they would want me. When I first came up and I was hitting third, that was because the [Milwaukee Braves] manager wanted to make sure I got to bat in the first inning. And, of course, later on when [Eddie] Mathews got hurt and didn't play well, then they dropped me down to fourth. So, it wouldn't make any difference. I just feel I would fit in regardless of whatever. I think I could still end up hitting my average of 35 to 40 home runs. I could play every day. I could steal a base when I got ready. I could do all right."

"Of course, the big question is: do you think you still would hit 755 home runs? More, less, or would it be about the same?"

"I don't know if that would happen, because I don't know if I would need to play that long," he said, laughing. "I would make a lot of money in just four or five years, and that's the thing. Would I have the incentive? Would I have the desire? Would I want to play a long time? I don't know. For years I didn't make any money and I was having good years. So, I don't know if I could [hit 755 home runs playing today]. That would be hard for me to say simply because they pay these guys so darn much money. They make these guys so rich for four or five years. I mean, hell, can you imagine all the money these guys make? I really can't count that high."

"What's the most you ever made for a season?"

"Just over $200,000 [actually $240,000 each in 1975 and 1976] when I was with the Brewers."

"And that was at the end of your career."

"Yes, it was. And then I remember somebody coming into the clubhouse when I was making $100,000-something dollars with the Braves, and it was one of the newspaper guys, trying to play mind games, and he said, 'Well, I want to talk to the guy who is making all this money in here. Who is he? There he is.' That's the kind of crap I had to deal with. I'll tell you."

"Well, you know I know about mind games," I said, leading us both to laugh.

"Here's my last question, and then I'll let you go."

"Oh, take you time. I'm in for the evening. That's fine."

"If you were in your prime today, how much money do you think you would be making per year right now?"

"Uh, let's put it this way, Terence: who's the highest paid player? Whoever that guy is, I could make as much money as that guy. Damn sure could. No question about it. I wouldn't see any reason why not. I don't think there's anything that he did that I couldn't do and couldn't do it better."

HANK, JACKIE, AND DESTINY

With Henry Louis Aaron right there disguised as the aching and tired man, I pushed his wheelchair into the hallway toward the unknown of whether this CNN interview would happen or evaporate.

He was an obvious choice for CNN to feature. Who better to talk about life, race—or even just baseball?

"Hey, Hank. How's it going today?" I asked over the phone in January 2009.

"Oh, how's it going, buddy," he laughed. "I was just watching you on TV a minute ago. You were talking about Deion Sanders. Yeah, yeah, just saw you not more than a few minutes ago. So how are you doing? You always do a great job on television."

"No complaints here, and thanks, sir. Yeah, you probably were watching me on that ESPN *30 for 30* show talking about Deion and Tim McCarver and those buckets of ice water."

(Serving as the main CBS Sports announcer during the 1992 National League Championship Series, McCarver criticized Sanders on air for playing for the Atlanta Falcons and the Atlanta Braves on the same day. A fuming Sanders doused McCarver with buckets of water with cameras rolling after the Braves won Game Seven.)

"You know who else Deion said he was looking for?" I asked.

"Who Schuerholz? I know he had no use whatsoever for Schuerholz."

"Uh uh, me."

"You?" Aaron laughed. "Oh, why was he after you?"

"He didn't like some of the things I was writing, and I got a call from Channel 5 to come down to the station. They had a camera crew following Deion around the hallways of Atlanta-Fulton County Stadium, saying, 'Where's Terence Moore? He's next,'" I said, as we both laughed. "I don't think he was serious because I was in the clubhouse several times, and he didn't do anything. He mostly was upset with Tim, and Tim wasn't happy getting those buckets dumped on him. I've talked to Tim [through the years about it], and he still isn't happy."

"Yeah, yeah. I'm sure Tim was upset because I *guess* it was water," Aaron said, laughing, "if that's what you want to call it, but Deion also got into it with [general manager] John Schuerholz. That's why they traded him. Deion didn't care too much for John Schuerholz. You saw on the show. [Deion] hated him. I got along with Deion, but I didn't have a reason not to because I wasn't looking for anything from him."

"Yeah, Deion is fine," I said. "A lot of that stuff he does is just to get his Prime Time brand out there. Deep down inside, he's a pretty good person. He just has his way of doing things."

"I think you're right. That was the whole thing when Deion was with the Braves and why he didn't get along with John Schuerholz. Deion pulled his own cards, yeah, yeah, yeah, uh huh."

The more I pushed the wheelchair down the hallway with the tired and aching man beginning to resemble Henry Louis Aaron in little ways, the more I remembered the beginning.

Then I thought about my time as The Hank Aaron Whisperer. That time ranged from our conversations of deep revelations to the wisdom he provided during my toxic decades as a Black sports columnist in the Deep South to this moment of me pushing the greatest baseball player ever in a wheelchair. This was destiny. In a flash, virtually everything from my past made sense, and Henry Louis Aaron was a running theme through much of it.

Just as fate merged Henry Louis Aaron with Jack Roosevelt Robinson, destiny combined both of them with me. I see it now in hindsight.

Even before I met Hank Aaron, I was familiar with "Hank Aaron." I hadn't a clue about the man, but I knew the player. I began watching Hank in the mid-1960s when I was maybe 10, and that was some trick.

My family and I didn't live anywhere near his Braves of Milwaukee or of Atlanta. Not only that, but I was in a city whose two Major League Baseball teams sat nearly a two-hour drive away on the north (Cubs) and south (White Sox) sides of Chicago. Such was part of the sporting life around South Bend, Indiana, where I was born in 1955 and raised through early puberty. South Bend's population was smaller than the crowd at Soldier Field in Chicago for the 1926 Army–Navy game (110,000), and South Bend's city limits had a couple of prominent entities: the University of Notre Dame and most of my relatives, which included both sets of grandparents, 10 aunts, seven uncles (before marriage), 42 first cousins, and a bunch of other kinfolks.

My parents, Sam and Annie Moore, hugged competition. It didn't matter if it involved basketball, football, bowling, or a bid whist card game. My brothers, Dennis and Darrell, and I followed their example. Fighting Irish football was our ultimate obsession as a family, especially with Notre Dame Stadium just a few kickoffs from our front door, but we cherished all things Chicago sports on the professional level, and it began with the Cubs. We pulled their games into our South Bend living room from WGN through the huge television antenna that Dad often needed to adjust by climbing on top of our roof. He twisted and turned the hunk of metal enough to make Ernie Banks and Billy Williams appear less fuzzy on our black-and-white screen. We also enjoyed many of the Cubs' opponents—the Black ones, in particular—and among them was Henry Louis Aaron.

No question, Willie Mays had the flair—complete with his cap flying toward the sky while chasing flyballs in center field or while rounding the bases before producing slides filled with dust and drama. I mentioned Mays because despite the extraordinary seasons during the mid-to-late 1960s of Roberto Clemente and Frank Robinson, society usually paired Mays with Aaron throughout my early youth as the top challengers for the unofficial honor of best overall baseball player in the major leagues.

I preferred Hank Aaron.

There was something mythical about the serene guy for the Braves with the noisy Louisville Slugger. He killed the Cubs. Followers of other teams said the same of somebody so ferocious at the plate that he was known as "The Hammer," but according to the statistics and common sense, Hank couldn't wait to face Chicago's National League team. His highest career batting average against any opponent was his mark of .326 versus the Cubs.

Even so, the Winds of Wrigley in Chicago conspired to get even with Hank but only for a moment. He told me the hardest ball he ever hit turned into an out in August 1969, when the gales from nearby Lake Michigan blew Hank's drive—rushing toward the apartment building on Waveland Avenue behind the left-field bleachers—back toward the ivy-covered walls and into the glove of Williams, the Cubs' left fielder who was as shocked as Hank.

The Homer That Wasn't kept the record books from featuring 756 next to Hank Aaron's name regarding career blasts instead of 755, but he shrugged at the memory decades later during our conversations. As I kept pushing Hank in that wheelchair through the hallway of his nursing home disguised as a rehabilitation center, I kept thinking: *Never would I have imagined as a young Cubs fan that I was headed toward spending much of my adult life understanding Hank's psyche more than any sports journalist ever.*

Then again, since Jack Roosevelt Robinson was among the primary role models for Henry Louis Aaron, I knew the mind-set of Hank Aaron the person more than I realized while growing up. That's because I knew Jackie Robinson.

Not officially.

It's just that, unofficially, I lived in a household full of Jackie Robinsons, which meant I was surrounded by Hank Aarons, too. The combination made me an expert-in-progress on how to survive and prosper as an African American in the midst of racial conflict generated by mind games.

Decades later, I needed to use every bit of that training at *The Atlanta Journal-Constitution*, where the mind games were on steroids during my Jackie Robinson days as the first Black sports columnist in the history of the Deep South. In addition, without me realizing it as a youth, that training was building the foundation for my ability to understand the inner soul of Henry Louis Aaron and for him to sense I was equipped to do so.

Here's why I was equipped: my parents, Annie Graham and Samuel Moore, were four and nine, respectively, when they moved to South Bend after their families left the South during The Great Migration of Blacks to the North in the early 1940s. They married in 1954 and they had mostly a racially tranquil existence during the early part of their lives in South Bend, which was the antithesis of Kokomo, located 86 miles to the south, where more than 100,000 folks gathered on July 4, 1923 for the largest Ku Klux Klan rally ever. Even beyond Kokomo, the state of Indiana earned its reputation during the 19th and 20th centuries as the southern-most northern state with the lynching of African Americans and ultra-right-wing politics.

South Bend was the glaring exception. You could attribute much of that to Notre Dame, a liberal anchor in the city since 1842 and the most prominent Catholic institution in the world not named the Vatican. University president Father Theodore Hesburgh was part of the Civil Rights Commission from 1957 to 1972 and he marched with Dr. Martin Luther King Jr. along the way to helping the U.S. Congress pass the 1964 Civil Rights Act.

As was the case for my brothers and me, my parents always went to integrated schools in South Bend, where Jim Crow didn't exist. But then Dad took his first train ride. He was in his late teens and he was off to the U.S. Army during the early 1950s with his best friend, Fred Ware. They left South Bend for basic training at Fort Campbell in Kentucky, which is south of Indiana, and Dad's whole racial outlook changed forever. They were told to get up and go to the back of the train. My father rarely showed anger regarding anything and he never did when discussing that racial incident. Like Hank, Dad preferred mellow. And, like Jackie, along his way to breaking baseball's color barrier on April 15, 1947 and like Hank, during his pursuit of Babe Ruth's record in the early 1970s, Dad used slights from Whites (and people in general) as motivation to make them look silly as he survived their mind games and prospered in the aftermath.

So, this was typical: after Dad's train ride to Fort Campbell became segregated out of nowhere, he departed to spend the next few days, weeks, months, and years turning into a sergeant first class among his group of paratroopers, and the majority of his troop was White.

Sam Moore wasn't finished with his Jackie and Hank moments. When he returned to South Bend from the U.S. Army in January 1955, he went back to the job he had before he joined the military, which was working at Indiana Bell as a janitor just to get inside its totally White world in pursuit of becoming that company's version of Jack Roosevelt Robinson.

South Bend wasn't Kokomo, but it was part of the United States of America for a Black person. In other words, racism took a different form in South Bend beyond burning white crosses on front lawns, but it was still racism. The preferred tactics for northern racists involved mind games. I discovered as much by listening to my parents. More importantly, I learned how to respond to this more prevalent form of racism (which I would experience often for decades, especially during my 25 years as Black columnist at *The AJC*) by watching my parents.

They were so like Jackie...and Hank.

"Now that Barack is in the White House, oh, man," Hank said during a phone conversation in January 2009, "some of these people are coming out of the closet, I'll tell you."

"Oh, man. I was just talking to my dad about that last night. He's a news junkie like you," I said, laughing. "I agree, but here's what we were saying: they've always been there, and now they're just..."

"Uh huh. Not to cut you off, but one guy," Aaron said, "this one guy made a remark about Obama after he won, and I heard him on television. He said, 'Obama either is going to be liberal to the people who got him elected...' so you know what he wanted to say when he's talking about those people, but he had to catch himself at the last minute—or he said, 'Obama is going to be an Uncle Tom to somebody in the White House.' Another person called this guy out on television for what he said, but he said he refused to apologize. I just said, 'when it comes to dealing with us, some of these folks ain't worth a hill of beans,' I'll tell you. That's one of the things that makes me wonder about whether things are going to change in this country. These attitudes toward us—after all the things you have to go through, they still make you feel like a second-class citizen."

As an Indiana Bell janitor who never missed a day, never was late and never did less than what he was supposed to do, Sam Moore knew his employers would have to end their discriminatory ways someday. He sought to make it so by spending his work breaks reading all of the books on electronics he could buy from a bookstore or borrow from a library. He read even more when he came home. He kept applying for every job opening inside the Indiana Bell building that didn't involve a broom or a pail, but the rejections kept coming. So did the mind games. To which Dad always said, "Whatever." He eventually became one of the first Black electronical engineers for Indiana Bell. Later, by the late 1960s, he became the first Black supervisor for AT&T in the Midwest and he was one of just two African Americans in the country holding that position for the company.

Then there was Dad's promotion to AT&T manager. With my father in management, AT&T transferred our family from South Bend to Cincinnati in 1968 and then to Chicago in 1971 and then to Milwaukee in 1972. Along with all the moves, the mind games never stopped coming for Sam Moore, our personal Jackie, who usually was the first—and frequently the only—Black at most functions throughout his rise at AT&T.

On November 22, 1963, when we still lived in South Bend, Sam Moore flew to Cincinnati for one of his frequent AT&T training session in the city. As usual, he was the only African American in the company's packed conference room when somebody walked in with the announcement: "We just got word that President Kennedy was shot and killed in Dallas." As Sam Moore sat there, trying to comprehend the loss of somebody who most Blacks thought was sympathetic to their plight, everybody else around him rose to cheer loudly and wildly. The sadder Dad looked, the giddier they became.

Another of those mind games Dad used to recite occurred more than a decade after JFK's death. The setting was Milwaukee, where my father completed his journey at AT&T from the floor (literally) to the penthouse as the manager in charge of the company's operations in Wisconsin, Indiana, and Illinois. He was the first and only Black manager at AT&T's Milwaukee headquarters, where the mind games accelerated for Sam Moore. Dad walked into his office, and his boss entered the room from across the way to say, "You know what? The only colored guy I would allow in my house would be Sammy Davis Jr."

The boss stared at Dad for a reaction. The boss was disappointed. With Sam Moore showing no emotion on his face, Dad responded with deeds instead of words by leaving to doing his job.

"Boy, oh boy, Terence. You'd be surprised by some of the mind games I've had to go through now even with the Braves," Aaron said during a phone conversation in January 2009.

"Yeah, back when you were farm director?" I asked.

"Yeah, we talked about that, but did I tell you the story about Ted Turner wanting to give me the office? The office story? Maybe I did, but I don't think so. That's one of the ones I'm talking about."

"You know I would remember something like that," I said, laughing, "can't wait to hear that one, but, oh, man, I gotta get to this basketball game for my little godson, Julian, but hold onto that for a moment."

"Okay, you around tomorrow?"

"Yeah, yeah, I'll call tomorrow. About this time?"

"That'll be fine."

Even before Dad's Jackie Robinson roles with Indiana Bell and AT&T, he joined a group of Blacks to integrate the South Bend golf courses during the late 1950s. He also was a prolific bowler and he became the first African American to win South Bend's singles championship, which he did in 1963. Golf was Dad's passion, though. At the time of his death at 84 in 2016, he was a 7-handicapper with three holes in one. He also spent his last breath, knowing he had laughed last regarding a slew of racial incidents.

Maybe, just maybe, when Sam Moore was forced to sit in the back of that train, while heading to Dixie for Army basic training in Kentucky from South Bend, maybe the angels were doing their thing. Maybe several of the White folks riding in the front of the compartment were among those destined to take orders from Dad as their commanding officer.

South Bend also was the national headquarters for a savings and loans company called Associates, and Annie Moore was its female Jackie Robinson. She was the first Black employee at Associates of any kind during her rise from custodial work in the building to filing clerk. When we moved to Cincinnati in 1968, the mind games went from mild to malicious for Annie Moore as the first and the only Black person at the Associates' regional office. She often came home to speak of Martha, a middle-aged White woman who resented three things about her early 30-something African American coworker: she was named the lead cashier in the place, she had a bigger desk, and she was darker than all of Martha's relatives.

There were always little things. With my parents back then sounding like Jackie and Hank—without my two brothers and me knowing it— they told us to take those little things seriously, but Dad and Mom added we should follow their lead by protecting our mental state before responding to those little things in a calm yet decisive manner.

Among the worst of those little things for Annie Moore at Associates in Cincinnati happened when Martha, carrying her ever-present plastic smile, strolled up to say, "You see this key?" Then Martha waved the metal object in the air near Mom's face before she added, "This key goes to your drawer. I can open it anytime I want." Then, with that ever-present plastic smile still in place, Martha walked away, glancing over her shoulder seconds later for Mom's response.

Annie Moore had no response, but she later delivered a blow-by-blow of Martha's mind games to Harvey, the head of the department.

"I'll take care of it," Harvey said, meekly, giving Mom only the satisfaction that Martha's sabotage threat was on record.

When Annie Moore wasn't deflecting Martha's little things, she was dealing with the ugliness of customers, such as that angry White farmer in overalls from nearby Kentucky. The man glared at the only African American in the building, sitting behind the register at her desk, and his face turned various shades of red as he flung the payment booklet for his John Deere tractor across the table toward her before it dropped to the floor with a thud.

Martha chuckled. Annie Moore ignored Martha, the farmer, and the payment booklet as she kept typing through the madness.

The next time the farmer arrived to pay his bill, Mom kept typing from behind the desk that featured the farmer's previous act of ignorance. He glanced around to see an empty office elsewhere and then he looked back at Mom. He waited as Mom continued to do her other job, which involved typing. He was going to wait for assistance from a White person.

Five minutes passed. Then 10, 15.

Finally, the farmer couldn't bear to wait any longer. He asked Annie Moore if she could process his payment. She took his book, wrote out a receipt, accepted his money, handed his book back to him, turned her back, and kept right on typing without saying a word. Jackie would have been proud. The same goes for Hank.

Like me, my youngest brother, Darrell, was just appreciative Mom and Dad gave us the blueprint for handling those little things and mind games when the racial spotlight is blinding your face. Darrell went to the University of Wisconsin, where he was the only Black baseball player for the Badgers when he arrived on campus during the fall of 1977. He was one of the first Wisconsin Black baseball players ever. For sure, he was the only African American baseball player to become a four-year letterman at the university, and that included 1981, when he was named the Badgers' Most Valuable Player. He battled his version of racism disguised as mind games inside and outside of the Wisconsin locker room, including jokes at his expense. A coach had him stand up before the team to tell them one day after a practice what it was like to be the only Black person on the roster.

His teammates still didn't get it totally until the Wisconsin baseball squad went to Baton Rouge, Louisiana, during March of 1978 to play LSU. That's deep in the heart of Dixie. This wasn't the spring of 1947, when Jackie Robinson took his first road trip with the Brooklyn Dodgers as the first Black player in Major League Baseball history. It was close, though.

Just like Jackie, Darrell was the only Black *player* in the ballpark. Unlike Jackie, Darrell was the only Black *person* in the ballpark. "I'm an 18-year-old Black kid in left field at LSU with all of these White fans everywhere, and for nine innings, they had folks up in the stands that wouldn't stop," Darrell said, recalling the scene with hurt and anger in his voice. "They called me n----r, spear-chucker, sambo, blackie. They were in my shorts for nine innings. And I'm literally in the outfield crying the entire time. So every time I came back into the dugout, I would tell my teammates what was going on, and they thought I was making it up. They didn't believe me because they couldn't possibly imagine anything like that could take place."

The more Darrell returned to the dugout with wetness in his eyes, the more the other Badgers understood his pain. Finally, when the game reached its final inning, the Wisconsin players became the collective 1970s version of Pee Wee Reese, Jackie's old teammate who was the Dodgers' shortstop while serving as team captain. During Jackie's 1947 rookie season, the Dodgers made a road trip to Cincinnati, baseball's southern-most city back then, and here's where legend takes over with help from the movie 42. Those at Crosley Field threw racial slurs at Jackie playing first base against their Cincinnati Reds as soon as they saw the No. 42 on his back. To slow the verbal daggers, Reese left his defensive position and then trotted over to Jackie. Just as Moses parted the Red Sea by raising his staff, Reese held off the racists by wrapping his arm around Jackie's shoulders.

Darrell's teammates had a different approach. "Just before we were moving toward the end of that LSU game, all of my White teammates were like, 'Darrell, you cannot follow us. You have to stay in the dugout, okay? We're going to take care of this,'" Darrell said. "My teammates went up into the stands with baseball bats, and those people just ran like cowards because my teammates were going to beat the living crap out of them. I know all of the crap I went through as an 18-year-old kid and then I have to catch myself. Compared to Jackie Robinson and to Hank Aaron, I only went through a snippet of the stuff they had to endure. I know how awful I felt. I know how helpless it felt, but I still had to go out there and do my job. It gives me mad respect for Jackie and Hank because I'm dealing with name calling, but they were dealing with death threats. Their intestinal fortitude had to be off the chain. The similarity is: you have to be mentally strong in all of these types of situations."

Yes, indeed, and I know. Courtesy of Dad's transfers by AT&T, I went to three different high schools in three different states within three years, and since my parents' first goal was to get us into the best school district possible, we often were in predominately White (if not all White) situations. I was the first Black player for my high school baseball team in Cincinnati and the first for my high school baseball team in Milwaukee, where I also became the only Black on the football team. Regarding the latter, we went undefeated my senior year, and I led the team in tackles as an inside linebacker. Midway through what became a Milwaukee City Conference title season for us, our White head football coach either forgot I was the only Black on the team—or he didn't care. Right before we left the locker room for the opening kickoff to face an all-Black opponent, the head coach ended his pregame pep talk by saying, "So let's go out and get those n-----s!" Two of my teammates pulled me aside to apologize for the head coach and for the non-responses from his assistant coaches. Those coaches never apologized. They never said a word.

While I was a prominent player for the football and baseball teams at my Milwaukee high school, I also was the first and the only Black person on the high school newspaper and I became its news editor. Later, I was the first Black writer for the Miami (Ohio) University student newspaper, which is the oldest one west of the Alleghenies, and I became its first Black editor of any kind when I ran the sports department. I worked for the Miami (Ohio) newspaper from my first day on campus in September 1974 through my graduation day in May 1978.

I was the first Black sports reporter ever for *The Cincinnati Enquirer*, when I joined the paper a week after I graduated from Miami (Ohio). I was the first Black sportswriter on a full-time basis in the history of the *San Francisco Examiner*, when I went there in March 1980. I became the first African American to cover an NFL team as a regular beat for a major metropolitan newspaper when the *Examiner* gave me the Oakland Raiders beat during the summer of 1980. Three years later, I became only the third Black general sports columnist in the history of major newspapers and I was the first ever in the Deep South when I joined *The Atlanta Journal-Constitution* in January 1985. Six years after that, I became just the second African American to vote for Baseball Hall of Famers as a member of the Baseball Writers

Association of America, and no Black person in history has voted for Baseball Hall of Famers longer than I.

When I connect those dots, I was destined to become The Hank Aaron Whisperer, but I didn't know it.

That poster was a sign. Well, there were two posters.

When AT&T transferred Dad from South Bend to Cincinnati in 1968, we made the transition from Cubs fans to disciples of the rapidly developing Big Red Machine, and I quickly became a Pete Rose die-hard. Even so, I retained my fascination with Hank Aaron, which is why I used my allowance that November at 13 years old to purchase posters of Rose and Aaron, and the posters were made by the same company. They were gorgeous. Through the years, I made sure they remained perfectly intact, and they graced my walls during those family moves from South Bend to Cincinnati and then from Cincinnati to Chicago and then from Chicago to Milwaukee. Both posters joined me during all my stops from newspaper to newspaper, and even though I didn't have them matted and framed until I reached Atlanta, I was lucky. They still looked brand new even through my subsequent Internet and television career.

During my youth, anything involving Pete Rose and Hank Aaron was sprinkled with pixie dust. They had those commercials that spoke directly to me during the late 1960s and early 1970s when we lived in Cincinnati. The Roses promoted Gulden's Spicy Brown Mustard, so my parents weren't allowed to buy any other mustard than that one. I've spent decades still using it. In fact, my cupboard always features a couple of jars of Gulden's, representing different flavors but always with the same thought when I grab one of them: it's Pete's mustard.

He also did commercials for OH HENRY! candy bars. How ironic, especially given his future chase of that Great White Ghost. Just like Babe Ruth had nothing to do with the creation of the chocolate bar called "Baby Ruth" (started in 1921, when Ruth led the Yankees to the first of their record 40 American League pennants), Hank Aaron was born 13 years after George Williamson combined peanuts, caramel, and fudge to form that first OH HENRY! candy bar at his Chicago company. I only cared about the commercial, which began with Hank standing at home plate. After he swung you heard the crack of his bat as he looked toward the outfield, presumably at one of his 755 home runs, as he began running toward first base. That crack of that bat was followed by a female's voice yelling in sort of a singing tone, "Oh, Henry!" The narrator would follow with something like, "Oh Henry! candy bar. It's a hit every time."

While Rose was baseball's all-time greatest competitor (regardless of his various gambling issues), Aaron was baseball's all-time greatest player. I loved them both. Following Dad's first transfer in 1968, my family and I were able to see Hank up close and personal after we moved from South Bend to Cincinnati. Our hometown Reds were in the same division as Hank's Atlanta Braves.

Is this heaven? No, it's Cincinnati.

Rose. Johnny Bench. Tony Perez. Lee May. They were the main cogs in the early version of the Big Red Machine after we arrived within those city limits, and they played in the funhouse of Crosley Field with its hill as a warning track in left field, the huge scoreboard in center that was in play, and the sun/moon deck as the right-field bleachers. Better yet, whenever the Braves came to town, we always had the chance to sit in the stands to watch Hank, the guy who sauntered in total peace to the batter's box regardless of the situation. The guy who never wore batting gloves. The guy who preferred a simple helmet without flaps. The guy who lacked drama before, during, and after his swings except for the way baseballs left his bat for open spaces or for landings beyond fences. The guy I had no idea would use me someday as his unofficial spokesperson after he evolved into the new Jackie.

Just as Henry Louis Aaron pulverized the Cubs, the old team of our hearts, he did the same to the Reds, the new team of our hearts. But as long as the Big Red Machine crushed the Braves, I didn't mind

Hank doing his thing. His .319 career batting average when facing the Reds was his best mark against any team not named...ahem...the Cubs, but he scored more runs (271) and he slammed more home runs (97) against the Reds than anybody. In general there was something about the city of Cincinnati and Hank. For one, he played his first major league game on April 13, 1954 at Crosley Field, where he went 0-for-5 for his Milwaukee Braves during a 9-8 loss. For another, he ripped the first home run ever at Riverfront Stadium on June 30, 1970. For yet another, he tied Babe Ruth with No. 714 at Riverfront Stadium on April 4, 1974.

There also was something else.

I kicked myself over Sunday, May 17, 1970. Back then, the Reds gave two free tickets to three games that season for any high school, middle school, or elementary school student in the Greater Cincinnati area with straight A's for a semester. With that as motivation, I easily reached perfection on my report card. You had to lock in your choices for games at the start of the season, and one of the available dates was Sunday, May 17, 1970, when Hank would collect his 3,000th hit against the Reds during the second game of a doubleheader. It wasn't a home run. Nor was it one of his signature drives to an outfield alley or a smoker past an infielder. It was a relatively harmless grounder up the middle, where Reds second baseman Woody Woodward backhanded the ball, but Woodward had zero chance of nailing Hank at first.

That was despite Hank's 36-year-old legs. Although he was in the final stretch of his career, he began the afternoon hitting .344 and he led the major leagues in home runs with 15, in RBIs with 37, and in slugging percentage at .744. So, not surprisingly, his wrists were quick enough on an inside fastball from Reds flame thrower Wayne Simpson for that infield single, and Hank became the first player ever with 3,000 hits and 500-plus home runs.

Baseball Hall of Famer Stan Musial was there. He left his box seat for the field to congratulate Henry Louis Aaron for his accomplishment.

Not that I saw it—nor did others beyond the 33,217 fans who gave the Reds their biggest attendance for a home game in 23 years. That Hank moment happened before you could find nearly every Major League Baseball game on television or through streaming capabilities. It was only on the radio, and I listened to every word for the most part—and I kept chastising myself. *Why? Why? Why didn't I call a psychic or something, so I could have chosen that date before the season with my straight-A's tickets?*

I figured this was a decent compromise: my next straight-A's game fell on Wednesday, July 1, 1970, the day after the Reds were scheduled to open their brand-new Riverfront Stadium against the Braves of Hank Aaron. He spent Tuesday, June 30, 1970, christening what was the first major league ballpark featuring an all-artificial surface with a home run in the first inning as we watched on television. Given that Riverfront-making history involving Hank, my brother, Darrell, and I could barely sleep that night in anticipation of likely seeing one of our favorite baseball players not on the Big Red Machine slam another homer the following night in Game Two of the series.

Hank didn't play, but the Reds won. Oh, well.

Four years later, we joined everybody else beyond Atlanta-Fulton County Stadium to watch the ultimate Hank moment on television. It came after we moved to Milwaukee for the last of Dad's transfers by AT&T. The moment involved a humble Black man preparing to pass a White man elevated to near deity for owning the most sacred of all sports records—lifetime home runs. We were among the majority of African Americans who treated that night of Monday, April 8, 1974, like the afternoon of Tuesday, April 15, 1947, when Jackie Robinson made segregation in baseball yesterday's news.

Folks gathered around the radio for Jackie. For Hank we had our color television—or so we thought we did. Earlier that day, the jumbo-sized Magnavox downstairs in the family room began giving us nothing but horizontal and vertical lines that wouldn't cooperate. As for the sound, what sound?

Speaking of Magnavox: long before the ball and the bat that would produce Hank's record-breaking 715th home run left for the Baseball Hall of Fame in Cooperstown, New York, he went on a promotional tour around the nation for five years. That's because prior to Hank surpassing Babe Ruth's record, he signed a deal with Magnavox to make that tour happen. In contrast, we didn't have an agreement on Monday, April 8, 1974, with the Magnavox folks or with anybody else to make those horizontal and vertical lines go away before the first pitch that night.

So with our version of ballpark food steps away in the refrigerator or on the stove, the five of us—Sam and Annie, along with Dennis, Darrell, and myself—were glued to the 19-inch Philips television that nevertheless gave us splendid black-and-white images from our kitchen.

It was Aaron versus Ruth. For us, it *really* had become a Black-and-White situation.

"Get the video camera," Mom yelled, gesturing to nobody in particular when it was nearly Hank's at-bat in the fourth inning against Al Downing of the Los Angeles Dodgers at Atlanta-Fulton County Stadium.

"He's going to hit it now," Dad said, sounding like somebody who knew his sports, which he did. In addition to his wonderful golf and bowling games, he was our first Little League coach. He preached trying to drive the ball up the middle, and "everything else will come," including home runs, and that was sort of Hank's approach. Well, that, along with what he told me through the years about his hitting philosophy: "See the ball and then hit the ball."

I raced downstairs for the video camera. It was a state-of-the art machine to us, even though its 8mm film didn't produce sound, and "high definition" wasn't a phrase or a thought at the time. I checked, then I checked some more to make sure the video camera worked properly for Hank's moment. It would become our moment—along with the moment for all African Americans and for anybody else wishing to view the culmination of a guy who just kept doing his job to accomplish something huge despite *everything.*

In that fourth inning after Downing hung a slider on the inside part of the plate, Aaron unleashed his wrist-dominated swing of greatness, and NBC announcer Curt Gowdy began shouting his words for posterity as the ball raced toward the bullpen in left-center field: "There's a long drive, ball hit deep...deep...and it's gone! He did it! He did it! Henry Aaron is the all-time home run leader now! Listen to this! He did it!"

The only thing we heard from Gowdy was nothing.

As soon as Hank swung, with the ball barely a few centimeters into the air, soaring toward the top of our television screen, Mom triggered the nonstop yelling and stomping in our kitchen. Somehow, I kept filming—from Downing's throw to Hank's swing to everybody's joy.

That said, when two young guys jumped from the stands to run behind Hank circling the bases, my brother, Darrell, screamed, "Look at that. Are they going tackle him, or are they trying to take him out?" Our joy subsided for a moment within the moment. Darrell, along with the rest of us, knew about Hank's battle involving racist letters and death threats, but more than that, we knew Gowdy had it wrong when he kept saying, *"He did it."*

We did it and we did it through Henry Louis Aaron.

On Monday, April 8, 1974, there were three main centers for Hank's No. 715, and they all were legitimate. You had Atlanta, of course, where Hank was finishing his ninth season as the primary (and often the only) reason for those in that southern hotbed of college football to care about their attendance-challenged Major League Baseball team in town. You had Mobile, Alabama, where Hank took his first breath as one of eight children for the Aarons of Herbert Sr. and Estella before he fulfilled his desire to become a Boy Scout along the way to serving as a cross-hitting outfielder and third baseman for the local Black Bears in a semipro league.

You also had Milwaukee, where Hank left his baseball heart, and it was love at first sight for both parties. We discovered as much soon after AT&T transferred Dad and the family from Chicago to Milwaukee in March 1972. Our move happened two years after Major League Baseball relocated the Pilots from Seattle to Milwaukee to become the Brewers. More strikingly, especially when you consider the historically loyal sports fans of Wisconsin, our move to Milwaukee occurred seven years after the Braves trampled over the baseball psyche of the entire Cheesehead Nation by bolting for Atlanta.

It didn't take long for us to discover Milwaukeeans liked the Brewers, but they loved the Braves, the ones who spent their second year in town debuting a rookie for the ages in 1954.

So it went:

Vince Lombardi.

Bart Starr.

Hank Aaron, maybe followed by just about any other starter for those Green Bay Packers powerhouse teams of the 1960s.

When we arrived in Milwaukee during the spring of 1972, that was the pecking order of greatness for Wisconsin's all-time sports figures in the minds of the Cheeseheads we encountered around school, on the job, in print, or from flipping around the television and radio dials of the local stations.

The Milwaukee Bucks of Kareem Abdul-Jabbar and Oscar Robertson were an NBA powerhouse. Al McGuire's Marquette Warriors ranked among the elite of college basketball teams every season. Win or lose (mainly lose), Camp Randall Stadium was packed and loud in Madison for University of Wisconsin football games. The Packers were bad, but among Cheeseheads, they were still the Packers.

Even with all of those things and even though it was seven years after the Braves bolted Schlitz for grits, we discovered Wisconsin folks still hadn't recovered from that breakup mostly out of nowhere. They remembered how the Milwaukee–Henry Louis Aaron relationship exploded on September 23, 1957, after his pennant-winning homer at Milwaukee County Stadium sent the Braves past the St. Louis Cardinals in 11 innings. They remembered how Hank was carried off the field during the subsequent celebration by his teammates. They remembered how the Braves won the World Series days later over the New York Yankees after Hank hit .393, with three home runs and seven RBIs. They remembered how Milwaukee, the rest of the state, and Cheeseheads everywhere were into all things Braves and Henry Louis Aaron.

Well, such was the case until news leaked during the next decade that the 1965 season would be the Braves' last in Milwaukee. Team officials used waning attendance during the early 1960s as an excuse for their leaving, but this was more about ownership anticipating bigger paydays in the South, which was virgin territory for Major League Baseball at the time.

Bud Selig was among those bitter over the entire situation as a native Milwaukeean who owned a car dealership in town. He cherished the Braves as much as anybody. He even befriended Hank along the way. When the Braves left for Atlanta, Selig worked with other local leaders to get another major league team to replace the Braves and he accomplished his goal while becoming its owner. The truth was that nobody could replace the Braves—not in the souls of Milwaukeeans, but they got the Brewers anyway.

They also got something else.

Less than seven months after the Cheeseheads reminisced about the glory days of the Milwaukee Braves as they watched Henry Louis Aaron seal his baseball legacy in Georgia instead of Wisconsin on April 8, 1974 with his 715th career home run, they got Hank back.

Sort of.

This was the 41-year-old Hank without the quick wrist and slim belly. He finished 1974 hitting 20 fewer home runs than he did the previous season, and his batting average dropped to .268, which was 37 points below what would become his lifetime average. Nevertheless, the Braves honored Hank's request to finish his career in Milwaukee. He did so in 1975 and 1976 with the Brewers owned by old pal Selig, who helped engineer the whole thing.

Decades later, Hank shared a couple of things with me that weren't known to the public about the close of his Braves career during the fall of 1974. They were things that remained secrets among the masses through his death. First, he could have joined another team back then instead of the Milwaukee Brewers: the Boston Red Sox. Second, he would have retired as a player after the 1974 season with the Braves but only if they gave him the front-office job he wanted. The Braves didn't.

"When you decided to leave the Braves after breaking Babe Ruth's record, it was kind of an amicable thing, I guess, where you wanted to end it with the Brewers," I asked Hank over the phone during the summer of 2012. "Or were there any bad feelings on your part when you left the Braves?"

"What happened in my case, I was ready to retire. That's No. 1. There was no hee-hawing, nothing about it. I was ready to go. Either I could get the job I wanted here [with the Braves], or if I couldn't… that was the only thing I was willing to do [to stay in Atlanta after breaking Ruth's record]. I wanted to have a job [and not play]. There was a description of what I wanted to do [to join the Braves' front office after the 1974 season]. I didn't want to be at a place where somebody would say, 'Well, you go here,' and I was told by somebody and I don't care to call the name, [and they said] well, 'Hey. Hank, you will be able to look at all the paper that comes across my desk.' Well, hell. I don't want to look at somebody's paper across their desk," Hank said before getting both of us to laugh. "That was something I didn't want to do. So, I had the opportunity to go to two, three different clubs. Red Sox was one because, I guess, [the Braves] started in Boston. And I had a chance to go back [to Milwaukee with] the Brewers and I chose the Brewers because I felt like if I went back to Milwaukee, I would have nothing to prove. I had played there in Milwaukee for a long time, and Milwaukee fans were always good to me, and I just always felt like if I had the opportunity, that's where I wanted to finish my career. But there was no animosity between me and the Braves. When I left here, I left here, and that was the end of it. It was all over with. I played here for how many years. They paid me. I was treated well, and that was the end of it, you know? I wasn't looking for anything.

"Of course, Bud Selig and I, along with people from the Miller Brewing Company, met here in Atlanta for three-and-a-half hours, my wife…and Bud wanted me to come back to Milwaukee and finish my career there. I said, 'Thank you. I will.' But I looked him dead in the eyes, and I said, 'Bud, you're not getting the same ballplayer that left Milwaukee.' He said, 'I understand.'"

My brothers and I didn't understand. We remembered the old Hank. We also remembered the National League, along with watching great baseball along the Ohio River, and we were destined to see none of those things at Milwaukee County Stadium.

Despite AT&T transferring Dad from Cincinnati to Chicago in August 1971 and then to Milwaukee the following spring, we remained loyal to the Big Red Machine we left behind. In contrast to the Brewers, the Reds were in the National League, the same one that featured the Henry Louis Aaron who intrigued us despite torturing our Cubs when we lived in South Bend and the same one that featured the Henry Louis Aaron who earned our respect through his ability to go from great to greater against our Reds during our Cincinnati stay.

This wasn't *that* Henry Louis Aaron during the 1975 and 1976 seasons at Milwaukee County Stadium, where my brothers and I made frequent trips to the bleachers during the summers. We were sports junkies. We saw the Packers when they played in Milwaukee during the regular season, but we spent more time at the MECCA, the downtown basketball arena. Our family owned partial season tickets to see Abdul-Jabbar and The Big O with the Bucks, and we had others for the entertaining Marquette Warriors who were March Madness threats every year. Although we embraced the Bucks and the Warriors, we had no feelings for the Brewers, an awful team with even worse uniforms, and they played in the American League.

Even so, we went to Brewers games as baseball fans, and those Milwaukee County Stadium brats with the Secret Sauce were awesome, and Bernie Brewer slid into balloons after home runs. Then the Brewers got Hank, but it wasn't Hank. Whoever that was looked more like your father's oldest brother getting amnesia, then stumbling into the Brewers clubhouse, squeezing into the No. 44 of one of their uniforms more suited for a Sunday afternoon softball league game for a keg of beer, and making the starting lineup of a shaky team that was mostly hoping to have enough players to fog up a mirror.

We saw the guy wearing No. 44 for the Brewers receive a standing ovation at Milwaukee County Stadium whenever the public-address person mentioned his name. Still, this was not a good look: Hank Aaron, going from those usually stylish Braves uniforms—showcasing the team's name in cursive with a tasteful mixture of red, white, and navy blue—to boring home Brewers uniforms not worth describing and powder blue road uniforms with mustard socks under the stirrups and eventually something like a hippie's version of a baseball glove on their caps. All of that was a better look for Hank than whatever you saw after he climbed into the batter's box as the Brewers' designated hitter. He finished with 22 home runs during his Milwaukee homecoming, and despite all of the Brewers games my brothers and I attended, we never saw him hit any of them. We cherished Henry Louis Aaron anyway. That's because we still remembered our Hank of Wrigley Field, Crosley Field, and Riverfront Stadium.

JACKIE ROBINSON

As I pushed the tired and aching man farther down the hallway, I saw others in wheelchairs and still others on walkers or canes (but only if they were among the fortunate). And it hit me again. *Rehabilitation center? Nah.* This was a nursing home, especially when I peeked into other rooms to see the tired and aching man was spry and bubbly by comparison. Something kept happening, though. I thought it was a fluke, but after a while, I realized it was a series of miracles. The more I pushed the tired and aching man down the hallway, the more it became apparent the sight of the tired and aching man was the best therapy for everybody, including the tired and aching man.

"Hey, Hank."

"How you doin,' Mr. Aaron?"

"I see ya, I see ya."

"There goes Hammer."

Joy kept replacing sorrow around us, but this wasn't the tired and aching man fulfilling Matthew 11:5, which says, "The blind receive their sight, and the lame walk, the lepers are cleansed, and the deaf hear, the dead are raised up, and the poor have the gospel preached to them." This was Hank 11:5, which says, "I'll just be myself, and The Good Lord willing, that will be enough."

With the Gospel According To Aaron at hand, we steadily moved down the hallway. They smiled, and he smiled bigger than that. They threw a compliment his way about everything you could name—his philanthropy, his business endeavors, his 755 home runs, his ability to look so much better than most folks in a wheelchair despite his tired and aching body—and he usually responded with a Henry Louis Aaron favorite: "Why, thank you. Thank you very much."

Maybe, just maybe, I thought to myself, *maybe we might do this CNN interview after all.* But the hallway remained long, the rain kept pounding, and the phone kept ringing from the producers about goodness knows what. So between asking the tired and aching man, "Is everything okay," I kept pushing while drifting back in my mind to our conversations on his hero, the one whose autobiography was so great the first time I read it in 1973 as a junior in high school that I memorized large passages of its 270 pages. Only the Bible spoke more to my heart. The author was Jack Roosevelt Robinson. Then again, it could have been Henry Louis Aaron, the socially conscious soulmate of Jackie, and I discovered as much the more I evolved into The Hank Aaron Whisperer.

Jackie was the sports legend-turned-American prophet who became more extraordinary with each decade—not only to Hank, but also to me and to anybody else who understood Jackie ranked among the greatest persons in American history. His baseball thing was second to his inspirational thing. Somehow, despite the world kicking and screaming around Jackie after he took the field on April 15, 1947, with the Brooklyn Dodgers to become the first Black player in Major League Baseball history, he walked with dignity. He transformed courage into a man wearing No. 42 as a bull's-eye. Throughout his attacks he followed the instructions of Dodgers general manager Branch Rickey by saying little or nothing, but that was only in the beginning. He spent the rest of his life never uttering anything less than what he thought.

Sounds like Hank.

When Jackie retired as a player after the 1956 season, he spoke even bolder. He became a crusader for baseball to end its unofficial ban against Black executives, managers, and coaches (which never happened on a full-time basis during his lifetime) and he was a staunch advocate for civil rights (which somewhat occurred when the U.S. Congress passed the Civil Rights Act in 1964 and the Voting Rights Act the following year). He also was significantly active in helping those with drug addictions conquer their inner demons since his oldest son, Jackie Jr, spent years suffering from those issues.

Then Jackie died on October 24, 1972, and his autobiography was published four days later. Months afterward, I read it and I kept hearing passages in my head from the Black National Anthem such as, "Out from the gloomy past, 'til now we stand at last, where the white gleam of our bright star is cast." The following also screamed Jackie, Jackie, Jackie: "God of our weary years, God of our silent tears, thou who has brought us thus far on the way. Thou who has by Thy might, led us into the light. Keep us forever in the path, we pray."

Jackie's book expressed those thoughts of hope out of adversity for African Americans, and his words became more dynamic after my first reading of his autobiography led to me returning to those pages many other times. Magic came to mind. In Jackie's book the pixie dust began for me with the opening sentence: "My grandfather was born into slavery and although my mother and father, Mallie and Jerry Robinson, lived during an era when physical slavery had been abolished, they also lived in a newer, more sophisticated kind of slavery than the kind Mr. Lincoln struck down." Then came the how-to passages from Jackie on ways to survive and to prosper as a Black man among racists, both overt and covert, which struck a nerve with me. So did the climactic ending, which made this more noteworthy: the book was told by Jackie to Alfred Duckett only months before Jackie died at 53 from a heart attack.

Well, that was Jackie's official cause of death.

Unofficially, with blindness spreading in a hurry across Jackie's eyes, he succumbed to heart issues, but he also battled diabetes and years of physical and mental stress on and off the baseball diamond. He was every bit of another song called "My Way" long before it left Frank

Sinatra's lips. That's because Jack Roosevelt Robinson went through the bulk of his adulthood doing things his way—wrapped in passion and executed with precision. It was all in Jackie's book. The potency of this work for the ages started with its title, the one that gave me goose bumps whenever I thought about it.

I never had it made.

That title spoke of Jackie, but it also referred to Hank, to me, to my parents, to my brothers, and to other African Americans who went long stretches as The First, The Only, The Tiny Few, or a combination of all three regarding the number of Blacks involved with a White-dominated anything you could name.

In so many ways, Hank Aaron stayed Hank Aaron his entire life, but he also evolved into Jackie Robinson. During the 49 years that Hank lived after Jackie's death on October 24, 1972, fate made it official: they were the same guy.

"Hank, I'll be honest with you," I said during a phone call in April 2016. "I always have mixed emotions whenever Major League Baseball has these Jackie Robinson Days. It's a joke. On the one hand, yeah, it's a great thing for obvious reasons, all of that stuff. On the other hand, it's like they're trying to get away with not having hardly any African American players anymore. I mean now less than 8 percent of the players are African Americans, and it keeps dropping every year. What do you think Jackie would say about these baseball folks giving him this day? Seems like they're just pretending they want more African American players."

"I think that Jackie would think that the whole system, particularly baseball, is going backward," Hank said. "In a lot of ways, we're not making the progress that he would have thought we should be making. I think he would think that baseball isn't doing what it's supposed to do."

"Do you think Jackie would have been as actively involved with baseball as he was before his death? Or do you think he would have gotten to the point where he would have just said, 'It's kind of beyond hope at this point' because, I mean, this is pretty depressing."

"Yeah, it's embarrassing, really. It's hard to watch what's happening, and I think about it all the time. But to answer your question, Jackie would have been actively involved, trying to get to the bottom of it."

Hank spent much of the nearly 50 years after Jackie's death as baseball's loudest and most famous critic, which made sense. Jackie would have been Hank because Hank was Jackie, and Jackie was Hank, and Hank was obsessed with making Major League Baseball squirm over its 21st century epidemic of teams having fewer African American players on their rosters than that of the Brooklyn Dodgers on April 15, 1947.

You needn't go further than the Braves of Atlanta—the home of Dr. Martin Luther King Jr., the cradle of the civil rights movement, and the capital of the New South, featuring Historically Black Colleges of national acclaim to complement a massive and thriving African American population filled with sports fans. They once hugged the Braves of Hank Aaron, Dusty Baker, and Ralph Garr from the late 1960s through the early 1970s and of Chris Chambliss, Claudell Washington, and Bob Watson in the 1980s and of David Justice, Terry Pendleton, and Fred McGriff during the 1990s. All of those names were among the slew of prominent Black players on Braves teams after the franchise helped Atlanta advance faster than its southern counterparts in race relations by moving to town from Milwaukee, following the 1965 season. "When the Braves came here, it was more than just sports. It was the start of a movement. It was the first time you had Blacks and Whites mixed together in a significant way in Atlanta all sitting together at the ballpark, all cheering for Hank Aaron, a Black man," Andrew Young, the Dr. King lieutenant who became U.S. ambassador to the United Nations, a U.S. congressman, and Atlanta's second Black mayor, told me.

That same Atlanta saw its Major League Baseball team play more than a few seasons before Hank's death with zero African Americans. Just the thought infuriated Henry Louis Aaron—whether it involved his modern-day Braves or one of the other 29 major league teams, operating as if April 15, 1947, never happened.

In the spring of 1982, when I worked for the *San Francisco Examiner*, it was the 35th anniversary of Jackie breaking baseball's color barrier, and I did a week-long series of stories on the state of Blacks in baseball. The series exploded across the nation. According to my research, the numbers were dropping rapidly for African Americans on the field (with help from something sinister in Major League Baseball), and those numbers were virtually non-existent off the field, where Hank was the only Black front-office person in the game as the Braves' director of player personnel.

During my research for that series, Hank and I spoke for the first time through a series of long-distance phone conversations. Even then, he fretted over the start of what would become a significant decline of African American players in the game and he knew it only would accelerate. Much of what Hank told me in 1982 about the future of Blacks in baseball was what he continued to say forever. He just updated his fears along the way. In September of 2016 during a phone conversation, he told me: "Terence, I know you and I have talked about this many, many, many times about what's going on, what's really happening with baseball when it comes to Blacks in the game and about what I think is going on. Remember that? Remember what I told you a few years ago?"

I do, indeed.

After each of the many times during my years as The Hank Aaron Whisperer in which an inferior or recycled White managerial candidate was hired over a qualified African American one, and after each of the many times something similar occurred regarding a front office or a coaching position, and after each of the many times baseball had another huge dip of African American players on major league rosters, I remembered this: Hank told me to avoid the mind games from others. Instead, he channeled his inner Jack Roosevelt Robinson, and he did so by using me as The Hank Aaron Whisperer to deliver his message to the masses on how to handle Major League Baseball's mind games of the moment over something involving African Americans. They were pedestrian mind games. They were only slightly better than the ones Martha used to play during the 1960s by dangling that key in Mom's face at the Associates offices in Cincinnati, Ohio.

Baseball officials saved some of their best mind games for trying to explain the imploding number of African Americans on team roster.

• They'd rather play football or basketball.

• Given the emphasis now on travel leagues and the equipment and the other costs involved with youth baseball these days, the sport is just too expensive for the average African American family.

• We'd love to have African American players, but you know what? We just can't find them anymore.

Yeah, well, regarding the reasons for the game's rapid decline in African American players in recent decades, my 1982 "Blacks in baseball" series for the *San Francisco Examiner* told a different story. It was a prophetic one, and Hank knew what I uncovered in the series since he contributed to the revelations way back then. So much for baseball's 21st century mind games.

There also were baseball's Hank-directed mind games in 1999. During an awkward try by major league officials to muzzle the new Jackie, who was becoming increasingly more vocal as a critic of the game he loved over its treatment of African Americans—I knew since the new Jackie usually contacted me at *The Atlanta Journal-Constitution* to deliver his powerfully blunt messages—those major league officials concocted this plan. Hank was way ahead of them though. So much for baseball's 21st century mind games. So he kept nodding to stifle a giggle whenever major league officials told him they would spend the 1999 season celebrating the 25th anniversary of his record-breaking

715th home run. They suggested they would do more than just bake their supposedly "Dear Mr. Aaron," another birthday cake the size of old Atlanta-Fulton County Stadium, which actually happened. Around Aaron's birthday, major league officials joined others to bring a who's who crowd (and that gigantic cake) to downtown Atlanta to honor Hank turning 65. Then-president Bill Clinton was there at the Hyatt Regency. The same went for country music legend Charley Pride, along with former Hank teammates Phil Niekro, Sonny Jackson, and others. Sammy Sosa was among baseball's stars of the present in the crowd, and Ernie Banks was among Major League Baseball's stars of the past.

I was there, too. "After all these many years, going back to when I was basically boycotted by teams for being outspoken about baseball's pitiful record hiring minorities, they're finally doing this," Hank said, telling me that spring of 1999 from his office at Turner Field about major league officials informing him of their plans to celebrate 715. He mentioned that previous recognition by folks in the game regarding his record-breaking home run had been sparse or non-existent. "They're just feeling guilty from all those years that should have been mine."

Then there was this: several weeks after Hank's birthday bash, Major League Baseball announced that each of its 30 teams would hold a ceremony during the season in Hank's honor.

That never happened. "I haven't heard from Cincinnati, the New York Yankees, the Cubs, or the White Sox," Hank told me in mid-September with only two weeks left in baseball's 1999 regular season. "No Philadelphia, no California Angels, and you know the Dodgers aren't involved with this. They're the worst when it comes to minorities. None of this surprises me because in this regard baseball always makes a few steps forward and several steps backward."

Hank spoke in a ho-hum tone during that part of our conversation because he knew what this "celebration" involved from the start. This was an attempted bribe by Major League Baseball officials, but it blew up in their faces because Jackie was Hank, and Hank was Jackie, and

Hank gathered a group of minorities together that summer of 1999 to meet in Milwaukee with then-baseball commissioner Bud Selig, Hank's pal from his Wisconsin days with the old Milwaukee Braves of the early 1950s through mid-1960s.

With Selig across the way in his Milwaukee office, where he ran baseball's affairs from his hometown, Hank and his guests discussed one of baseball's worst blights, which was having Hank as its only African American executive at the team level. They discussed the lack of Black general managers. They discussed the 42 managerial changes since 1992 up to that point and that Tony Perez of the Cincinnati Reds and Jerry Manuel of the Chicago White Sox were the only minority hires. They discussed Len Coleman announcing he was leaving his post at the end of the year as baseball's highest-ranking Black official as National League president, and even if Coleman stayed around, Hank suggested to Selig that the Queen of England would have more power regarding baseball decisions than Coleman.

Aaron chuckled, then he continued to tell me in September 1999, "Bud's trying, but what happens is that the people who run these teams will tell you one thing, and then they'll head back to their country clubs. [They] laugh to all their buddies while getting a back rub, [saying], 'They can't tell us what to do.' People in baseball can say they're going to do this and that, but when will they do it?"

Sounded like Jackie. Fate demanded nothing less.

Fate set in motion this Hank-Jackie alliance by starting with Jackie, who was Rosa Parks more than a decade before she refused to move to the back of a city bus in Montgomery, Alabama. While Parks' stance occurred on December 1, 1955, U.S. Army lieutenant Jack Roosevelt Robinson kept ignoring the commands of a bus driver on July 6, 1944, in Waco, Texas, to scoot from the front to the rear of that vehicle at Camp Hood. Jackie received a court-martial.

Three years later Jackie became that only Black face in a mass of whiteness on the field of any Major League Baseball ballpark. The whole planet studied his every move, while he tried to hit, field, and run against professional players despite death threats and racist messages.

Sounded like Hank.

Jackie eventually spent his decade with the Dodgers through 1956, never wavering from his convictions, and he had many of them. "I was 26 [as a rookie with the Dodgers]," Robinson wrote in his autobiography, "and all my life back to the age of eight when a little neighbor girl called me a n----r, I had believed in payback, retaliation. The most luxurious possession, the richest treasure anybody has, is his personal dignity."

Sounded like Hank.

When Jackie retired from the Brooklyn Dodgers after the 1956 season, Henry Louis Aaron had an entire career remaining since that was just his third year in the major leagues. Jackie's mission was to spend the rest of his post-playing existence as a noisy advocate for everything from civil rights to ending baseball's resistance to having Blacks do more than just take the field. He kept speaking truth for his time from the late 1940s through his death in October 1972, and Hank watched, studied, and admired; then he remembered and he applied.

Hank was the only one. Literally. Although the power of Jackie's memory always kept Hank leaning toward courage, other prominent African American baseball players from the 1950s and 1960s preferred cowardice. Like Hank, they had a choice involving Jack Roosevelt Robinson: they could show they loved Jackie by living and touting his principles—even beyond their playing careers—or they could do what they did, which is they decided to keep their mouths shut over the injustices against African Americans everywhere inside and outside of baseball for fear of White America labeling them as radical or worse.

Fate engineered this. Hank broke Babe Ruth's record nearly 27 years to the day Robinson shredded baseball's color barrier on April 15, 1947 with the Dodgers.

Fate also made the two most significant Black men in baseball history share a room together 11 months after Jackie's debut in the major leagues. Actually, fate did more than that. Fate made one of those Black men idolize the other. That's why during this chance meeting that really wasn't due to fate, the idol (Jack Roosevelt Robinson) hadn't a clue his worshiper (Henry Louis Aaron) was a worshiper or even that his worshiper sat a hook slide away. The worshiper remembered everything.

When Jackie visited Hank's hometown of Mobile, Alabama, in March 1948, Jackie was 29, married with a baby boy, and 15 years older than his worshipper, who was a skinny 14-year-old teenager whose biggest thrill up to that point was joining the Boy Scouts of America. "Well, of course back then, my parents expected me to go to school, and I had read about how Jackie Robinson and the Dodgers were going to play an exhibition game in Mobile, and Jackie was speaking, I believe, at a drugstore," Hank told me during the spring of 2014 as joy spread across his face. Through each word, he raced further back in his mind to the poor yet loving home of Herbert and Estella Aaron as one of their eight children. Everything was tranquil, and before reading the news about his idol, the worshiper prepared for another typical time on the other side of the tracks in the farthest part of the South.

During summers, weekends, and evenings without homework or chores, Hank played sandlot baseball, but he looked clueless to those into fundamentals. He was a cross-handed hitter. Due to his family's budget (which often was no budget), he used sticks as bats and bottle caps as balls. None of that factored into this moment because this was a weekday during the spring, and Hank's usual destination that time of morning involved Central High School and thinking about reading, writing, and arithmetic.

This time Hank was thinking about Jackie, Jackie, and Jackie. "As I was leaving the house, I said, 'Now I'm not going to have this opportunity again,' so I said, 'I better take my chances on listening to Jackie Robinson now,'" Hank told me before he laughed his laugh, the one that surged with energy from the bottom of his soul into the hearts of those nearby. "I got a front-row seat, but listen to this." Hank laughed again and then he said, "Next to me on the front row was my father, but it was worth it. I don't need to tell you what happened when I got home after that, and it really was worth it by doing that. Yeah, Jackie was my hero. He always has been and not only because of the baseball he played but simply because of the person he was."

Sounded like Hank. Then again, Jackie was Hank, and Hank was Jackie, and they both spent large chunks of their baseball careers prospering despite those death threats and racist slurs. They both handled adversity with dignity. They both spoke loudly and boldly about discriminatory practices, not only in baseball, but also around the world. They both were told by "friends" to keep quiet, especially when they drifted toward social issues and politics. They both responded by covering their ears, but they both kept doing what they were doing and they both did so more loudly and boldly than before.

Finally, when Hank and Jackie passed the seventh-inning stretch of their lives, they both saw their critics get amnesia and treat them as if they were cherished by everybody from the first through their sixth inning. Neither Jackie nor Hank was that person. They weren't cherished forever by a lot of folks—let alone everybody—but when it came to that and their fake lifetime admirers, who surfaced when they both were gray and wobbly and declared harmless by those who otherwise viewed those ungrateful (or worse) Black guys as dangerous in their younger and vibrant years, neither Jackie nor Hank could care less.

They did it their way, and it was striking. Hank was Jackie, and Jackie was Hank. Even so, given the 15-year age difference between idol and worshiper and given that Hank sought to mimic Jackie's ways in nearly every way, Hank always knew as an adult through studying Jackie's life what was coming during the next half generation of his life.

As for Jackie the player, Hank admired Jackie's ability to combine the psychological with the physical to steal home—even when the pitcher, the opposing players, and everybody else in the ballpark knew he was charging toward the plate without stopping on that pitch. As for Jackie the citizen, Hank became more captivated because he saw Jackie remain Jackie after he made the transformation into a silver-haired lightning rod for criticism when he sprinted from dugouts to politics.

That all led to Hank, Jackie, fate, and the pregame ceremony before Game Two of the World Series between the Reds and the Oakland A's in Cincinnati on Sunday, October 15, 1972. More importantly, that combination pushed Hank closer to becoming Jackie, and it caused destiny to work with fate to keep me evolving into The Hank Aaron Whisperer.

It began with Jackie and politics. Two years after Jackie retired following the 1956 season, Hank saw Jackie anger many Whites over his letter to Dwight Eisenhower, in which Jackie told the Republican president and former supreme allied commander during World War II: "As the chief executive of our nation, I respectfully suggest that you unwittingly crush the spirit of freedom in Negroes by constantly urging forbearance and give hope to those pro-segregation leaders like Governor Faubus who would take from us even those freedoms we now enjoy."

Then Hank saw Jackie anger many Blacks, when Jackie supported Eisenhower's vice president, Richard Nixon, against Democratic candidate John F. Kennedy during the 1960 presidential campaign. Just like Hank, Jackie didn't make his decisions by licking a finger before sticking it toward the wind. Just like Hank, Jackie researched like crazy before he delivered his opinions on the big stuff and Jackie figured Nixon would support the civil rights movement more than Kennedy, a relatively unknown national figure who Jackie viewed as an out-of-touch elitist from back East. He also disliked JFK's habit of looking away from those speaking to him. Jackie said in his autobiography, "I did write him a note advising him to look people in the eye."

All of Jackie's niceties toward Nixon stopped after Dr. Martin Luther King Jr. was arrested on October 19, 1960, weeks before the election. Dr. King was charged with joining 51 others in refusing to leave their seats at the lunch counter of a segregated Atlanta department store. Given the viciousness of the South back then, King, as the nation's civil rights leader and the most recognizable Black man in America (or uppity N to those in the Jim Crow judicial system), was slated for months of hard labor in a Georgia prison.

Jackie pleaded with Nixon and his handlers to get King out of jail. Jackie even gave them the phone number to the place. The Nixon folks wouldn't budge, but those around Kennedy did. They freed King through their connections, and Kennedy slipped into the White House with help from African American voters who remembered his response to the King situation. Jackie fumed over Nixon's snub of King. Even though Jackie was a Black Republican, he cherished King and he joined the March on Washington in 1963 while also huddling with King on other civil rights matters.

Hank followed the drama from afar involving Jackie, Nixon, and King. And after Jackie had a second consecutive falling out with a Republican presidential candidate (far-right winger Barry Goldwater in 1964), Hank saw Jackie spend the 1968 presidential campaign working in the camp of Hubert Humphrey, the Democratic vice president running for the highest office. The Republican candidate in 1968 was Nixon. By then, Jackie had gone from fan to foe of the guy who would become the 37th U.S. president over Humphrey. That tied into Hank,

Jackie, fate, and the pregame ceremony before Game Two of the World Series on October 15, 1972. Courtesy of President Nixon and the cluelessness of Major League Baseball officials, the ceremony was a disaster for just about everybody not named Jack Roosevelt Robinson.

The disaster began days before the ceremony, when Jackie received a call about throwing out the first pitch for that Game Two of the World Series from Major League Baseball commissioner Bowie Kuhn, a lawyer by trade and a lousy person at race relations. I have my personal Kuhn stories, but I'll defer for the moment to Thursday, April 4, 1974, when Hank was Jackie, and Jackie was Hank, and when one of Hank's Kuhn stories involved another baseball game in Cincinnati. This time it didn't occur around the World Series. It was during Hank's pursuit of Babe Ruth's career home run record. It was Opening Day in Cincinnati for the Reds and the entire 1974 Major League Baseball season, and even beyond the Hank situation, Opening Days were unofficial holidays in Cincinnati, home of baseball's first professional team in 1869. That brings me to my Destiny, Part I regarding that Jackie 1972 World Series situation. I became a die-hard fan in 1968 of the fabled Big Red Machine after AT&T transferred Dad and the rest of my family from South Bend, Indiana, to that rabid town for Skyline Chili and everything baseball.

Due to another AT&T transfer, we lived in Milwaukee for Cincinnati's 1974 Opening Day, but I listened through WLW on my radio. That was Destiny, Part II regarding that Jackie 1972 situation. The Atlanta Braves were visiting Riverfront Stadium, and Henry Louis Aaron was just a swing away from tying Babe Ruth's 714 for lifetime homers. The moment happened after Hank flicked his famous wrists against Reds pitcher Jack Billingham in the top of the first inning, and within seconds The Hammer and The Babe were one in the record books as the ball dropped over the left-field wall.

"Hey, Hank," I said during a phone call in the summer of 2004.

"Hey, Terence, how you doing?" Hank asked while laughing.

"Oh, pretty good."

"Well, I'm kind of busy, but you know I always can talk to you for a little while. If I have to leave, then you just call me back, and we'll talk longer."

"Okay, that's fine, but I just had a quick one for you: it looks like Barry Bonds could do the home run record thing on the road at some point. I was curious: back when you were going for the Babe Ruth record, was there any concern in your mind that you would hit [No. 715] on the road instead of at home. Did you have a preference?"

"Well, I did at the time because mine was a little different than his. The commissioner was so involved. Everybody else was so involved. So I thought I wanted to do it in Atlanta."

"And I guess as you got closer to the record, at what point did you say to yourself, 'I'm definitely going to do it at home instead of the road?' Or did you have a feel one way or the other?"

"I had no feelings really. I had no control over that because my motto was to do the very best that I could do at all times. But I was hoping it would work out, and it did work out that way, where I did do it at home."

"Right, right. Then, of course in Cincinnati, when you hit 714 in Cincinnati, did you think at that time you probably would hit another one in Cincinnati, or was that still something that was kind of unknown in your mind?"

"I never thought about hitting the first one. But it's like everything else. Once you get to the plate, everything is a chance. You know?"

"And I guess the other thing is, did you ever think to yourself, *If I hit it on the road, I might have trouble with fans* or anything like that?"

"I never thought about it really. In fact, after I tied the record on the road [in Cincinnati], the fans were as jubilant as they were as if I hit it in Atlanta. So, all the things I was receiving [as far as racist letters and death threats], I also had thousands of people that were on my side. So I never thought about that. I just thought all the things I was working against at that point was strictly from the standpoint of newspaper people just writing false remarks. They were just saying some false things."

"And you know that's kind of a parallel to what you're going through and what's happening to Bonds. It looks like the fans are kind of turning toward him. You know, he just got elected to the All-Star Game. It's almost like the fans are saying now, 'Well, now that you're getting close to the record, we're going to support you a little bit.' It's almost like the same way with you. When you were getting close to the record, like you said, the fans in Cincinnati, which is a very conservative town, they were becoming more supportive, too. Not just in Cincinnati, but maybe in America in general."

"Uh huh. Well…you may be right about that. I think that generally that's true."

"Do you think that when you're going for a record like that and you're on the road, do you take any extra precautions at all for safety? Or did any of that enter into your mind that, *Man, I might have to protect myself* and run in the dugout or do something along those lines?"

"I'm sure [Bonds'] protection is coming from the commissioner—as [my protection] was—and also the city. The Braves. I had protection on the road and everywhere else. Not only that, but my kids also had protection. But you know, I always thought the safest place for me—no matter what else was going on—was on the baseball field. I always felt very protected, as if there was nothing ever was going to happen to me. I felt very protected."

"So I guess the scariest time would be going to the ballpark or being at the hotel, something like that."

"Well, in some ways. But you never know about somebody being just an outright nut and do something to you, no matter where you are. And most times they probably can't get down to the baseball field. But when you're just walking around somewhere, going from your house to the car or from your car to the grocery store—anywhere—you never know what somebody might do. You always have some nut in the crowd who wants to make headlines. The president, all these guys, they ain't got people following all around them for no reason," he said, laughing.

"So, when you were going for the record, did you ever have anybody away from the baseball park. Did you ever have anybody come up to you on the street and say anything derogatory or threatening?"

"Oh, I had some folks in Chicago say something when I was getting on the bus. It's been so long, but they did walk up to me on the bus and say something. But here again, I was in safe heaven because I had a lot of friends," Hank said, laughing. "And they didn't have a chance. I don't know what they said, but they did say something derogatory. They didn't tell me exactly what it was."

"What city are you in, by the way?"

"I'm in West Palm Beach, Florida, having breakfast with some friends of mine and getting ready to go back to the house, and about 4:00, I'm going to play some golf."

"You can't beat that now."

"It is hot. It is hot," he said, laughing.

"I'll let you finish breakfast and cool off," I said, laughing. "Talk to you later."

"Okay, Terence," he said. "Bye-bye."

After Hank pulled even with The Babe in Cincinnati, the next day was an off day for the Reds and the Braves during what was a three-game series, and Braves manager Eddie Mathews wanted to rest Hank for the final two games on Saturday and Sunday. Eddie and Hank played well together as future Baseball Hall of Fame teammates for that same Braves franchise in Milwaukee and in Atlanta. Even as Braves manager, Eddie didn't make Hank decisions without Hank approving, and neither Hank nor Eddie had issues with the Braves officials wanting to save Hank and the record for their home opener that Monday night on national television against the Los Angeles Dodgers.

The truth was if Hank's chase of the record went a few games beyond that Monday night, Braves officials would have dropped to their knees in praise of the baseball gods. They needed bigger home crowds. Since the franchise's eight-year-old move from Wisconsin, sellouts had been rare in Georgia. Braves officials knew ongoing local headlines of "Hammer Close to Passing Babe" would keep producing stuffed houses at Atlanta-Fulton County Stadium, but Kuhn wasn't amused. That off day, he reminded the Braves of his warning to team decision makers during spring training. Back then, he told them they had to play a healthy Hank Aaron against the Reds throughout the three-game series or he said they would face "serious consequences."

To make sure the commissioner wasn't bluffing, Mathews wrote Aaron's name on the Braves lineup card for Sunday's game, but it didn't matter. Hank went homerless during that series finale in Cincinnati, and there was a made-for-Hollywood script on Monday night from Dixie. When the Braves returned home, the whole world was watching, at least those tuned to NBC's *Monday Night Baseball*. From our Milwaukee kitchen, my family joined the viewing masses. Pearl Bailey sang the national anthem, and Sammy Davis cheered in the packed stands of 53,775 people with then-Georgia governor and future U.S. president Jimmy Carter. Other celebrities. Other politicians. Other baseball personalities. Everybody was there inside of Atlanta-Fulton County Stadium in anticipation of catching Hank's moment.

Everybody but Kuhn.

The commissioner said he couldn't get out of his previously scheduled meeting in Cleveland, Ohio, that night with the Wahoo Club of the Indians. I don't recall speaking to Hank about Kuhn's preference for making sure fans in one of the least-consequential baseball cities in America back then were satisfied with his appearance as opposed to attending what became one of the two most consequential moments in baseball history.

The other? Yep, Jackie's debut with the Dodgers.

Hank and I did speak often about two of my three personal Kuhn stories, including the one that caused Hank to laugh for just shy of an eternity. During the early 1980s, I covered the Giants for the *San Francisco Examiner*, where I continued my lifetime as ranking as The

First, The Only, or The Few as an African American doing anything in the media. I was the *Examiner's* first full-time Black sports reporter. Not only that, but when the newspaper sent me to the cover my first World Series in 1980, Larry Whiteside of *The Boston Globe* was the only other Black writer there. It figured. We went the longest time as the only two Black reporters in the country covering a Major League Baseball team as a beat for a major metropolitan newspaper. In other words, I stood out in the press box.

That brings me to Destiny, Part III regarding that Jackie 1972 situation. During the summer of 1981, newspapers remained kings of the media, especially in the Bay Area. Along with the *Examiner*, the other dailies sent their San Francisco Giants beat writers to every home game, and there were frequent appearances by general columnists and feature writers. Electronic media members were regulars, too. On this typically crisp night for a Giants home game, it seemed everybody with the ability to get a media credential in northern California was there at Candlestick Park, when one of the Giants public-relations persons stood in the middle of the press box to say, "Commissioner Bowie Kuhn is in the suite next door and he'd like to greet the media between innings in a receiving line."

Most folks responded, including me.

Technically, Kuhn and I had met five years before but only through radio. While home in Milwaukee for summer break from college at Miami (Ohio) University, I heard Kuhn was a telephone guest that night on my favorite sports talk radio show in town and I got through for a question. It involved the 1976 All-Star Game, sitting a couple of weeks away, and Cesar Geronimo from my Big Red Machine wasn't on the ballot. In addition to patrolling center field in his Gold Glove style, Cesar sizzled at the plate. *Why wasn't he on the ballot?* The commissioner gave me mostly an "I feel your pain" answer before he added at the end of his words of nothingness, "You've got to have a system, and that's just the way the system works."

When I spoke to *that* Bowie Kuhn, he couldn't tell over the radio airways if I was the color of The Hammer or The Babe. As I edged closer to *this* Bowie Kuhn in the distance of a suite at Candlestick Park, I saw his routine. He shook the hand of the media person, then he delivered a phrase or two with a smile, and then he looked toward the next person heading his way. Everybody in line was White. Well, except for one.

When Kuhn got to me, he said, "Good to see you" and then he switched from the conventional handshake he used for everybody else to a soul brother-like maneuver he maybe discovered through watching clips of a *Super Fly* movie. While he shook my hand for the longest time with what he thought was a cool grip for a young Black guy, he kept nodding and flashing that look Blacks often get from Whites that supposedly says, "I understand." Then he gave me a few pats on the shoulder as I moved along.

That handshake thing.

That Wahoo Club thing.

That Hank 714 thing.

Those things came after the Jackie Robinson disaster of a thing for Major League Baseball that was the pregame ceremony before Game Two of the 1972 World Series in Cincinnati.

Still, those things put into perspective what happened back then. During early October 1972, Jack Roosevelt Robinson watched Kuhn deliver the commissioner's version of a soul brother handshake to him through words, when Kuhn asked Jackie to throw out the first pitch before Game Two. Jackie declined, but he didn't do so without an explanation. Since Hank was Jackie, and Jackie was Hank, Jackie told Kuhn that he wouldn't feel comfortable doing anything with the World Series or Major League Baseball since he planned to keep ripping the game as much as possible over its hiring (or non-hiring) practices regarding African Americans.

Baseball's racial history remained shameful. Stretching from the time the National League became the first of baseball's two major leagues in 1876 through that moment Kuhn tried to end Jackie's sour attitude toward the game by using the sweet talk of a phony gesture of having the mouthy African American throw out the first pitch before a World Series game, there never had been a Black manager. There never had been a Black third-base coach, which often was the spot back then that led to managerial jobs. There also never had been a position in a major league front office for any African American, including for a former Black player with considerable baseball and people skills such as Henry Louis Aaron.

Fate took over again for Jackie and Hank. While Kuhn tried and failed to play mind games with Jackie through that first-pitch offer, Hank remained two seasons from catching and exorcising Ruth's ghost. Two years after that, when Hank retired from playing the game in October 1976 with the Milwaukee Brewers, he nearly became the Jackie Robinson of baseball front offices as a Braves executive. I wrote "nearly" because a few weeks before the end of Hank's last season as a player, Braves owner Ted Turner hired Bill Lucas as the game's first African American general manager. Lucas was Aaron's brother-in-law, and after slightly less than three years on the job, Lucas died in May 1979 at 43 of a heart attack and a cerebral hemorrhage. That left Hank during the spring of 1979 as baseball's highest (and only) ranking Black person in baseball for a while.

Nothing about Hank's future role with the Braves was conceivable in October 1972, when Jackie declined Kuhn's offer about that first pitch, but the commissioner wouldn't give up. He countered by telling the constant thorn in baseball's side, "What if I told you we're working on those issues?"

Before long, Jackie nodded, but he didn't walk away saying, "When it comes to soul brothers, this Bowie Kuhn guy isn't so bad after all."

Jackie was setting up Kuhn, along with baseball. The only thing the world saw in the beginning before Game Two was Jackie reversing himself by spending that sun-splattered afternoon in Cincinnati throwing out the first pitch. There also was that other Jackie moment. Kuhn sought to muzzle Jackie forever regarding the game's ongoing racism by having baseball turn the pregame session into a celebration of the 25 years since Jackie shattered its color barrier. Before the sellout crowd at Riverfront Stadium of 53,224 fans— mostly nervously distracted (along with me watching at home from Milwaukee) by our heavily favored Big Red Machine dropping the opener in Cincinnati the previous day to an A's team without megastar Reggie Jackson— baseball had an interesting group on the field.

Red Barber served as emcee, which made sense. He began his broadcasting career during the 1930s with the Reds and he sat behind the mic as the Brooklyn Dodgers' play-by-play guy on April 15, 1947, when Jackie left the home dugout at Ebbets Field and walked into history. Members of the late Rickey family were around, which made sense. Rickey signed Jackie for the Dodgers as their general manager and gave baseball's most important rookie ever instructions on how to survive on and off the field through the short run of his career.

Pee Wee Reese was there, which made sense. He was the Dodgers shortstop credited with silencing the racists in this same Cincinnati on May 13, 1947, when the Dodgers played the first game of their second road trip featuring baseball's first and only Black player. In the middle of vicious slurs hurled Jackie's way at first base during the bottom of the first inning, Reese, the southerner from nearby Kentucky, supposedly trotted from his position to place his arm around Jackie to tell the crowd through actions instead of words, "This is my guy, and he should be yours, too."

As for the others present, Dodgers president Peter O'Malley made sense because under patriarch, Walter, his family owned the team during Jackie's debut. Larry Doby made sense as the first Black player in the American League. Joe Black made sense as one of Jackie's former teammates. Chub Feeney made sense as National League president. The presence of Jackie's widow, Rachel, and his other family members and friends made sense.

The following made zero sense. It involved Kuhn strolling to the stand-up mic on the artificial turf at Riverfront Stadium, where he prepared to do his version of attending the Wahoo Club in Cleveland on April 8, 1974 or delivering a strange-looking handshake to a young African American. As millions watched on the NBC telecast, along with the suddenly attentive folks in the ballpark, the commissioner said, "Jackie Robinson is something special, special as an athlete, special as a husband and father, special as a human being."

That was all good and accurate. A few seconds later, Kuhn said, "As most of you know, President Nixon…"

Wait. What?

The same President Nixon who Jackie disowned 12 years before? The same President Nixon, who as vice president and running for the Oval Office for the first of his two times, ignored Jackie's pleading in October 1960 to pick up the phone and help King Jr. get out of an Atlanta jail along the way to a Georgia prison? The same President Nixon that everybody with eyes and ears knew Jackie Robinson couldn't stand? Kuhn continued to say that same President Nixon "named Jackie to his all-time All-Star Baseball Team."

Who cared? Jackie certainly didn't.

Kuhn kept suggesting through his speech that Nixon wouldn't mind anointing Jackie as Czar of the Earth someday. It included the commissioner saying he was requested by the commander in chief to read a telegram: "It is especially fitting that today in the midst of baseball's most exciting event, the World Series, we pause to honor Jackie Robinson." Jackie kept his head down, presumably trying not to clench his teeth before the cameras, as he studied nothing in particular on the ground.

Nixon? This was so tone deaf, so Bowie Kuhn, so baseball.

After the commissioner spent all that time pleading with Jack Roosevelt Robinson to throw out the first pitch before Game Two, Jackie agreed and he opted to participate during this ceremony supposedly in his honor, but Jackie knew the truth: this mostly was baseball officials trying to fool the public into thinking, *Look what they're doing for Jackie. Despite their lily-White operations, guess they really do care about Black people.*

The commissioner made the ceremony more awkward when he gave Jackie a symbolic trophy for whatever reason, but the worst of the worst involved Kuhn delivering his huge PR platform on national television to Nixon four months after reports surfaced of a political scandal at some place called Watergate. If that wasn't awful enough, "Tricky Dick" ranked among Jackie's least favorite persons in the solar system. All that did was make Jackie's final words in public even more powerful for the ages. After Kuhn finished embarrassing himself by relaying almost three minutes of Nixon propaganda, Jackie spoke next.

He needed just 63 seconds. The last 10 mattered the most. He thanked Reese, the Rickey folks, and then his family. After a few generalities about the Dodgers and baseball, he said the words that struck his listeners the most, especially Henry Louis Aaron. What followed was Jackie setting up Kuhn and baseball. What followed was the foundation for Jackie as Hank and Hank as Jackie.

So, even though Kuhn, other baseball people, Nixon, and much of White America expected to hear The Good Jackie—the one, in their minds, who always kept his head bowed and his mouth zipped when folks hurled insults his way for having the audacity to try to play Major League Baseball while Black—The Bad Jackie took the unofficial stage. The Bad Jackie was the one in their minds who wouldn't make them feel good about themselves. The Bad Jackie was the one who would accept their mostly insincere apologies by agreeing to do something such as throw out the first pitch of a World Series game but then continue to use every chance he got to expose the racism not only in baseball, but also throughout society.

The bright rays on the warm autumn day accentuated Robinson's brownish eyes and his famously snowy head. His voice boomed, too, which meant he didn't sound or look like the dying man that he was. Among other ailments, he nearly was blind from the diabetes eating through his body. "I'm extremely proud and pleased to be here this afternoon," Robinson said.

Nevertheless with seemingly the whole universe watching, hanging on every syllable, listening for more of The Good Jackie, Jack Roosevelt Robinson said out of nowhere, "but must admit I'm going to be tremendously more pleased and more proud when I look at that third-base coaching line one day and see a Black face managing in baseball. Thank you very much."

Even though folks didn't drop the mic back then, Jackie basically did just that.

The crowd applauded…politely. Baseball responded by returning to its White business as usual (only with quiet disgust in the shadows over The Bad Jackie sliding spikes high for a final time to deliver a shot to somebody's jaw). Hank also responded, but he did so by pulling those last 10 seconds of Jackie's final speech in public close to his heart and mind. As a result, this was inevitable because it also was fate. Nine days after The Bad Jackie said exactly what everybody needed to hear, which was baseball was going backward 25 years after he brought it forward with his name on a major league lineup card, the inevitable yet unthinkable dominated news reports: Jack Roosevelt Robinson was dead. He was 53, and they said it was a heart attack, but it was so many things, including his struggles as The Bad Jackie.

Of course, thoughts on The Good Jackie dominated the airways and the newsprint on Friday, October 27, 1972, when he was laid to rest at Cypress Hills Cemetery—a couple of pop flies away from Ebbets Field.

His farewell was epic. Before Jackie's mile-long funeral procession crept to his resting place—from Riverside Church in Manhattan through Harlem and then to Brooklyn—more than 2,500 packed the pews to hear the eulogy from Jesse Jackson. "In his last dash, Jackie stole home. Pain, misery, and travail have lost. Jackie is saved," Jesse Jackson said. "His enemies can leave him alone. His body will rest, but his spirit and his mind and his impact are perpetual and as affixed to human progress as are the stars in the heavens, the shine in the sun, and the glow in the moon. This mind, this mission, could not be held down by a grave."

Several of Jackie's former teammates were pallbearers. Reese was among them, and others included Jim Gilliam, Don Newcombe, Ralph Branca, and Joe Black. Joe Louis was in the sanctuary. So were celebrities, ranging from comedian Dick Gregory to fabled television host Ed Sullivan. Among baseball notables, there was Doby along with A's All-Star pitcher Vida Blue and Banks and Willie Mays, among the game's greatest sluggers ever.

And somebody else was there: Henry Louis Aaron.

The Jackie homegoing. The final 10 of his 63 seconds overall in Cincinnati during his last public address. The ability to deliver his thoughts on anything and everything without fear. The love of righteousness. The courage before, during, and after he left the home dugout at Ebbets Field on April 15, 1947. The dignity, always the dignity. The ability to turn a visit to Mobile, Alabama, for an exhibition game into the biggest thrill of a lifetime for a young Black admirer who would become his idol in spirit and soul. After Jackie's casket was lowered into the ground for eternity, Hank kept remembering all things Jack Roosevelt Robinson in an endless loop and then he knew what he had to do.

Hank told me the story. There we were 35 years after Jackie's death, sitting in a private area of the Atlanta Braves' home ballpark of Turner Field during the spring of 2007, and Henry Louis Aaron got emotional recalling how he approached Banks and Mays after Jackie's funeral. "The three of us had a platform to stand on. We needed to voice our opinions," Hank said. "Willie being in New York, Ernie being in Chicago, and me being where I was [Atlanta], we needed to make sure we didn't give our stamp of approval on certain things that were happening."

Hank, like Jackie, had issues with baseball shrugging during the early 1970s over hiring Blacks as team executives, on-field managers, and the frequent manager-in-waiting position of third-base coach. There also was Hank and other prominent Black players of the 1950s and the 1960s discussing something more sinister between themselves: baseball's quota system. Hank and his African American peers joined even non-minorities through the years and decades to believe those who ran baseball monitored and controlled the number of African American players in the major leagues, and none of this was done for benevolent reasons.

Unlike Hank, neither Mays nor Banks was Jackie, and, goodness knows, Jackie wasn't either one of them. All four of those Baseball Hall of Famers preferred it that way. Just as noisy as Mays and Banks were with their bats to make a collective 38 All-Star Game trips while ripping 1,172 home runs between them, well, that was as silent as Mays and Banks were with their mouths on Black issues in baseball and around society, especially if conflict was involved. Unlike Hank and Jackie, Mays was considered harmless by the masses. I mean, he was "The Say Hey Kid," always ranking as the people's choice among all races, colors, and creed even after his playing career in 1973. The same went for Banks. Known as the eternally smiling Mr. Cub, he spent 19 years playing on Chicago's northside through the 1971 season promoting nothing but baseball (instead of civil rights or the need for the game to hire Black executives, managers, and third-base coaches). "Let's play two," Banks used to say, as opposed to "Let's join Hank in making Jackie proud by following in his spike marks."

When Hank revealed his Mays and Banks story from October 1972 in public for the first time during our chat in the spring of 2007, he did so with a couple of thoughts in his mind: little had changed in baseball and in society, and he was willing to fight those battles alone. Hank delivered one of his contagious laughs across the way from me, and then he added his final thought on his plea to Willie and Ernie about carrying on Jackie's legacy. "Quite naturally, those guys decided they weren't going to do it," Hank said. "I decided that, not only do I owe it to myself, but I owe it to Jackie Robinson."

Hank officially became Jackie.

BLACKS IN BASEBALL

As I pushed the tired and aching man farther down the hallway of the nursing home disguised as a rehabilitation center, maneuvering the wheelchair as if I were handling somebody more valuable than a head of state (which I was, since this was Henry Louis Aaron), the accolades for Hank kept coming and so did my calls and texts from CNN. *Are you on your way?*

Not even close, I wanted to respond, while laughing away that question and the follow-up ones. Instead, I didn't respond. As we finally reached the doorway for the trip to the golf club, the tired and aching man looked ready for me to swing the wheelchair around, head back down the hallway, and slide under a comfortable sheet with a fluffy pillow nearby. The rain came faster and harder with no end in sight. The car company sent the best for Henry Louis Aaron.

This time, I would have settled for no more than their fourth- or maybe fifth-best choice. The car service ordered by CNN sent a huge SUV that needed something just shy of a fireman's ladder for the average person to climb from the ground to the seats.

I also had another problem—the driver.

He was an African American male in his mid-40s and when he came around the front of the car to join us from his driver's seat he suffered one of the biggest attacks of stardom I'd ever seen. "Oh, Mr. Aaron. This is such an honor," he said. "I'm your biggest fan and I was born and raised here in Atlanta and I'm just so excited to meet you."

Once again, the tired and aching man in the wheelchair evolved into Hank Aaron again, smiling and nodding before saying, "Why, thank you." Even so, I was not amused, not with that problem of the distance between the sidewalk to the top of the SUV's floor, not with CNN still calling and texting from the golf club, not with the rain falling like crazy, and not with this biggest of Henry Louis Aaron fans failing to do anything to help the situation at hand.

The driver did pop open his massive umbrella for all of us. That was a start.

Between pushing the tired and aching man from his room toward the direction of those waiting CNN cameras, I drifted back to the start of Hank's post-playing career. Hank became Jackie so much that he rarely missed an opportunity as a baseball executive to rip the game for its past and present issues with African Americans both on and off the field. He also blasted major league officials over what he thought was a bleak future for Blacks in the game and he used me as his vehicle for relaying those messages.

Among Hank's pet peeves? It was the insistence of Major League Baseball officials, along with team executives and scouts, that they really did want more African Americans in the game. While forming sad faces, those baseball folks said they couldn't find them, hadn't discovered how to retain them, or believed African American athletes were more interested in football, basketball, and other stuff, or they said the dog ate the homework after somebody forgot to set the alarm clock.

Eight percent. *Eight percent!* On the high side, 8 percent represented the number of African American players in Major League Baseball during most seasons in the 21st century, and franchises often had rosters with zero African American players, including the Atlanta Braves, Hank's team of nearly 70 years as a player and executive. In contrast, when Hank broke Babe Ruth's home run mark on April 8, 1974, the percentage of African Americans in Major League Baseball was three times higher than 8 percent. His 1974 Braves were on the low side since he was one of seven African Americans on their 40-man roster, but that was still 18 percent, and that was more than twice baseball's 21st century average for teams.

"You look back over all of these things, and I've thought about this, when you talk about Blacks in baseball now today," Hank said over the phone during the summer of 2007. "I may have told you this a long time ago. I do remember telling it [to you], I believe. This is what Major League Baseball is trying to do, trying to make this what they call a World Series, and I say a World Series. I'm not talking about a World Series with the United States. I'm talking about a World Series of Mexico, the United States, all of them. That's exactly what's going to happen. That's what they want to do."

"That's interesting," I said.

"That's exactly what they want to do. They want to make this a World Series and they want to be able to have—just like for an example—I was just listening to TV last night and looking at this [pitcher Daisuke Matsuzaka, who left the Japanese professional league in November 2006 to sign a $52 million contract with the Boston Red Sox following a bidding war]. I was just listening to the commentators talking about this and then talking about that and I watched him pitch and I know enough about baseball to know that he ain't throwing no better than any damn body, no more than [Bob] Gibson. If they tell me he throws better than Gibson, then I'll [put money] on Wall Street. He ain't doing no more, but what they have done in baseball, they are trying to build up all of these Japanese players to get these players to play Major League Baseball. They're trying to get all of these [Latin American players] to come over here to play baseball. They're trying to get all these people from all over the world to come here to play Major League Baseball. They don't give a hoot, not one hill of beans, about a Black person. Not one thing about whether we play baseball or not. This game of baseball, and you have to look at it, that this game was so, it was just folding until Jackie Robinson came in and lifted it to another level with playing and trying to make it exciting for the fans—both Black and White."

Aaron then sighed heavily and slowly raised his voice, "Terence, it is amazing how this game has changed for the benefit of how they want [the public] to perceive it to be, you know? Yeah, just keep your eye on it. Watch what I tell you about this game. I guarantee you [what I say is true]."

It was true. By the 2021 baseball season, which began three months after Hank's death, the game's biggest star was Shohei Ohtani, a pitching and hitting sensation from Iwate Prefecture, Japan, located 6,700 miles, a Pacific Ocean, and several times zones west of Mobile, Alabama, the old stomping grounds of an African American who became the greatest Major League player ever. Now baseball has virtually no African Americans.

Courtesy of Hank's personal experiences as a player and as an executive in Major League Baseball since the early 1950s combined with my 1982 research for the *San Francisco Examiner* on the state of Blacks in the game to commemorate the 35th anniversary of Jackie Robinson breaking baseball's color barrier, Hank had splendid reasons to believe the game he cherished wasn't loving African Americans as much as it claimed. This vanishing act involving African American players in baseball happened too fast, too dramatically, and too blatantly after the 1970s for The Myth to be more than a myth by the 21st century.

About The Myth: To hear many folks tell it, especially those involved with Major League Baseball, African Americans rolled out of bed one day and just didn't like the sport anymore. They preferred football, basketball, and even wrestling—at least according to Calvin Griffith, the Minnesota Twins owner who likely wasn't a card-carrying member of the NAACP. During a 1978 gathering in Waseca, Minnesota, Griffith explained his reason for moving his franchise from Washington, D.C., to the Minneapolis area before the 1961 season by saying, "It was when we found out that there were only 15,000 Blacks here. Black people don't go to ballgames, but they'll fill up a wrestling ring and put up such a chant it'll scare you to death. We came because you've got good, hard-working White people here."

Forget The Myth. This was sinister and deliberate.

Hank and I often discussed the following: contrary to popular belief, Jackie Robinson didn't prove African Americans could play baseball after he entered the lineup for the Brooklyn Dodgers at Ebbets Field on April 15, 1947. Those who ran the game knew African Americans could play. (See the Negro Leagues, which included Satchel Paige, who Joe DiMaggio called the best pitcher he ever faced.) Those who ran the game also knew, if they weren't vigilant, African Americans would dominate their totally White league, which is what they wanted to prevent as much as possible.

Exhibit A: the 1960s, when baseball's biggest stars were named Hank, Willie, and Frank instead of Babe, Ty, and Stan, which meant those who ran the game knew they needed to do something about it, which they did.

Let's start with baseball's dirty little secret, and Hank laughed his wonderful laugh whenever we discussed what involved my Big Red Machine. It was the greatest Major League Baseball team of all time. If not, it was 1B to the 1A that would be the New York Yankees of any given stretch. I'll stick with my guys, though. Those Cincinnati Reds won more games during the 1970s than anybody in baseball along the way to six division titles, four National League pennants, and consecutive World Series titles in 1975 and 1976. They had a Hall of Fame manager (Sparky Anderson), three Hall of Fame players (catcher Johnny Bench, first baseman Tony Perez, and second baseman Joe Morgan), baseball's all-time hits king (Pete Rose), a five-time All-Star left fielder who led the National League in home runs twice and grabbed league MVP honors (George Foster), a nine-time All-Star shortstop with five Gold Gloves and two Silver Slugger Awards (Dave

Concepcion), a three-time All-Star right fielder (Ken Griffey Sr.), and a center fielder with four Gold Gloves (Cesar Geronimo).

The Big Red Machine was The Big Black Machine since it ranked among the darkest teams in baseball history. Rose and Bench were the only White players in the Machine's everyday lineup. Morgan, Foster, and Griffey Sr. were African Americans; Perez came from Cuba; Geronimo was from the Dominican Republic, and Concepcion was from Venezuela.

There also was the 1971 All-Star Game—considered among the best ever—and Reggie Jackson provided the biggest highlight after he slammed a rising home run that nearly cleared the right-field roof at Tiger Stadium in Detroit before it banged against a light tower. Jackson was African American, by the way. The same went for the game's starting pitchers (Dock Ellis for the National League and Vida Blue for the American League) and the game's Most Valuable Player, Frank Robinson, who homered with two RBIs during the American League's 6–4 victory. There were 17 African Americans overall in the 1971 All-Star Game, when Africans American players remained dominant around baseball throughout that decade, but 50 years later, when Hank died, African American players in the National Pastime were going, going, nearly gone.

This wasn't a fluke, not from what I discovered during the spring of 1982, when I acquired a smoking gun that was more like a smoldering nuclear bomb designed to take African Americans out of the major leagues in a hurry. To help me verify what I kept finding back then, I spoke with Henry Louis Aaron for the first time that May during a series of phone conversations.

To get to that moment, along with others that turned me into The Hank Aaron Whisperer, my journey toward becoming a confidant of an American baseball treasure began five years before that "Blacks in Baseball" series, when destiny picked up the pace toward helping me evolve into Jackie and Hank.

I was at *The Cincinnati Enquirer*, where I served as the first Black intern ever at the then-137-year-old paper during the summer after my junior year at Miami University in Oxford, Ohio, located 37 miles away to the north. Eight days after I graduated from Miami (Ohio) on May 7, 1978, I began working as the first full-time Black sports journalist in the history of *The Enquirer* and as only the second full-time Black reporter of any kind on the paper. Except for one racial incident involving those in the sports department—which I handled with Hank-like wisdom, even before I knew Henry Louis Aaron, the person—*The Enquirer* and I were a perfect fit.

Jim Schottelkotte, the paper's managing editor, hired me as both that intern and full-time guy, and whether it was me or anybody else in the newsroom, he fussed, he yelled, he demanded, but he also encouraged. He was Lou Grant, the grouchy yet caring news director from *The Mary Tyler Moore Show*, but in contrast to Grant, Schottelkotte had hair.

Then *San Francisco Examiner* sports editor Charles "Coop" Cooper called me out of nowhere during a late December night in 1979 at my Cincinnati apartment. Soon, courtesy of an interview the following week at a five-star restaurant in Sausalito, California, along with an offer before dessert to cover the San Francisco Giants and a slew of other things in the San Francisco Bay Area, I agreed to leave the Ohio River for the Pacific Ocean. Then came my last day at *The Enquirer*, when two White sports reporters couldn't stand it anymore. They were slightly older than I. Even though I never viewed them as racists, I knew since my summer internship at the paper that they were resentful the bosses allowed me to write frequently on The Big Red Machine, featuring all of those baseball gods I hugged as a youth. I also suspected the two White sports reporters weren't pleased when the bosses nodded after I asked if I could cover the big stories and games involving Indiana University sports. Bloomington was relatively close to Cincinnati, and the Hoosiers had Bobby Knight as their explosive basketball coach, along with colorful Lee Corso running an Indiana football team featuring several former Cincinnati-area high school standouts.

The combination heightened my rise as a journalist, including to the point of getting that call out of nowhere from the *San Francisco Examiner*. As I prepared to depart *The Enquirer* sports office for the last time, the two White sports reporters moved to the middle of the room, and one of them said loudly, "So I wonder how Terry got that San Francisco job." The other one responded by pointing to the back of his hand—as in his skin color—as in the two White sports reporters suggesting they weren't able to advance in the business as well as only the second Black reporter of any kind during what was then the 140-year-old history of *The Cincinnati Enquirer*.

They laughed. I wanted to—but only at them.

Instead, as I turned away without any expression, I left the building, and I remembered. I remembered Mom and Martha at Associates during my earlier life in Cincinnati. I remembered Dad and his boss in Milwaukee mentioning Sammy Davis Jr. to prove whatever his boss thought he was proving. I remembered my brother, Darrell, crying over the racist cowards in the stands at LSU. I remembered my high school football coach using the N-word during his pregame speech and never apologizing. I remembered the title of Jackie's autobiography: *I Never Had It Made*, along with long passages from its inspired chapters. Mostly, I remembered to ignore mind games.

During my first year with the *San Francisco Examiner* in 1980, I had a couple of beats: the San Francisco Giants and the Oakland Raiders, and my Jackie Robinson roles continued to multiply. I was the first full-time Black sports journalist in what was then the paper's 118-year history. I also became the first Black person ever to cover an NFL team on a regular basis for a major daily newspaper and I did so with the Raiders of Al Davis, who had a bunch of his Pro Football

Hall of Fame players and a Super Bowl victory for the franchise my first year on the job.

In my second year covering the Giants, they hired Baseball Hall of Famer Frank Robinson as the first Black National League manager. He became the game's first Black manager period in 1975 as player/ manager for the Cleveland Indians, and Frank and I talked often. The conversations were frequently deep, and it didn't hurt we were both African Americans. I followed Larry Whiteside of *The Boston Globe* as only the second Black person ever to cover a Major League Baseball team on a regular basis for a major daily newspaper. My dealings with Frank remained professional, but the obvious was always there, and it was unspoken: we both were Jackie in different ways. Frank told me he was too silent on racial issues during his playing days, ranging from the mid-1950s through the mid-1970s. He sat only behind Hank Aaron, Babe Ruth, and Willie Mays for the longest time in career homers. When I covered Frank, he spoke his mind on racial issues (usually with me as his messenger as a prelude to my role as The Hank Aaron Whisperer), but he lacked the fire of the Jackie I studied. He also had neither the depth nor the insight regarding everything you could name that Henry Louis Aaron would show me often during future years. Still, Frank was as strong as Jackie and Hank with his convictions.

So was Morgan, one of my former Big Red Machine guys, who played for the Giants in 1981 and 1982. Joe often used me to rip baseball's attitude toward African Americans as players and as potential front-office workers, where the numbers remained mostly extinct. For the *Examiner* I quickly became more than just the Giants guy or the Raiders guy. Given the glimpses in 1981 of the coming NFL dynasty to the San Francisco 49ers of Bill Walsh and Joe Montana and given the mania around Oakland created by BillyBall under crazy yet effective A's manager Billy Martin, I was able to bounce between everything and I was allowed to write whatever. Eventually, in 1983, without me asking, I became only the third Black person in the history of major daily newspapers allowed to write his opinion on a full-time basis as a general sports columnist.

To commemorate the 35th anniversary of Jackie Robinson breaking baseball's color barrier, I did a seven-day series in June 1982 for the *Examiner* called "Blacks in Baseball," and the package exposed (with the help from that smoldering nuclear weapon) that the game had a quota system designed to limit the number of African Americans throughout the sport over the course of years and decades. I was told as much from the prominent to the obscure throughout various levels of major league, college, and high school baseball, and everybody agreed to speak on the record.

That included Henry Louis Aaron.

Nearly a month before the first of my decades worth of conversations with Hank, I got a call in April 1982 at the *San Francisco Examiner* from a White baseball scout I knew from the Oakland area. "Listen, are you going to be at the A's game tomorrow? I've got something I think you need to see," the scout said, barely audible, presumably because others were listening nearby. I was excited. If this particular scout claimed his information was huge, it ranked between discovering the next Henry Louis Aaron or determining the sun would fall out of the sky.

"I wasn't planning to go, but I'll go now. What is it?"

"Well," the scout said, stretching out the word, before he paused. "It's something that needs to come out. I've been meaning to tell you about it for a long time, and you are the only person I know who will touch it. I'm just sick of what's going on, but you'll see what I'm talking about."

The next day, I sat at the end of an empty home dugout at Oakland-Alameda County Coliseum several hours before that A's game, waiting for the scout. When he arrived as scheduled, he looked around, making sure nobody else was in our universe before he moved in front of me. He reached into a folder, pulled out a sheet of paper, and then slowly pushed it my way. No, the scout hadn't signed the next Henry Louis Aaron because there will only be one of those, but as I studied the paper, I did nearly glance upward to make sure everything was in place around the clouds.

I held a computerized free-agent report in my hands from the Major League Scouting Bureau, which was used by 18 of the 26 major league teams at the time. According to the scout, while I examined the smoldering nuclear weapon in my hand, the other eight franchises that weren't a part of the bureau had similar categories on their free-agent reports.

Last name...first name...middle name ...position
Current address
Telephone...date of birth ...height...weight...bats...throws
Permanent address (if different from above)
Team name...city...state
Scout...date ...race...games...innings.

Wait! What? *Race?*

"Yeah," the scout said, still looking around to make sure he wasn't discovered as my Deep Throat. He wanted no part of baseball's Watergate—at least not directly. But indirectly, he left it to me. "As far as I know, they've always had race there, and you know why, right? They're trying to control the number of African American players in the game."

After a few more minutes, the scout hustled toward the other end of the dugout, saying, "I'll let you take it from here."

I took it to Coop, who studied every inch of the sheet while leaning back in his chair without uttering a word. Then, he moved forward toward me to say, "Wow, how do you want to handle this?"

I wanted to take a short break from the Giants and take a week or two to investigate. I wanted to do all of the reporting and all of the writing myself to keep leaks to a minimum for such a touchy subject. I wanted the *Examiner* to dedicate a couple of open pages on the inside of the Sunday paper to what I wrote, starting with coverage on the front page. "Let's do it like this," Coop said after listening and thinking. "Just forget about the Giants. They're nothing compared to this. I want you to take as much time as you need to see where this leads you. Two weeks, a month, I don't care, but do what you need to do to get everything you can. We'll play it up big. Let's plan on doing the whole thing over the course of an entire week. Terry, I have the feeling you're going to come up with a lot of explosive stuff, and it's going to be hard on you personally. But I know you can handle it and remember this: the *Examiner* will have your back no matter what happens. I'll have your back."

Coop did have my back like he always did, but except for racially motivated knuckleheads here and there, I was pleasantly stunned. Getting folks to cooperate regarding what was the first expansive investigation of its kind on the decline of Blacks in baseball was easier than I thought. My interviewing and reporting stretched from the major leagues to the minor leagues, and I also went deeply into what was happening to African Americans regarding baseball in colleges and high schools. Nobody I contacted disputed the ugliness of the bottom line—well, unless they were operating with less than sincerity—and the bottom line came in the form of this question: why is a slot for race on baseball's computerized scouting report?

The following raised more questions. Through my reporting, I knew the National Football League didn't have anything involving race on scouting reports for its yearly combine. Neither did the Raiders, the only NFL team that wasn't a member of the combine. The scouting book for the National Basketball Association also didn't ask for the race of players.

With every interview, I kept thinking about that smoldering nuclear weapon while hearing the voice of that White scout in the back of my mind. *"They're trying to control the number of African American players in the game."*

I needed answers and I started at the top. I called Major League Baseball headquarters in New York for commissioner Bowie Kuhn. As I dialed, I recalled the year before in 1981, when he gave me that soul brother handshake (or whatever he thought he was doing) at Candlestick Park in San Francisco to show he was down for the cause involving African Americans. I also recalled six years earlier, when I asked "Mr. Kuhn" my question as a die-hard Reds fan about Geronimo and the All-Star Game.

Maybe Kuhn still remembered me. It didn't matter because of the bottom line.

Why is a slot for race on baseball's computerized scouting report?

I dialed Kuhn's office and I told the receptionist who I was before I said I needed to speak to the commissioner on an urgent matter.

"What do you wish to speak to the commissioner about?" the receptionist said.

"The plight of Blacks in baseball," I responded, and soon afterward the secretary switched me to Kuhn's right-hand man who asked me the same question as the receptionist. Then, when I gave him the same answer while trying to say as little as possible until I spoke to Kuhn himself about the bottom line, his right-hand man added, "I'll pass it on to the commissioner."

Later that day, Kuhn returned my call. "Hi, Commissioner. I'm not sure if you remember me. I'm Terence Moore, a sports reporter for the *San Francisco Examiner*. I met you in the press box at Candlestick Park last season, and we were…"

"Sure, sure. I do. How do the Giants look this year?"

Whether Kuhn remembered me or not was questionable, but it also was irrelevant. After more small talk, I jumped to the bottom line. I asked the commissioner if Major League Baseball was trying to use certain tactics to control the number of Black players in the game.

"Oh, of course not," Kuhn said before he did his version over the phone of that crazy handshake to me during the previous year.

More specifically, he did what baseball folks have done forever when questioned about their attitudes regarding African Americans in the game: They return to April 15, 1947, by saying Jackie Robinson this and Jackie Robinson that, then they try to name every Black superstar who ever played in the major leagues, and then they toss in the name of Martin Luther King Jr. for good measure.

When Kuhn finished, I had another question: *why is a slot for race on baseball's computerized scouting report?*

Kuhn denied there was such a slot for race on those scouting reports, but then he caught himself, remembering his lawyer training, and he said, "I'm not aware of anything like that on the scouting reports."

I told him I would fax him a copy. "I'll look into it and then I'll give you a response," Kuhn said, who issued a statement to me the following day through a phone call from Bob Wirz, his director of information: "The commissioner says, 'I don't see where the classification of race on the forms serves a purpose.'"

That was it, but that didn't mean Kuhn ignored the whole thing. He couldn't and he didn't because he knew there was just one answer to the bottom line regarding a slot for race on baseball's computerized scouting reports. And he knew that answer wasn't good.

Baseball had a quota system. Period.

Less than 24 hours after my "Blacks in Baseball" series ran in the *San Francisco Examiner* during the last week of June 1982 (featuring me writing everything, including the two to three pieces for each of the five days of a series that would finish first in the 1982 California-Nevada Associated Press awards), I spoke with Oakland A's president Roy Eisenhardt about another matter. Then, after a pause, he told me Major League Baseball sent a confidential memo to all of its 26 teams asking them to remove race from their scouting reports and he said the Major League Scouting Bureau was told to do the same. "I had not noticed race on the forms before. I was shocked when you pointed it out," Eisenhardt said, reflecting back on my questions to him about the practice during my initial reporting on the series. "It certainly has no place on the forms. I think it was just a relic of time."

No, race on those baseball scouting reports was a flashing red light about the game's past, present, and future regarding African Americans both on and off the field. The majority of those I interviewed during the spring of 1982 said as much, and they were Black, White, and Hispanic. They were prominent and obscure. They were executives, players, scouts, statisticians, clubhouse workers, and others deep on organizational flow charts.

I spoke to a month's worth of baseball-related folks, and they were all willing for me to put their names in newsprint. In the end the consensus was: Major League Baseball had a quota system that either consciously or subconsciously remained in effect to limit the number of African Americans in the game. Those scouting reports with race as a category were only part of the evidence, and the momentum from that quota system would travel deep into the 21st century to make African Americans an afterthought in the game of Jackie and Hank. "There are quotas to be followed. No doubt about that," said Bob Thurman, who was one of just three full-time Black scouts in the 67-person Major League Scouting Bureau during the time of my 1982 interview. "That's why I didn't get to the major leagues sooner than I did in 1956 with the Cincinnati Reds. The quota system—it's something that has always bothered me about this game. Why color?"

Baseball Hall of Famer Marvin Miller, the executive director of the game's players association for its first 16 years, told me: "From time to time, you hear talk about a quota system, but it's hard to prove."

Miller was White, and so was William Weiss, an accomplished statistician for Minor League Baseball on the West Coast since the 1940s. According to Weiss, the number of African Americans in both the major and minor leagues was plunging, and he said during the spring of 1982: "It's been a gradual trend. One thing has occurred to me over the last 10 or 12 years, and that is when a decision has to be made between a White player and a Black player, the White player is usually chosen. If you have 10 teams in a league and you take away two Black players from each team, then that's 20 fewer Blacks in the league. Maybe that's why the trend isn't as noticeable. I'm sure you have a few individuals in baseball who might think along racial lines when decisions are being made."

That brings me back to Griffith, the Minnesota Twins owner who was just four years removed from his racist comments involving African Americans and wrestling when I dialed his office during the spring of 1987. He thought he was speaking in private back then, but a reporter was in the room to record words that Griffith later said he regretted saying. I called Griffith during the spring of 1982 for his thoughts for my "Blacks in Baseball" series. He still sounded like a guy dreaming of standing in the door of the home clubhouse at Ebbets Field on April 15, 1947, to keep You Know Who from entering. Griffith told me over the phone from Minneapolis that he wanted to make his team as White as possible. He said, "You look through the stands. How many Blacks do you usually see? Not many. Statistics prove they pay to see wrestling, boxing, and basketball. The truth hurts."

This also was true: in addition to Griffith's willingness to speak bluntly about his 19th century racial beliefs to a total stranger such as me during a random phone call, I discovered up close and personal through the decades that more than a few baseball folks were Griffith in body, mind, and soul. Either that or they remained on automatic pilot regarding their racial thoughts and actions. Nothing showed that more than my decades of encountering Griffith clones during other phone interviews, when the person on the other end couldn't tell they were speaking with an African American reporter.

While doing a profile at the *San Francisco Examiner* on Robinson, I called one of his fellow Baseball Hall of Fame members for reflections on Robinson's career. Robinson was Black, and the Baseball Hall of

Famer I had on the phone was White. After a few words of general conversation, I told the Baseball Hall of Fame player what I was doing. "That fucking n----r…He's nothing but a fucking n----r."

Alrighty then.

I told Coop and several other San Francisco Bay Area writing colleagues about the incident, and a couple of months later when I was at Candlestick Park, one of those colleagues told me that Baseball Hall of Famer was in the press box. "Well, I guess I'll introduce myself," I said, smiling, as that colleague laughed, saying he wanted to watch things unfold.

When I approached the Baseball Hall of Fame player, he was pleasant. We shook hands, and then I said, "I just want to thank you for the interview a few months ago. I'm the guy who called you for the story I was doing on Frank Robinson."

The blood left the face of the Baseball Hall of Fame player. Soon afterward, he rushed from the press box. I didn't use the Baseball Hall of Fame player's comments, by the way. Just like I never wrote about the Major League executives and managers, including Baseball Hall of Famers, who often referred to "colored" players whenever they spoke to me about African Americans on their teams or elsewhere in the game.

I did write about my phone conversation with relatively new Reds owner Marge Schott, and this was before she became known for her affinity for Adolph Hitler's domestic policies, among other things that made her the female Griffith. Nevertheless, Schott invited me to her estate on the exclusive Indian Hill side of town. When I climbed out of my car, she stood on her front porch, and her face indicated she was perturbed that I was much darker than Hermann Goring or Joseph Goebbels. We did the interview in her kitchen.

There also was a former baseball owner I bonded with over the phone. At the end of the interview, he invited me to spend an afternoon reminiscing about his life and his franchise at his massive complex. When I drove up the main driveway, he ran toward me in a rage, waving his hands, screaming, "Go around! Go around!" I went to the back entrance somewhat confused. Before he could explode again while rushing toward me from the distance, I said, "I'm Terence Moore, the sportswriter. We just talked on the phone."

The former baseball owner frowned, threw up his arms, and said, "Why didn't you tell me you were Black?"

Anyhow, in my *Examiner* piece, the commissioner's office refused to cooperate during our search for historical numbers on African Americans in the game, and among the defiant was Monte Irvin, a special assistant to Kuhn and one of the game's first Black players. I was tipped off that Irvin kept those numbers in his desk drawer. After I phoned Irvin, he confirmed what I knew. He said, "I complied the figures for my personal records, but somehow, they aren't there anymore. They just aren't there. I can't find them. So let's leave it at that. We don't need any more stories knocking Major League Baseball but stories saying things are moving along. I think baseball is doing just fine for Blacks."

On the 25-man Opening Day rosters on Major League Baseball's opening week of 1982, slightly less than 19 percent of the players were African Americans. That's a massive figure compared to the 8 percent one of the 21st century but not compared to this: the peak of African Americans players in the major leagues was around 25 percent in the mid-1970s.

There also were these ugly numbers in 1982:

- Robinson was the only African American manager in baseball, and there only had been three in history—all since he became the first one in 1975 with the Cleveland Indians.

- There were just 13 African American coaches in the major leagues out of 123 positions. There had never been a Black third-base coach, which was considered the next step to a manager's job back then.

- There were 32 Blacks in front-office positions (including secretaries) out of approximately 914 available positions. Atlanta Braves vice president Hank Aaron was the only African American in an executive role. In addition, at least 13 clubs had no Blacks in their front office. The Red Sox and the New York Yankees refused to cooperate for my survey, so those numbers were based on 24 of the 26 teams at the time.

- Out of the 568 full-time scouts in the game—including the Major League Scouting Bureau with 60 full-time scouts, two cross-checkers, and five supervisors—only 15 were African Americans. There were 14 major league teams with no full-time Black scouts, and only full-time Black scouts were allowed to sign prospects.

Which brings me to Morgan, an outspoken African American player who followed me from Cincinnati, where he won two National League Most Valuable Player Awards with the Big Red Machine, to San Francisco, where he continued his Baseball Hall of Fame career in 1982 at second base for the Giants. He was my Hank Aaron before I met Hank Aaron since Joe and I huddled often for long stretches to discuss racial issues involving baseball and society. During my research for the "Blacks in Baseball" series, Joe told me those scary numbers for African Americans in the game weren't by accident and he said they would get worse, especially regarding African American players. "If you're not looking for Black players, you're not going to find them, and they aren't looking for Black players," Morgan said. "Baseball has a quota system, and that's it in a nutshell, but you can start with this: how can you expect to sign a lot of Black players if you don't have a lot of Black scouts?"

Foster took it further. The standout African American left fielder on my Big Red Machine was playing for the New York Mets in 1982. He told me one of the most prophetic things. Hispanic players were represented by single digit percentages in the major leagues during the start of my "Blacks in Baseball" series, but they were at 32 percent by the time of Hank's death in January 2021. In contrast, the number of African Americans had sunk from that mid-1970s high of around 25 percent to 8 percent. That means Foster was clairvoyant in 1982 when he told me: "It's reverse discrimination. American Blacks are being phased out and replaced by Latin American players in some cases. I don't mean that in a negative way, but the Latin American players make eight and 10 times less many than many American Blacks. They're cheaper to sign."

It's called a quota system. "It's just the way some people in baseball establishment have been brought up," Bill White told me in May 1982, when he was a Yankees announcer at the time. Before that, he was an eight-time All-Star first baseman from the mid-1950s with the New York Giants through the late 1960s with the St. Louis Cardinals. He later rose to the highest-ranking position for a Black person in the history of professional sports management when he began a five-year term in 1989 as National League president.

Yes, *that* Bill White verified the existence of a quota system, when I did the research for my "Blacks in baseball" series. "Some of the people who are calling the shots in baseball today were trained by the original owners of the game back before Jackie Robinson broke the color line," White said. "The offspring of the original owners are creating the same results as before the color line was broken. This situation is partly the fault of Black players who were in uniform during the 1960s. We knew this was going on back then, but we just sat back and said nothing. We should have been screaming. Now it could be too late."

At that point, I knew I needed to go for the jugular. I needed Henry Louis Aaron.

With apologies to DiMaggio, who insisted before gatherings to be introduced as "the greatest living player," or to Willie Mays, who deserved that honor more than DiMaggio or anybody else not named Henry Louis Aaron, Hank was the greatest living player. He also was the definitive person to interview for my "Blacks in Baseball" series, and it didn't hurt he owned a PHD in racism.

Hank grew up in segregated Mobile, Alabama, before he played in the Negro Leagues. He made one of his minor league stops for the Milwaukee Braves in Jacksonville, Florida, during the early 1950s, when Jim Crow reigned. He entered the major leagues in 1954, the same year the U.S. Supreme Court ruled separate but equal was dead courtesy of its ruling on Brown versus the Board of Education of Topeka. Even so, Hank spent the peak of his baseball career during the 1960s with the likes of White, Robinson, and Morgan, watching the game operate as if separate but equal still lived. No doubt Hank fretted over the game's quota system, which began decades before I had that smoldering nuclear weapon—*Why is a slot for race on baseball's computerized scouting report?*—to prove it.

I needed Hank because even then I could see Henry Louis Aaron was Jack Roosevelt Robinson. Less than a decade before, he conquered death threats and hate mail to make beloved White hero George Herman Ruth secondary in the record book under career home runs. I needed Hank for my "Blacks in Baseball" series for another reason. During the spring of 1982, he was the highest ranking African American in the front office of any Major League Baseball team. He was months into his new role as director of player development for the Atlanta Braves, his team for 21 seasons before he spent his final two years as a player with the Milwaukee Brewers. His jump to management was courtesy of Ted Turner, the cable television maverick who bought the Braves in January 1976. Eight months later, Turner made Bill Lucas baseball's first African American general manager. (Hank's first wife, Barbara, was Lucas' sister.) Then soon after that, Turner hired Henry Louis Aaron for an unspecified role in the Braves' front office, following Hank's retirement as a player after the 1976 season.

While the other major league teams had zero Black executives, the Braves had two. Before long, there was just Hank in May 1979 after Lucas died at 43.

I needed Hank.

I got Hank in May 1982, and my first conversation with Henry Louis Aaron shouldn't have happened, but it did, and the process was flawless. Destiny demanded as much for the fan-turned-journalist who still used a wall in his home to display his Mona Lisa of a Hank Aaron poster he bought at 12 years old.

Destiny also got me past Susan Bailey.

Bailey was Hank's Rose Mary Woods, Richard Nixon's secretary with the reputation of protecting her boss no matter what. Rose Mary Woods was so loyal to the president that in June 1972, she said she stretched the arm and leg on the left side of her body so far apart in opposite directions behind her desk—while operating a tape-recording device and reaching for her phone—that she said she accidentally erased about five minutes of a damaging Watergate tape involving the commander in chief.

Hank didn't have secret recordings, but he had Bailey, who he cherished. She spent decades doing exactly what Hank wanted done, which was to say no in a forceful yet pleasant manner whenever somebody called to speak with Henry Louis Aaron regarding just about anything. I wouldn't know. In addition to operating as The Hank Aaron Whisperer, I was his Clark Kent as the only media person with ability to contact this Superman of a sports personality at any time. That partly was because I never had a problem with Bailey (you know, courtesy of Hank). As a result, I regularly had local and national reporters begging me to put in a good word for them with her, but they were on their own. Nobody told Susan Baily what to do.

When I contacted the Braves in May 1982 for Hank Aaron, I knew nothing about Bailey or her reputation. I just dialed 404-522-7630, the main number to the team's headquarters for as long as I could remember, and I asked to be connected to Hank Aaron's office. Bailey was on the other end. I introduced myself and told her I wanted to do something with Hank Aaron involving my series for the *San Francisco Examiner* on "Blacks in Baseball," specifically about the future of African Americans in the game, and she put me on hold for several seconds.

"Hello."

Destiny responded again. It was Hank.

I didn't know how much time I would have with the guy we cheered for like crazy as a family in Milwaukee on April 8, 1974, in front of our black-and-white TV set in the kitchen, so I got to the point. Well, almost. With my voice cracking from nervousness, I said we had something in common: a love for Jackie Robinson. I said Hank was speaking to only the second African American ever to cover a Major League Baseball team.

Just like that, Hank wanted to hear more about my groundbreaking things as a journalist, so I told him everything. I mentioned I was the first Black writer for my high school and college newspapers, the first full-time Black sports reporter for *The Cincinnati Enquirer*, the first full-time Black sports reporter for the *San Francisco Examiner*, and the first Black sports reporter to cover an NFL team on a full-time basis for a major newspaper.

"How old are you?" Hank said.

"Twenty-six," I said.

"You did all of that at 26 as a Black man working for newspapers?" Aaron said, chuckling over the phone. Then he said something I would hear often over the decades from Henry Louis Aaron, and every time he said it, I had to deal with the moisture in my eyes. "I'm proud of you."

Then we got down to business. I told Hank about baseball's computerized scouting reports with the word "race" screaming in the middle of them. Fresh on the job as Braves director of player development, Hank said he hadn't seen those forms, but he said he was disgusted by my news and he added he wasn't surprised. I told Hank about my research showing at least a 7 percent drop in African American players in baseball since the previous decade. I told Hank about Foster joining others by telling me baseball officials were planning to systematically replace African American players with Hispanic ones. I told Hank about the pitiful number of Blacks as major league scouts, coaches, and even secretaries in front offices. I told Hank about Weiss, a respected minor league statistician for four decades, joining Miller and other non-Blacks to conclude the same thing as former and current African American players: baseball was systematically ousting African American players from its game through a quota system.

I told Hank about White, a perennial All-Star player, who blamed much of the situation on himself and other African American players of the 1960s. I told Hank how White got emotional when he told me, "We should have been screaming. Now it could be too late."

"Oh, I agree with Bill. We should have been screaming. We could see what they were doing to Black players, and that's what Jackie would have done [as a player in the 1960s]. And after he finished playing, he still was out there screaming about the racism in baseball," Hank said, sounding comfortable speaking to a stranger over the phone about sensitive topics.

Then again, Hank and I had our Jackie Robinson connection, and destiny controlled our conversation.

Hank added: "Parents are seeing how Blacks are being treated in baseball once they retire and they are telling their kids to go into other sports. That's why I think there is a lack of participation in baseball on the part of Black kids. The number of Blacks in the front offices of Major League Baseball has always been scarce, and they remain scarce today."

A few days later, I reviewed my Hank notes. I discovered something I would notice here and there through the decades after the hundreds of times I would speak with Henry Louis Aaron. He would say something, but it wouldn't be exactly what he meant to say. They were little things—mainly due to his down-home style of speaking through his south Alabama drawl.

I did in May 1982 what I would do over the next four decades. Whenever I wasn't sure if Hank wished to say something exactly, I would check with him. So I called the Braves again and I reached Bailey again. I told her I needed to speak to Hank again. Just like before, there was Hank within seconds.

"Hello."

After I told Hank I just wanted to clarify something he said, he thanked me for calling because he said he made a mistake. He told me what he really meant to say, and before we hung up, he added, "You know what, Terence? After all these many years, you're the only reporter who has ever done that—just flat-out ask me if they were keeping me in context."

Hank never forgot that May 1982 clarification moment, along with others, and it accelerated our bonding, even though I had him at Jackie Robinson.

SIXTH INNING

BECOMING JACKIE AND HANK

Pull yourself together, dude.

That's what I wanted to say to the driver of the SUV from the car service sent by CNN to take the tired and aching man in the wheelchair and me to a nearby country club for our interview. Instead, I could tell the driver just wanted to enjoy the opening moments with one of his idols. If nothing else, the driver did a splendid job positioning his umbrella to keep the rain from soaking the three of us. So with Henry Louis Aaron dancing in the eyes of the driver, I gave him a few more seconds, almost another minute. I knew he represented thousands and millions everywhere. For the driver Hank Aaron was right there in the flesh, even though this also was a tired and aching man in a wheelchair. "Can you open the door for me?" I said, finally, determining this part of the driver's fandom was lasting way too long.

He apologized, yanked opened the front passenger door, and then he mostly stood there, still talking to Hank about home runs, ancient Atlanta Braves games, and Atlanta-Fulton County Stadium. I sighed to myself while beginning the impossible: trying to help a tired and aching man out of his wheelchair and then raising him up to an area nearly as high as the sun beyond the dark skies. I wanted to do so without bruising or breaking something (either on the tired and aching man or me) and I knew I'd get little or no help with the driver still talking Hank, Hank, and more Hank.

Yeah, I understood.

The tired and aching man in the wheelchair remained the greatest baseball player of all time, and I saw it in the driver's eyes.

I thought of my evolution with Henry Louis Aaron. I went from that 12-year-old sports fan who sacrificed his model car money for a Hank Aaron poster of magnificence to hugging every word of Jackie Robinson's autobiography to becoming Jackie and Hank, especially after I left the splendid vibes around the *San Francisco Examiner* in January 1985 for *The Atlanta Journal-Constitution*, my newspaper of racially motivated hell for 25 years. Hank often served as The Terence Moore Whisperer during those times. We were kindred souls on conflict and we were staunch disciples of the Bible and Jack Roosevelt Robinson.

I needed all of that.

Just like Jackie and Hank, I was a Black man in a unique situation, facing hostility at *The Atlanta Journal-Constitution* from those with sinister intentions through a heavy dose of mind games. Just like Jackie and Hank, I needed to respond by using more brain than brawn. Unlike Jackie and Hank, I had Jack Roosevelt Robinson and Henry Louis Aaron to help me survive. I used the lessons of Jackie through his autobiography *I Never Had It Made* and Hank through our numerous phone calls and visits.

When I came to Atlanta, Hank was in his eighth year as a Braves vice president overall and his third as their farm director. That followed his 23 seasons as a major league player, including his opening 21 with the Braves. It wasn't long before we grew our face-to-face relationship and it was a relationship that began three years earlier after a few phone calls I made to Hank for my *San Francisco Examiner* series on Blacks in baseball, which exposed a quota system in the game and other matters regarding the rapid decline of African American baseball players.

Hank and I had four decades of captivating, revealing, and frequently hilarious conversations. We also had similar personalities. For instance: Hank enjoyed lots of associates and acquaintances but only a handful of friends. While he was approachable, he preferred solitude. In contrast, regarding his convictions—such as his Christian beliefs, as well as he thoughts on the plight of African Americans, the welfare of all youth, and the consequences of his actions as a trailblazer for Black people as a whole—he spoke boldly and frequently and fearlessly to anybody who would listen.

We also had something else in common: Jackie's attitude, which meant we had the ability to survive our detractors while frustrating them. We discussed strategy often. "The one thing you can't do, Terence, is give in to them and give them the impression they're getting to you because that's what they want, and you'll frustrate yourself as much as anything else," Hank often told me—sometimes with more colorful words—during some of my roughest times at *The AJC*. "You just keep being you. Don't stop doing what you know is right, and the Good Lord will take care of the rest."

Amen.

Nearly without exception, Hank used me at *The AJC* as his voice to blast Major League Baseball for its treatment of African Americans on and off the field. Since I also did a ton of national and local television followed by Internet work during the latter years, I also spread The Gospel of Aaron through cyberspace and the airways. But I also possessed a fighter's mentality like Hank. Hank knew it and loved it, too.

"You keep fighting, keep going until you've had enough," Aaron said, referring to my role as a sports columnist at *The Atlanta Journal-Constitution* during the summer of 2006, three years before I would leave the paper after 25 years of mostly turmoil. "You do a great job, Terence. Everybody knows it. They know it, and you've been driving them crazy for years, and it's obvious they don't want to hear you tell the truth, and I don't know how much longer…well, the Braves want me to come back. They want me to come back. The commissioner [Bud Selig, Hank's old pal from his Milwaukee Braves days], he wants me to come back more than anybody. I've never actually left [the Braves' front office], but I played baseball for 23 years and I don't need it. I don't need the money. So, I'm satisfied, you know. Whatever I do, I'm going to do it for the sake of doing it, not because the commissioner wants me to do it. I'm only going to stay around baseball long enough to raise enough hell because I want them to do some things I want them to do and then I'm going to get to Florida. I've already talked to my accountant, and my wife and I—we've got a home there—and I'm going to try to spend more of my time there."

"It's a lot warmer than it is here," I said.

"Well, I just feel I don't need to keep putting up with this crap really. That's what I'm telling you the same. I'll do whatever I can, but I've had my share. I'm 72. I'll be 73 on February 5, and I don't know how much longer the Good Lord will be smiling upon me," he said, laughing, "but I'll keep moving until He tells me to slow down. Anyhow, if I'm in Florida or wherever, I will always be here able to talk with you whenever you want me to."

"Boy, I appreciate that."

As a journalist, I've always been Jackie and Hank, which means I've never had trouble expressing my opinion. I did so at Miami (Ohio) University as the guy who inspired this caption below his picture in the 1978 yearbook called *Recensio*: "Terence Moore, the infamous sports editor, in one of his typical poses. Terence was the rabble-rouser of *The Student* and always found himself in heated debate with coaches and readers." I did so through the summer columns I wrote for *The Cincinnati Enquirer* during the late 1970s. I also did so as a full-time sports columnist during the early 1980s for the *San Francisco Examiner*.

Even before my January 1985 arrival to Atlanta, where I quickly learned "The New South" was more of a slogan than a reality, I had my share of friction as a sports journalist who happened to be African American. At Miami (Ohio), which is overwhelmingly White, athletes told me coaches regularly posted my columns on their locker room walls—and not because they enjoyed glancing at my photo as the first Black writer ever for *The Miami Student*, the oldest college newspaper west of the Alleghenies, and as the only Black writer during my four years on campus. Still, I experienced only one blatantly racist incident in college as a journalist. I returned to my dorm room my senior year to find one of my columns taped to the door, and somebody used a red magic marker to write the N-word across my photo.

Among the worst racial episodes I had at *The Cincinnati Enquirer* (excluding those two insecure knuckleheads on my last day) occurred in Dayton, Kentucky, where I covered a horseshoe pitching contest. While doing interviews I was surrounded by three fairly large good-old boys who demanded I show them proof I was a reporter. My *Enquirer* ID complete with photo apparently wasn't good enough, and, no, they weren't using the language of folks destined to participate in the Million Man March someday. A middle-aged White woman moved over to calm things by a bunch until I could hustle to my car.

Before my time in Atlanta, I flew into the city during the summer of 1982 to cover the San Francisco Giants for the *San Francisco Examiner*. Before long I got a heavy dose of racism combined with jealousy and mind games, which foreshadowed things to come in that same city. With newspapers still thriving during that summer of 1982, all four major dailies in the San Francisco Bay Area joined the *Examiner* in sending reporters to cover the Giants home and away. My competitors loved pack journalism, which meant they traveled together, dined together, and socialized together, but I kept to myself. Since they were significantly older than me, I had nothing in common with them. I also broke a ton of stories while they were doing whatever they were doing together.

I did follow the tradition in sports journalism back then of staying at the same hotel as the team you covered, and after a game during that Atlanta trip, I went to a deli near the lobby to order a sandwich. The other Giants beat writers were at the nearby bar but only until they spotted me. They stumbled my way, and the leader, turning redder by the moment, leaned over as I sat at my table, and he said loudly, "You think you're one tough n----r, don't you? I'll show you how tough you are. You ain't that tough, n----r!"

The other Giants writers grabbed him, laughing as a group, and then they retreated but not all of them. Minutes later, one of the group members returned, not to apologize, but to say, "Come on, Terry. You're younger than the rest of us. We can't keep up. I'll tell you what [looking around]. Why don't you and me team up against the other guys?"

I smiled, got my sandwich, and left.

So, it was like this after I left the *San Francisco Examiner* for *The Atlanta Journal-Constitution* in January 1985. The upset Miami (Ohio) coaches over what I wrote for the student newspaper. The two insecure knuckleheads at *The Cincinnati Enquirer*. The rednecks of Dayton. The N-word. Yes, the N-word that was uttered during a pep talk by my high school football coach, and that was printed across my column taped to my college dorm room, and that was mentioned several times over the phone by a Baseball Hall of Famer about another one, and that was yelled in my face by another writer covering the Giants.

You could wrap those moments together and you could multiply them by Hank's 755 home runs, but they still ranked in the lower minor leagues of derogatory episodes compared to the major league high heat I faced on a consistent basis after I left California for Georgia.

Somehow, I lasted at *The Atlanta Journal-Constitution* from January 1985 through April 2009, and I know how: thank God for the lessons I learned by watching and listening to my parents handle racially-motivated mind games in their workplaces for decades. Thank God for my spiritual beliefs. Thank God for what I learned from Jack Roosevelt Robinson. Thank God for Henry Louis Aaron.

Given *everything* I would encounter at *The AJC*, I needed to become Jackie and Hank in a hurry. When I joined the paper in January 1985, I was only the third Black general sports columnist in the history of major newspapers and I was the first Black general sports columnist for a major newspaper in the Deep South, which meant I was the first Black person ever allowed to give his opinion as a sports journalist for a major newspaper in the Deep South, which meant I was the Jackie Robinson of that situation. Given my direct approach to opinion writing in a region that never experienced anything close to such a thing from a Black person in print, over the airways, or any place else in the media on a consistent basis, I was headed for a brutal stay in Atlanta.

But I wasn't going anywhere. To me I had a God-given assignment and I had encouragers within days of my arrival. They were huge encouragers, ranging from Henry Louis Aaron to other civil rights legends who lived inside of Hank's neighborhood in southwest Atlanta or nearby. Not coincidentally, I first heard from Andrew Young, among Hank's closest friends. Young was Atlanta's mayor and he was the former United States ambassador to the United Nations after he served as an Atlanta-area congressman in the U.S. House of Representatives. He also was one of the top lieutenants for Dr. Martin Luther King Jr., a native of the city, and Young followed Maynard Jackson as Atlanta's second Black mayor. During my opening week at *The AJC*, Young called me at the paper to declare his support. So did Jackson, who became one of the first Black mayors in the country for a major metropolitan city after his 1973 election in Atlanta. Before long, I got a call from Reverend Joseph Lowery, another one of Dr. King's lieutenants, and Lowery was president of the same Southern Christian Leadership Conference that Dr. King founded.

As was the case with Aaron, those other civil rights legends remained loyal and available throughout my stay at the paper. More significant, they delivered a similar warning to me from the start. They suggested life for African Americans in the so-called "City Too Busy To Hate" (along with that happy talk around the country about The New South) meant many Blacks had gone from cotton fields to corporate offices around Atlanta, but they also suggested the following was true: the fire hoses and the attack dogs had been replaced by mind games, mind games, and more mind games.

I fulfilled one of my bucket list items pertaining to my first month in town. I stopped by Hank's office at Atlanta Fulton-County

Stadium to introduce myself in person. I also asked the man himself to autograph the poster I purchased at 12 years old, and it was the one I treated like an oil painting from another century. It featured Henry Louis Aaron as a stately Black baseball player, slightly crouching with his bat while looking over his right shoulder inside of his 1960-ish Atlanta Braves uniform.

I thought more about meeting Hank in the flesh than anything that might signal the start of 25 years of *The AJC* craziness, when the sports editor called me into the office of the paper's head editor. I discovered later that head editor was nicknamed The Big Bulldog by those around the newsroom for his obsession with University of Georgia sports. It was February 1985, the day after I wrote only my second column, and the column involved the Georgia Bulldogs. I said the university should oust basketball coach Hugh Durham since he faced 27 alleged violations of NCAA rules and since this was 15 years after his Florida State team had similar issues. On Sunday, February 17, 1985, I wrote: "If the NCAA jury looks southeast this summer and turns thumbs down on the University of Georgia basketball program, athletics director Vince Dooley will have three options and one duty. About the options: He could cover his eyes, click his heels and hope Cedric Henderson turns into 6 feet, 9 inches of air. He could sigh over the basketball probation rendered by the NCAA judges, then praise the 21-year-old sanctity of his football program [give or take a booster or three]. He could fire the coach. His duty? Fire the coach."

"What do you have against the University of Georgia?" said The Big Bulldog, forcing a smile from behind his desk after the sports editor and I were greeted in his office by two other men in dark suits.

"Nothing," I replied, wondering where this was going. Seeing those two men in dark suits, I guessed it wouldn't end well.

As The Big Bulldog nodded after my answer, the sports editor eased into a tone that sounded nothing like the guy who spent the two previous years trying to convince me to leave the *San Francisco*

Examiner for *The AJC* while resembling a pesky used car salesman. I finally agreed to head south with help from a nice salary bump along with a mightier signing bonus to seal the deal.

This time, the sports editor sounded like Ward Cleaver from those *Leave It To Beaver* TV shows when the concerned father huddled with one of his confused sons in the den. "Well, we've had a discussion and we have wonderful news to share, and what we want you to do is: turn in your columns a few days early, which helps you, really," the sports editor said with his eyes darting between The Big Bulldog, myself, and the two other men. "By doing that, we can check your columns over just to help you out and we can give you some suggestions. It will be a wonderful setup for your own benefit."

Days before my departure to Atlanta, Charles "Coop" Cooper, my *San Francisco Examiner* sports editor, begged me over dinner through watery eyes not to leave for Atlanta after my five years of award-winning journalism in San Francisco. "You're going to ruin your career," Coop said, claiming my "blunt-writing style" would sort of… ahem…disturb the gentle folks of Dixie, and then there was that other thing on his mind. "I'm sure you realize I hired you since you were on the verge of becoming a great, young sports journalist…They're hiring you in Atlanta because they want a Black face in the sports section. They have no idea how direct you are or they think they can control you. I still don't get why you're leaving. You have a great future here, but if you want to go, you would be a lot better off considering some of those other places."

In addition to the earlier offers from *The AJC*, I had an offer from a new concept for newspapers called the *USA TODAY*. I had ones from the *New York Daily News* and *Newsday*, as well as from *The Kansas City Star*, the *Detroit Free Press*, along with a standing one to return to *The Cincinnati Enquirer*. In addition, I had my ongoing conversations that began in high school with *Los Angeles Times* sports editor Bill Dwyre. There also were my dealings since college with *The Washington Post* sports editor George Solomon, who joined Dwyre as two of the most significant names in the business.

My chat with Solomon included an introduction to Ben Bradlee, the famous *Post* editor who led the paper five years earlier during its Watergate days of Bob Woodward and Carl Bernstein. I sat nervously across from Bradlee in his office. With Solomon in silence nearby and with artifacts from the Kennedy family around the room, Bradlee turned to Solomon after delivering brief instructions to somebody who finished poking his head through the door and said, "What is Terence going to do if he doesn't join us for an internship?"

"He's got a job with *The Cincinnati Enquirer*," Solomon said. Bradlee twisted around in his chair, looked at me, and said with a laugh, "But there are no good newspapers in Ohio."

Actually, *The Cincinnati Enquirer* was pretty good during my stay in the late 1970s, and I went to a great newspaper after that in California called the *San Francisco Examiner*. Something just intrigued me about becoming the Jackie Robinson of sports columnists in the birthplace of Dr. King. At the *San Francisco Examiner*, I already was the only full-time Black sports columnist in the country for a major newspaper at that time. So, I figured, with God's help (and maybe with that of Henry Louis Aaron and other notable African Americans in Atlanta), I could enhance that role in a region where Blacks historically were told to keep their thoughts to themselves, especially regarding White folks.

This also intrigued me: *The AJC* sports editor said I would become one of the primary faces in his sports section within two years. Among others, the paper had regionally-revered sports columnists in Furman Bisher and Jesse Outlar, and they were as southern as sweet tea. They also were about as old as your tallest Georgia pine tree and they began working for the Atlanta newspapers long before Rosa Parks refused to move to the back of that bus in 1954 in nearby Birmingham, Alabama. Translated: this young Black guy from the Midwest via San Francisco would be a shock to the system of your average *AJC* readers.

According to the sports editor, Outlar was close to retirement, and as soon as the old man was out the door, the sports editor said *The AJC* would give me his slot, and "That will give us a chance to promote the hell out of Terence Moore even more."

Even though the *San Francisco Examiner* offered me a bunch to stay, I heard Black history whistling "Dixie." *I could help change things*, I said to myself, as a Yankee who spent his lifetime growing up in the Midwest, where I thought I knew about mind games. (Spoiler alert: given what I would experience early, often and forever at *The AJC*, I didn't know a flip about mind games.) As a bonus, I figured I could go from a phone relationship to a face-to face one with Henry Louis Aaron, the ultimate Jackie disciple of *my* Jack Roosevelt Robinson.

That part worked. As for the newspaper part, not so much. Well, not at all, but I wasn't totally naïve to some of the horrors to come.

I knew from colleagues with connections that Coop was omniscient about the situation. With *The AJC* sports staff growing into one of the largest in newspaper history during the 1980s, those running the operation wished to fix a problem. They lacked a prominent Black person in the sports section and they wanted to attract African American readers around a city that was becoming known as the Black Mecca. They wanted what they believed was the best African American sports journalist in the country to write columns. Sort of.

They didn't say this part out loud: even though sports columnists usually gave their opinions, *The AJC* bosses wanted an African American who would write feature stories disguised as sports columns and keep his mouth shut. They wanted a Black face. That is all.

Coop told me all of that. "You can always come back," Coop said during our last meal as employer and employee, and he wasn't the only person telling me to do more than Tony Bennett, who sang he left his heart in San Francisco.

The majority of those I trusted in the business urged me to keep my heart, body, and soul in Northern California or just about any other place outside of the Atlanta newspapers. I appreciated their concerns, but I didn't embrace them. As soon as I crossed the eastbound part of the San Francisco-Oakland Bay Bridge during the middle of January 1985, I had this thought, and it kept getting louder in my subconscious the closer my Datsun 200 reached the Alabama-Georgia state line: *Charles Cooper probably is right. Don't trust these folks, but no matter what happens, I'll only leave The AJC on my terms. Either that, or they'll have to fire me and they better do so with good reason!*

That's how Jackie and Hank would respond, along with my parents, who perfected the art of prospering through racism before my very eyes. Even so, I only gave Mom, Dad, my two brothers, and my relatives the big picture of my challenges there. I knew if they heard the blow-by-blow, they would fly to Atlanta to drag me by my ankles through Tennessee and Kentucky until we crossed the Mason-Dixon Line.

I saved the details for Hank and others.

They knew the depth of the racist phone calls and hateful messages I endured for 25 years. They also knew my endless battles with the mind games from *The AJC* bosses, and those mind games were designed to get me to quit, to destroy my career, or to do both. Those mind games came from upper-management officials, along with whoever the sports editor was at the moment, and the slew of designated terrorists that were the assistants under the sports editor. Some of those assistants were supportive. Dinn Mann topped the list and he hired me nearly a couple of decades later for a lengthy stay as a national sports columnist when he ran Sportsonearth.com and MLB.com.

To Hank and to my other insiders, I referred to *The AJC* bosses as the Dixiecrats, harkening back to the late 1940s, when Southern conservative, White politicians left the integration-minded Democratic Party of Harry Truman to keep their segregated ways. The Dixiecrats promoted their racism as a party only during the 1948 presidential year, but their philosophies remained. Over my 25 years at *The AJC*, my Dixiecrats came and went, and several weren't Southerners, but Dr.

King said he encountered some of his worse racism from Northerners in Chicago. A few of my Dixiecrats were African American, but so was Uncle Ruckus, the internally racist Black character who hated Black people in *The Boondocks* cartoon series.

With the exception of Mann and some others, the Dixiecrats dominated my stay at *The AJC*. They were obsessed with me because I was their Black sports columnist who wouldn't stay on his side of the tracks by having the audacity to keep giving his opinion—and strong ones—even about White folks and the University of Georgia. Worse, in the minds of the Dixiecrats, I was their Black sports columnist who kept combining with Henry Louis Aaron to make national news by hurling fastballs when discussing racism and social injustice.

It didn't take long for me to determine all of those things along with this: in the minds of the Dixiecrats, the more national exposure their Black sports columnist got (especially with Aaron in the middle of it), the harder it would be to get rid of him, but they tried. They never stopped trying. In contrast, after I joined *The AJC*, it didn't take long for me to notice the other four sports columnists gave their opinions, and they were allowed to operate without mind games. But they were White.

That brings me back to February 1985, when *The AJC* mind games began during my meeting in the Big Bulldog's office. As everybody nodded in the room, including the two men in the dark suits, the sports editor said again they wanted me to turn in my opinion pieces days in advance and he added it was "just to help you out," presumably to make sure my comma usage was okay. I declined their offer, which led to silence except for the sports editor taking a slow puff on his cigarette.

Just like that, I knew the Dixiecrats hadn't done their homework on my "blunt-writing style" that Coop said would scare them to death, but when I left The Big Bulldog's office, I kept writing what I was writing. I did negative and positive columns on University of Georgia sports teams and I did the same regarding everything and everybody else in local and national sports. I did opinion pieces on social injustice in sports—usually with African Americans as a central theme given my Jackie Robinson role as a Black sports columnist in the cradle of the civil rights movement—and I offered solutions.

The Dixiecrats couldn't stand it. I prepared for the lunacy that packed my office voicemail no matter the day or the hour.

"Moore, you are a vicious, Black racist. If a White person said the same things you say about White people to the Black race, they would be fired by *The AJC* in a heartbeat. But because of *The AJC*'s political correctness, you're allowed to keep your job and spout this vicious, racist rhetoric about Blacks and African American coaches and Blacks this and that and the lack thereof. Come on, it's just, it's just ridiculous. You just [are] continuingly attacking White ballplayers and continuously praise African American or Black athletes. You're just a racist. Why don't you write a column and be honest? 'I am a Black racist, and I'm proud of it.' Go ahead. Be up front about it. You are a vicious Black racist, I'll tell you. Comments by you and other people have turned me into a White racist. Your vicious Black racism makes it okay for me to be a White racist because you get away with it. So why can't I be a White racist? And that's what I am. That's what I've become because of your vicious, Black racism."

"You're a fucking n----r, a goddamn n----r. You want to take away the MVP award from Judge Mountain Landis, who saved Major League Baseball, and you want to give it to Hank Aaron, because he's Black. And, by the way, the greatest player ever to play the game was Babe Ruth because in addition to his 714 home runs he won almost 100 games as a pitcher, including three World Series games. So, he's the greatest Major League Baseball player ever, but you would never acknowledge that because you're a n----r. You're a goddamn n----r. You're a bigot. You hate White people. You viciously hate White people. You're a goddamn n----r. Go back to Notre Dame, you fucking Catholic bastard. Go back to Notre Dame. You talk about Notre Dame and then you come down here and you say, 'I'm glad they didn't get the Super Bowl.' Unbelievable ingrate. What a fucking ingate you are. Go play in traffic, you goddamn n----r. You fucking piece of shit. You carpetbagger, Catholic carpetbagger, you fucking piece of shit."

Those were two of the kinder, gentler ones.

To keep my sanity, I often thought about how the racial jabs I received were the poor man's version of what Jackie and Hank got on a heightened level during their barrier-busting times as players and during their decades afterward as prominent civil rights spokespersons. Here are some Hank mentioned to me, and I later found them in print:

> Dear Hank Aaron,
> I got orders to do a bad job on you if and when you get 10 from B. Ruth record. A guy in Atlanta and a few in Miami Fla don't seem to care if they have to take care of your family too.

> Hey n----r boy,
> We at the KKK Staten island Division want you to know that no number of guards can keep you dirty son of a bitch n----r—alive.

> Dear Hank Aaron,
> How about some sickle cell anemia, Hank?

> Dear Hank Aaron,
> I hope you get it between the eyes.

By the time Hank passed Babe Ruth's 714 career home runs on April 8, 1974, he was receiving 3,000 letters per day. The ones carrying death threats were put in plastic bags before they were sent to the FBI. He eventually got a plaque from the U.S. Postal Service for accumulating more pieces of mail overall (930,000) than anybody outside of politicians.

I joked with my closest friends during my opening couple of months at the paper: "I'm not sure if this racist stuff I'm getting is coming from outside or inside *The AJC*." After the steady diet of mind games from the Dixiecrats worsened over the next year or so through 1986, I stopped saying that as a joke, and then those mind games raced to a level that fluctuated between nasty and dangerous for the rest of my stay there. The Dixiecrats wanted me gone.

During the summer of 1987, a White sportswriter at *The AJC* huddled with me in the back of the sports office. "I know what they promised you and I don't want you to get blindsided," he said. "I heard a bunch of the assistant sports editors talking, and they were saying you would make a good beat writer, covering one of the professional Atlanta teams."

Since I wouldn't leave, the Dixiecrats were plotting to switch me from giving my opinion as the Jackie Robinson of sports journalism in major newspapers to writing game stories on the Braves, the Falcons, or the Hawks. I kept that in the back of my mind, but I kept writing what I was writing, and the Dixiecrats kept thinking they needed to get nastier. Even though the Dixiecrats wanted me gone, they had a dilemma. It was their dilemma for 25 years. They wanted me gone, but they didn't want to trigger the following headline from their peers across the country: "First Black sports columnist in the history of the Deep South harassed into leaving The City Too Busy To Hate and home of Dr. Martin Luther King Jr. by the Dixiecrats of *The Atlanta Journal-Constitution*."

The Dixiecrats also knew about Hank and me. It terrified them.

In sum, from the Dixiecrats' perspective, one of the most important persons in sports history lived in Atlanta, and he shared his thoughts on controversial issues such as race in America with only the Black columnist they wanted gone, and he wasn't a fan of *The AJC*.

The Dixiecrats were their friendliest toward me when they needed something in the paper regarding one of Hank's No. 715 anniversaries, Hank's thoughts on Barry Bonds and steroids, or Hank's eulogy of a baseball legend.

When my column involved Hank on those other subjects such as racism, they rushed to their playbook on mind games. "Outside of yourself, I don't have anything to say to those folks at that newspaper really," Hank told me in the late 1980s from his office at Atlanta-Fulton County Stadium. "If I talk to them, I talk to [*The AJC* writers] and I'm courteous because I'm that way with everybody. But I'm not looking to talk to them. You got my numbers. You call me any time at the office or tell Susan [Bailey, his secretary, personal assistant, and gatekeeper] you're looking for me or you can get me at the dealership or just call me at home. You still got that number, right?" I did and called that number often.

Soon after Aaron came to Georgia from Wisconsin in 1966 with the Braves, his respect for the Atlanta papers (separated between the *Constitution* and the *Journal* until 2001) fluctuated between dislike and worse than that. He said the local writers twisted his words as a player in the beginning and later as a Braves executive. He said they pounded him with potshots over his honest tongue, especially regarding social issues. In 1974 when Hank played for the Braves, he went from his normally even-tempered self to smashing a basket of strawberries into the face of Atlanta reporter Frank Hyland for writing Hank "double-talked" by telling Hyland's paper, *The Atlanta Journal*, that Hank didn't wish to become the Braves manager in 1974 and by saying the opposite in the aftermath to a national television commentator.

Hyland didn't mention Hank's reason for changing his mind. After Hank's original conversation with Hyland, Braves general manager Eddie Robinson suggested to another Atlanta reporter that the city wasn't ready for a Black manager despite having Jackson as its Black mayor and Young representing much of Atlanta in the U.S. House of Representatives. Given that, Hank reversed course on the subject to tell that national reporter something like, "Why not me?"

Hank also had no use for Outlar. When I told Hank during one of our initial meetings after my arrival from San Francisco that I was slated to take Outlar's place in stature at the paper, Hank rejoiced as if he'd just slammed No. 756.

Outlar wrote things, saying Hank was just a mouthpiece for civil rights leaders, which Hank took as the cheapest of blows. That's because it was. Henry Louis Aaron spent his life proclaiming loyalty to Jack Roosevelt Robinson, the epitome of a civil rights leader. Then, after Jackie's death in October 1972, Hank said to anybody who would listen that he'd honor his hero by taking over his social justice agenda regarding baseball and life.

A mouthpiece for civil rights leaders? Hank *was* a civil rights leader. Despite Outlar's cluelessness on Hank's sense of destiny, Bisher was Hank's least favorite person at the Atlanta papers. "Every chance he gets, he takes a jab at me, and they let it happen. It's been that way since I stepped foot in this town, just totally against me, and I'm sick of it," Hank told me in the mid-1990s.

Within days of anything in the media about Hank Aaron ripping baseball or society for its treatment of African Americans (usually written in *The AJC* or said over the airways by me as The Hank Aaron Whisperer), Bisher would pounce to counter.

In June of 1987, Hank told me he was joining civil rights leader Jesse Jackson and his Operation Push organization in calling for a Fourth of July boycott of major league games over baseball's hiring practices. The Philadelphia Phillies triggered Hank's anger by firing nondescript John Felske as manager and by hiring the recycled Lee Elia. They both were White. Hank told me, along with others gathered for his words on the situation, "I know what [the Phillies] are going to say. They're going to say that [Elia] is an organizational man, that he knows the organization, and we hired him because of that. I know things aren't going to change overnight, but what I'm looking for is some fairness in decision-making on the part of owners."

Hank's words barely left my computer keys before Bisher responded with the following in his column: "Once more Jesse Jackson and Henry Aaron have teamed up on a baseball target, this time the Phillies. Jackson's aim in life is clearly stated. He is the man who would combine church and state by putting a 'Rev.' in the White House. Politicians will use any ploy to keep their name in print. But Aaron, here is a man on the payroll of the Braves, a rival of the Phillies. That the Phillies should fire John Felske and replace him with Lee Elia should be none of his concern. Baseball has certain rules about crossing the line of club relationships. 'What I'm looking for is some fairness in decision-making on the part of owners,' [Aaron] said for some reason." Four years later, in February of 1991, Hank published a book called *I Had a Hammer*, detailing some of his racial issues as a player through conversations with Lonnie Wheeler, one of my former colleagues at *The Cincinnati Enquirer*. Bisher decided he needed to respond and, after he mentioned deep into his column that he once authored his own Henry Aaron book, Bisher added Hank was just trying "to get more attention." Then Bisher wrote: "Aaron's most cogent contributions to baseball have been with a bat. He would have liked to have been a big-time executive, but he didn't like taking a cut in pay. He has had the title of farm director, director of player development, and now is listed as 'senior vice president and assistant to the president,' who is Stan Kasten. How much he has assisted is kept within the family. His main service to the Braves has been titular rather than active. In a sense, he has been a pensioned artifact, playing the role of a professional Hank Aaron, Home Run King."

Hank called me, fuming. As we discussed Bisher's latest piece, which suggested Henry Louis Aaron didn't know how to stay in his place, something occurred to me during what was then my sixth year at *The AJC*: I was in my final stage of becoming Jackie and Hank.

What Bisher wrote about Hank was what the Dixiecrats thought about me, which was that I had gotten too big for my britches: *Don't try to upstage the White columnists. Keep your mouth shut and your computer keys from moving, especially whenever you have the urge to give your opinion about race, getting rid of White folks in authority, the Georgia Bulldogs, or anything else we might find offensive, which is why we wanted you to turn in your columns days in advance, so we could help you out.*

The Bisher-Hank thing and my Dixiecrats thing sounded like a passage from Jackie's autobiography, which I re-read often, along with the Bible, as antidotes to those *AJC* mind games. Jackie wrote: "It is not terribly difficult for the black man as an individual to enter into the white man's world and be partially accepted. However, if that individual black man is, in the eyes of the white world, an 'uppity n----r,' he is in for a very hard time indeed. I can just hear my liberal white friends and a lot of Negroes, who haven't yet got the word that they are black, protesting such an observation."

I wouldn't follow the Dixiecrats' script. If I did, it would have been like Hank choosing to hide inside a closet at his southwest Atlanta home instead of deciding to chase Babe Ruth's ghost despite those death threats and racist messages. Even during my early years at *The AJC*—particularly in the fall of 1987, when I knew a showdown was coming between the Dixiecrats and me involving Outlar's retirement—I already was Jackie and Hank, which meant I placed conviction over capitulation. The Dixiecrats detected that, which is why they wanted me gone even more so.

They had one tactic left. Mind games 2.0.

With Outlar's retirement nearly at hand in 1987, the sports editor told me he had a surprise for me. "It's something wonderful. You'll love it," he said between puffs on his cigarette. In addition to Bisher, Outlar, and myself, *The AJC* had two other general sports columnists (both White, of course), and the sports editor said one of those two other columnists "has agreed" to critique my columns "to help you out." I was caught off guard, but I tried not to show it.

When I went into that columnist's office, he opened his briefcase and he had a stack of *The AJC* sports sections featuring my columns smothered with red marks everywhere. One of the things that columnist told me "to help me out" was that I should always end my columns with something positive or maybe a quote or perhaps both. What he essentially was saying is that it would turn my columns more into feature stories to help the Dixiecrats get rid of my blunt opinions, even though that columnist didn't follow his own advice.

I was done with that.

The sports editor later called me into his office. He leaned back in his chair from behind his desk and he said he was "disappointed" I wasn't going to those sessions with that other columnist who was trying to "help me out." While frowning between cigarette puffs, the sports editor added, "We've got a problem. Everybody says you're blasting everybody on the paper, and it's in the press box, and...they say it's everywhere, Terry. And they're saying it's bad. Everybody says you're bad news and they don't like working with you."

Rage threatened to sprint from my little toes to the tallest hair on my head, but I caught myself. I thought of every conflict I faced and conquered, spanning from my pre-teen days around South Bend, Indiana, to our moves involving three different states in three years and three different high schools to Miami (Ohio) University, and then to working in Cincinnati and San Francisco. I thought of Jackie and Hank.

Everybody? So, everybody says I'm bad news?

I hadn't a problem with most of *The AJC* writers or even with many of the assistant editors in the sports department. *Blasting colleagues in public?* Several folks at *The AJC* were typical of journalists everywhere: they were constant grumblers and they fired arrows in the shadows at fellow writers and editors. They did so in press boxes, in vehicles, or planes traveling to sporting events and in the taverns they loved to frequent after surviving deadline.

I never was that guy. *Who's saying these things?*

"Everybody, Terry," the sports editor said, puffing his cigarette, studying my face for a reaction that never came. "It's everybody."

Courtesy of those conversations with the sports editor, I became even more disciplined at doing what I would do for my next two decades at *The AJC*. After an average day of mind games from the Dixiecrats, I went home and I documented everything in detail right down to something like the last puff from the sports editor's cigarette. I even befriended an individual in *The AJC* personnel department. After our huddles on the latest batch of mind games from the

Dixiecrats, that individual would shake his head between expletives and then he would copy whatever I had to offer for placement in a file cabinet with his personal key.

When things got rougher in my latter years at the paper, I sought legal advice. I was told I would win the battle while losing the war and I realized as much. The media remained a predominately White industry, and despite my resume complete with brilliant references, I still would be that Black guy who had some kind of racial problems in Atlanta.

The legal advice was to leave, but I was Jackie and Hank, which meant I kept writing what I was writing.

Shortly after that meeting with the sports editor, I was off to Miami, Florida, to write about the surging Hurricanes in college football. Ralph Wiley was there, too. He was a *Sports Illustrated* writer and he authored best-selling books such as *Why Black People Tend to Shout: Cold Facts and Wry Views from a Black Man's World.* When I was at the *San Francisco Examiner* during the early 1980s, Ralph and I became friends when he worked across the bay for the *Oakland Tribune* as the second Black person ever to write a full-time general sports column for a major newspaper. Thom Greer was the first in the late 1970s with the *Philadelphia Daily News.* Then I was the third in 1983 at the *Examiner.* Ralph pulled me aside in the media dining room of the press box of the Orange Bowl to say, slightly above a whisper, "You know you're scaring those White folks to death down there, Terry. You're not in San Francisco anymore."

We laughed, and then Ralph turned serious. "Do you know Roy Johnson of *The New York Times?*" Ralph asked. "Roy is a feature writer for *The New York Times,* and they're working behind your back to hire him, trying to replace a Black man with another Black man. Now that's messed up. You have to do what you feel comfortable doing, but whatever you do, watch your back."

Ralph wasn't the only journalist mentor of mine with such a warning. I called Tom Callahan, the sports editor at *Time* magazine. Tom was White. We worked together at *The Cincinnati Enquirer*, where he was a hard-edged columnist and deep thinker. He knew some of the Dixiecrats, calling them "classic little rednecks" and then he said, "Get out. It won't get better, Terry, but knowing you as a principled guy, you're going to stay, and I understand. Since you're going to stay, you need to take the approach of the Marines…You're already dead."

As long as I worked at *The AJC*, even if it was for something like 25 years, the Dixiecrats would terrorize me. So I figured I might as well go down swinging by keep writing what I was writing.

Sure enough, a few days after my Miami trip, which was the first week of December 1987 and slightly less than two years after I left San Francisco, *The AJC* sports editor called me into his office. He said he would get right to the point, and I was prepared. From start to finish of the meeting, I documented every syllable, every gesture, and every puff, and he didn't seem to care. The sports editor began by saying the paper wanted to turn me into a general assignment sportswriter, adding, "You write two or three great columns, but then you write one or two that ain't so great, and to be a columnist at this paper, all your columns have to be great. Everybody here writes great columns, but you don't. Now…if you went to a place like the *L.A. Times*, you would be like great there, but you're not great on a consistent basis to write columns here."

I stared at the sports editor without saying a word or showing a hint of emotion either way. "Okay, we're hiring another Black guy to take your place," the sports editor said, raising his voice as he leaned toward me. He eased into a biting tone, saying, "How does that make you feel, Terry? We hired another Black guy to take your place. We think he's going to be more cooperative than you've been. He's never written a column before. So he's going to need a lot of help, so he won't act like you. How does that make you feel? I would tell you his name, but I won't." The sports editor paused, looking down, then he glanced up to say, "It's Roy Johnson. Roy Johnson of *The New York Times*. He's going to take your place. How does that make you feel?"

I stood up and I said in a calm voice to the sports editor to put everything in writing. After he screamed from behind his desk, "We're not putting shit in writing," he lowered his tone: "We need you to do us a favor. Roy won't be here from *The New York Times* for a few more weeks. Can you…uh…continue to write columns until he gets here?" I already knew what that was about. "Clumsy" was the operative word to describe the Dixiecrats' view of African Americans in Atlanta and of African Americans in general. The Dixiecrats figured it didn't matter who had the Black face in their sports section. They figured African Americans in Atlanta just wanted somebody's (anybody's) Black face in *The AJC* sports section on a regular basis after I started the tradition nearly two years before.

Hank and I later discussed many of my issues at *The AJC* in 2001.

"We've talked about this before. There have been more than a few times they've tried to get rid of me," I told Hank.

"Uh huh. You need to write a book."

"Yeah, someday I will because this, I mean, when they hired me, they just wanted to hire a Black guy they thought was good. They didn't do any research. The way I approach writing my opinion now is the way I've always done it. I don't take any prisoners. So, when they hired me, they found out real quickly I wasn't the kind of Black guy they wanted."

"Uh huh. Uh huh. They wanted somebody who would just roll over. Do what they tell you to write and how they want you to write it."

"That's exactly right. That's exactly right," I said as we both laughed. "When that didn't happen, that's when they got crazy, and all my friends in the business, Black and White, were telling me to get outta there, all that stuff. But I just became defiant. I just said to myself, *Look. If these guys are going to get rid of me, they better come hard and correct. I'm not going anywhere.* Besides that, I like Atlanta."

"I don't blame you, you know. It's like a lot of Black people I tell in baseball. I say, 'When you take a job, you gonna have to put up with a bunch of crap, but don't quit. You make sure you make them fire you. Don't just walk away because if you walk away, you give them an excuse to say whatever they want to say, you know. Make them fire you.' I told, God rest his soul, somebody all of that long before he died. He had to deal with a bunch of crap, and I said, 'Whatever you do, make them fire you.' He didn't do it. He quit instead of getting fired, and it was hard for him to get back in the game. So you're absolutely right, Terence. You're doing the right thing. Really, they don't have a reason to get rid of you. That's the thing. That's what's eaten at them. If they don't have a reason, they just can't come out and say, 'Well, we just don't like the way he writes.'"

"Exactly."

"Hang in there, buddy."

I did. When Johnson joined the paper as a sports columnist during the early part of 1988, I was still there. I never got anything in writing from the Dixiecrats, which I requested mostly as a scare tactic, and I never reported to the assistant sports editor I allegedly was supposed to contact for my new general sports assignment job. Without ever following up with the sports editor or anybody else, I just kept doing what I was doing as a general columnist and I also kept writing what I was writing.

How convinced were the Dixiecrats I'd be gone after my December 1987 meeting with the sports editor, featuring that fist banging against his desk, those curse words, and the flashing eyes? Well, Phillip M. Hoose published a book in 1989 called *Necessities: Racial Barriers in American Sports,* and his research began long before that. On page 21 of the chapter entitled "The Media," he wrote: "At this writing, among general-circulation newspapers, there is one black sports columnist in America, Roy Johnson of *The Atlanta Journal-Constitution,* who took over the column from another black, Terry Moore."

Johnson ended up leaving *The AJC* after barely a year. With Hank applauding, I was still there. So was that dilemma for *The AJC* bosses.

• • •

In April of 1989, I wrote a column blasting the ongoing racism in the NFL involving Black quarterbacks, and Rodney Peete was my focal point. He left Southern Cal with nearly every significant record you can name for the Trojans. He finished his senior year behind only Barry Sanders in the 1988 Heisman Trophy voting and he ended 330 points ahead of third-place finisher Troy Aikman, UCLA's quarterback who lost twice to Peete-led USC teams, including once just days after Peete was hospitalized with the measles.

The Dallas Cowboys made Aikman the No. 1 overall pick in the 1989 NFL Draft, and Peete was taken 141st in the sixth round by the Detroit Lions. Blatant. Awful. Typical.

I wrote all of that. "Even though this year's NFL draft is nearly two weeks and 3,189 Deion Sanders stories old, the thought of Southern Cal's Rodney Peete having to wait until the sixth round for his phone to ring remains unfathomable. Then, all of a sudden, you remember two things: (1) Rodney Peete is Black. (2) Rodney Peete is a quarterback. End of mystery. Nothing causes NFL officials to suffer amnesia faster than when a Rodney Peete comes along. After somebody snaps them out of their momentary funk by reminding them of the impressive college resume of a Rodney Peete, they start the excuses. They claim a Rodney Peete wasn't considered a top quarterback prospect in the NFL because (pick two or more) he wasn't tall enough, didn't have a strong enough arm, was such a great athlete that he was projected as a wide receiver or a defensive back. At Southern Cal, where Trojans have starred on football fields for more than a century, Peete broke 17 school records, some running, some passing. He led the Trojans to the Rose Bowl after a 10–1 finish last season. In all, eight quarterbacks were picked ahead of Peete in the draft, and of the eight, only Troy

Aikman finished in the top 10 of the Heisman Trophy voting last year…"

The Dixiecrats killed the column.

I knew I had to walk into the sports editor's office on the day my Peete piece didn't appear. *So why did you kill it?* "Because it didn't make sense, Terry. You don't really believe that shit, do you?" he said, laughing. "Everybody knows Rodney Peete can't play, everybody. I know you don't mind embarrassing yourself, but we did you a favor on that one. [Peete] ain't that good. The editors were passing [the column] around and laughing. We have high standards. None of the other [columnists] write shit like that. So, no, we weren't running it."

Peete played 15 NFL seasons, by the way.

The sports editor took a puff from his cigarette then he stared at me as I left his office without saying a word. I sought an audience with the relatively new overall editor of the paper. He'd always been among the Dixiecrats but only in other capacities. Even though I knew this meeting was worthless, I wanted it for my files on dealing with *The Atlanta Journal-Constitution*, which were expanding by the mind game. I couldn't see any of my bosses that afternoon, but I did several days later.

The conversation was brutal.

After I told *The AJC* official about the ugliness displayed by the sports editor during that conversation over the killing of my Peete column, that official squinted as he leaned forward in his chair a few feet away. Then he said in a soft yet threatening tone, "Why are you still here on the paper? I don't get it. I talked to, well, none of us get. Nobody likes you. *Nobody*, and if you stay, we will make life miserable for you. I can tell you that."

"When you say you will make life miserable for me, what does that mean?" I asked without blinking.

The AJC official moved back in his chair and then he said with disgust growing across his face, "Look. Just take some time off. Take, take, take, you can. Just take as much time as… We'll pay you not to write until you find another job, and I'll even help you go someplace else."

I wasn't going anywhere. As the years became decades, I kept writing what I was writing, and the Dixiecrats kept trying to get rid of me without leaving any fingerprints. This was the epitome of institutional racism. The Dixiecrats came and went—stretching from the sports department through mid-level bosses to the head of the paper—but they continued *The AJC*'s disdain for that Black sports columnist who still had the audacity to write hard-edged opinions, frequently in cahoots with Henry Louis Aaron. So the mind games also continued, but these mind games fluctuated between imaginative and sinister.

To the Dixiecrats, they hadn't a choice. They had that old dilemma, which was trying to get rid of a Black sports columnist without telling the world it was because they didn't like his opinions. Then they had a new dilemma, and this one made them crazier than the previous one: it involved my rising celebrity in print through cyberspace and over the airways. Despite those mind games by the Dixiecrats, I kept growing bigger outside of their little newspaper bubble than the White columnists they always promoted over me. Not only that, but from the early 1990s through my *AJC* departure in April 2009, I also was the most noted person on the paper both locally and nationally.

After *CNN/SI* launched in 1996, its bosses called me to do opinion pieces on air for the network on a regular basis. I spent the middle of that decade as the cohost of the drive home show on weekdays for Atlanta's first sports talk radio station. I became one of the ESPN regulars for their *SportsCentury* series on legendary athletes, including Henry Louis Aaron. I began spending several Sunday nights per month doing work for the local ABC affiliate. I was part of a Saturday night show every week for the NBC affiliate. There also was that time before an Atlanta Hawks game, when a young radio announcer just hired in the local market approached me to say, "I just want to tell you: I don't always agree with you, but you do a great job with your columns: well-written, stimulating thought. You're a dual threat, for sure. In addition to newspapers, you have a splendid future in electronic media."

The guy's name was Sean Hannity. Yeah, *that* Sean Hannity, who later became one of the celebrated right-wing hosts on FOX.

That was just the 1990s. Through it all, the Dixiecrats couldn't stand it. They developed those new mind games, but as always, they had to unleash them with care. Well, they tried.

I leaned on what Jackie Robinson wrote in *I Never Had It Made*: "If a black becomes too important or too big for his racial britches or if he has too much power, he will get cut down. They will cut him down even when the power the black has doesn't come from the white man…Name them for me. The examples of blacks who 'made it.' For virtually every one you name, I can give you a sordid piece of factual information on how they have been mistreated, humiliated."

After the early 1990s, there was a different *AJC* sports editor, but it didn't matter. He was a longtime Dixiecrat at the paper. Whereas the earlier sports editor took a sledgehammer approach to delivering his mind games between puffs on his cigarette, this one preferred a smiley face. So, that spring of 1996, I went into that sports editor's office with notes in hand and I told him about the lopsided numbers regarding the placement of my columns on the front sports section compared to the three White columnists. I gave him the notes. (Well, it was a copy of the notes because I kept the originals for my *AJC* files). I also told him about the three straight weeks of my column on the back page of the Sunday sports section.

The epitome of The Burying happened in April 1997 after Tiger Woods blew away the field for his first victory at The Masters in Augusta, Georgia. Two days later Woods appeared on Oprah Winfrey's show with his father, and Tiger said he invented a name for himself as a kid. Since his father was African American and his mother was Asian, he said he went by Cabilanasian. I wrote about the whole thing the following day in an *AJC* column entitled, "Wake up, Tiger, this is America, and that means you're Black."

That column was buried on Page 8 just above an ad for Honda lawnmowers, but at least Henry Louis Aaron found it. He was a fan of the golfer and of the columnist and he called me with words of praise, adding near the end, "Terence, you just keep giving them hell."

Somebody else found the column.

"Hello, Terence? This is Oprah Winfrey," said the caller on the other end of my home phone, and it really was Oprah. "I'm a great admirer of your work. You're one of my favorite sports columnists. I read your piece on Tiger today and I really enjoyed your perspective and I wanted to see if I can have you on Tuesday's show next week to discuss it more."

I agreed to do Oprah's show, of course.

I also got a phone call later that day from the sports editor with the smiley face, and he complained about the avalanche of nasty messages they were getting at *The AJC* regarding my Woods column. He wasn't upset that most of those messages were from folks still fighting the Civil War. He said with a perturbed tone that was a contrast to his smiley face, "It's not fair, Terry. It's just not fair to the rest of us that we have to answer these calls over something you write. You're not in here, and we have to deal with this."

With help from my Oprah appearance, I moved toward the 21st century as a magnet for requests to do even more national and local television, and the Dixiecrats just got angrier. They revved up the mind games, especially since their three White columnists were getting nothing along those lines.

On Sunday, August 13, 2000, I wrote: "Atlanta should never get another Final Four. Atlanta should never get another Super Bowl. Atlanta should never get another anything from outside of this anachronistic state until its Confederate flag flies only in museums. Period.

"Enough of politicians smothering this ugly issue with pretty words. Forget those playing mind games by claiming the Confederate flag represents heritage instead of hatred. If that Confederate flag literally doesn't become history around here, Georgia should pay a hefty price for its ignorance. That hefty price should include Atlanta getting shunned by those who actually know the South lost the Civil War."

That was the column that helped Georgia state representative Tyrone L. Brooks and others months later to finish their mission to have the Confederate battle emblem removed from Georgia's state flag. The reason I knew that column was a huge contributor to the flag-changing process was because Brooks called to tell me as much. That also was the column that made the Dixiecrats lose their minds over my presence in their world because that was the column that forced them to adopt the Malcolm X approach toward seeking ways to get me out of their sight: by any means necessary.

That Confederate flag column led to more buried columns for me in the section over the next few months, and there also were too many little mind games from the Dixiecrats to mention.

Then came The Big One.

Following the terrorist attacks of September 2001, the Dixiecrats restructured parts of their departments. Virtually none of that juggling involved sports folks or anybody involved with writing commentary for the paper. Nevertheless, the sports editor with the smiley face used his right-hand man for his dirty work. That right-hand man was a notoriously joyless soul, but days after the New York twin towers collapsed, that right-hand man called me on the phone at home, just as I was heading to Bible study, and he said with a rare burst of glee, "Hi, Terry. I have some good news for you...You are no longer a sports columnist," the right-hand man said, his voice rising over the phone. "You need to report to the newsroom tomorrow for your assignment as a member of the war on terrorism unit. If you have any questions, just give them a call. Pretty simple, and I really have nothing more to add, but any questions for me, Terry?"

The sports editor said "they," as in the Dixiecrats, discussed everybody on the newspaper, and "they" determined it would be "fantastic" for me to go from sports to one of the new teams they were forming on 9/11 coverage. "You'll be great," the sports editor said. "I know you love writing about politics and what not, things of that nature, and it'll be a perfect fit. I mean, these are different times. Oh, my gosh, we all have to be flexible, and this is just something, well, it's something that has already been decided, and you can…"

When I found out the three White sports columnists were remaining in the sports section, I told him I was remaining a sports columnist. He said something in response fairly loudly for somebody who normally had a smiley face, but I wasn't listening. I kept walking. I went to the managing editor and I repeated what I told the sports editor about not changing roles. Then, after hearing more Dixiecrat gobbledygook, I hinted of going nuclear for the first time during my stay at *The AJC*. I told the managing editor I easily could get the Black community involved and I added I would tell the same to *The AJC*'s overall editor and to the publisher. I mentioned the big names, including Mr. Jackson (Maynard and Jesse since Jesse and his people were close to the pastor at my powerful Atlanta church), Mr. Young, Mr. Lowery, and Mr. Aaron, and that was for starters. Then I suggested that headline was closer to reality than ever before: "First Black sports columnist in the history of the Deep South harassed into leaving The City Too Busy To Hate and home of Dr. Martin Luther King Jr. by the Dixiecrats of *The Atlanta Journal-Constitution*."

I never reported to whomever I was supposed to report to for *The AJC*'s war on terrorism team and I kept writing what I was writing. Even though I outsmarted the Dixiecrats during their attempt to turn me into a war correspondent or something, they were determined even more to get me out of there, especially since I continued to grow in national and local stature. They couldn't stand it, which led to this: instead of dialing my home this time, the sports editor's right-hand man with the joyless soul called me into the office for more "good news." He said I was *The AJC*'s new pro sports columnist.

I told them that sounds like they didn't want me writing about Georgia Tech, the University of Georgia, or other college teams.

The right-hand man with the joyless soul erupted, banging his fist on the desk similar to the bully of a chain-smoking sports editor who hired me. With the reddest of faces he said, "Yes. That's *exactly* what it means. You write too many negative columns about Georgia football and you write too many negative columns about Georgia Tech football. Yes, Terry. That's why we're doing this. You won't be able to write about Nolan Richardson running off at the mouth anymore. Yeah, that's what this means. That's *exactly* what this means."

The Richardson the assistant sports editor referenced was the University of Arkansas basketball coach who routinely turned into Jackie and Hank by talking about social issues while leading his Razorbacks to national glory. I wrote several columns through the years with Richardson on the shockingly low number of African Americans coaching football and basketball despite teams heavily populated by Black athletes, and most of those columns were buried, of course.

I knew the latest Jim Crow move by the Dixiecrats wouldn't last, and Henry Louis Aaron agreed. A few days later, before I introduced Hank as a speaker at a hotel ballroom in downtown Atlanta, he said, "You just keep doing what you're doing, Terence. They're just trying to intimidate you, buddy, and in the end, the Good Lord will take care of everything."

I knew he was right. I also knew several ESPN officials, including a producer I'd known for years. During the spring of 2002, he called me to say, "Terry, how long have you been at that newspaper?"

I told him 17 years.

He paused over the phone before saying, "Well, they're not doing you any favors down there. We want you to be a big part of this new show we're starting, but they won't let you do it, and it's hard to understand why. Maybe you can go talk to somebody in upper management."

The name of that ESPN show? *Around the Horn*, which remained a regular on ESPN for the following two decades. By sabotaging that deal, the Dixiecrats kept me from becoming part of the show's original crew while throwing away an opportunity for *The AJC* to grow revenue through free advertising on national television just about every weekday. That's how obsessed the Dixiecrats were with getting rid of that Black SOB still writing stuff they didn't like in their paper.

Nearly a year later, when *Around the Horn* flourished—with sports columnists giving their opinions from the prominently displayed newsrooms of *The Boston Globe, Los Angeles Times, The Dallas Morning News,* and elsewhere—I got a call from the sports editor with the smiley face. "Listen, we've been thinking and we've talked about some things and we decided to go ahead and let you do that ESPN show," the sports editor with the smiley face said, pausing for my reaction, but I was silent on the other end of the phone. Then he said in a hurry, "But, but, but here's what we want to do. We can go ahead and do the show here and everything, but we need to get our other columnists involved and…"

In a matter of seconds, the sports editor with the smiley face brought the Dixiecrats all the way out of the closet. He said what I already knew. They blew up that ESPN opportunity to keep me from outshining their designated faces (the White sports columnists) even more. It was way too late for that. Before long an ESPN producer friend called me with an opportunity to spend five years as one of the regular panelists on *The Jim Rome Show*, which paid me a significant sum to spend a week at a time doing telecasts from southern California, and the Dixiecrats couldn't stand it. In addition, I operated as the

Atlanta point person for ESPN in 2007 during Michael Vick's year-long issues with the Atlanta Falcons, the NFL, and dogfighting. I spent that year on nearly every media outlet with a satellite discussing Barry Bonds' chase of Hank's home run mark of 755. I had an increased role on the local ABC affiliate every Sunday night while doing the Falcons postgame show for the local Fox affiliate. I filmed a slew of interviews with NFL Films for their various projects shown on the NFL Network and ESPN. I got a regular role on ESPN's new show called *Classic Now*, where I appeared three to four times per week.

Barry Bonds broke Hank's career home run record with No. 756 in San Francisco on August 7, 2007. Henry Louis Aaron remained Henry Louis Aaron in the aftermath. Despite requests from ESPN to *The Washington Post* to CBS News, he said he would only give his thoughts to The Hank Aaron Whisperer, and it was great stuff as usual.

It was too great for the Dixiecrats.

Just as I prepared to send *The AJC* my exclusive column on Hank's response to Bonds' homer, I got a message from one of the assistant sports editors. He said they just wanted me to transcribe my conversation with Hank and send them only the quotes for publication. Mind games. I said I wouldn't do the transcription thing. The assistant sports editor said if I insisted, they would have to run my column (my planet-wide exclusive on Henry Louis Aaron giving his only thoughts to anybody on Barry Lamar Bonds chasing and then breaking Hank's sacred and hard-earned record of 33 years) on Page 2. The assistant sports editor said they wanted to put one of their other columnists (White, of course) on the front page, and that columnist was in New York covering a meaningless Braves regular-season game.

I told the assistant sports editor that *The AJC*'s decision makers would embarrass themselves if they did that, and through an exchange of emails, I repeated as much to the managing editor. I told both of them this whole thing was blatant and I told both of them I wasn't backing down.

They backed down. Sort of. They ran both columns on the front of the sports section, but mine was placed at the bottom of the page. In contrast, after that same Hank column was grabbed by every wire service you can imagine, it was prominently displayed by media outlets everywhere. Everywhere but Atlanta.

Courtesy of several more incidents over the next two years from the Dixiecrats that went beyond outrageous, I finally decided my Jackie and Hank role was over at *The AJC*. Destiny said so. In April of 2009, I sat in my dining room, thinking about *The AJC* horrors, along with the rapid decline of newspapers, and then the phone rang. It was from the head of AOL Sports, and he said he wished to hire me as one of their national sports columnists. I'd get a $25,000 per year raise with the ability to do whatever I wanted, and he added, "I love all of the TV work you do. We encourage that, and you do a fantastic job with your writing and commentating on ESPN and everyplace else. That helps us get our brand out there." (In addition to AOL, I eventually wrote sports columns for Forbes.com, CNN.com, Sportsonearth.com, and MLB.com with no drama and with none of them featuring anything close to their version of the Dixiecrats. I also kept writing what I was writing for each of those Internet sites.)

The next day, *The AJC* announced a huge buyout package for employees 55 or older with my experience. I was so out of there, but after I announced my two-week notice, the mind games continued. The Dixiecrats warned me several times not to try to write a farewell column on my last day in April 2009 because they said it was against *The AJC* policy. Six months after I left *The AJC*, Furman Bisher retired. Not only did he write a farewell column, but the Dixiecrats gave him a farewell section, along with tributes throughout the paper. I laughed.

I also called Hank.

> "Hey, this is Terence. How's it going?"
>
> "Well, hello, Terence. How ya doing, buddy," Hank said, laughing.
>
> "I'm doing very well, thank you."

"Where are you calling me from? Just saw you doing something on ESPN and good job! Yeah, good job, as always."

"Well, thank you. And, well, I'm here in Atlanta and I was going to tell you I escaped The Evil Empire, *The Atlanta Journal-Constitution.*"

"Oh, you did?"

"Yeah, I've been telling people. I was describing this to my dad the other day. It's like good news, great news, and greater news," I said, and we both laughed. "The good news is I'm no longer at the paper anymore. Because as you know, it's like all newspapers these days. Things are terrible, and they're getting worse."

"It sure is. I was just making a comment about [newspapers] the other day. It's horrible, especially with that paper, and you're the only person I read to get the true, get the insight."

"Yeah, yeah. Nobody's reading papers, but the better news is: I took the buyout, so they have to pay me my full salary through the end of April of next year."

Hank laughed and said, "Well, congratulations."

"Thank you, and then the best news of all is, I'm now a national sports columnist for AOL Sports. They'll pay me way more than what I was making at *The AJC.* I can do whatever I want. I can travel whenever I want to travel. I pretty much can call my own shots. It's like going from the Flintstones to the Jetsons," I said, laughing. "And I won't have to deal with anything close to the craziness we've been talking about for the last 25 years."

"That's putting it kind of mildly," Hank said, laughing. "Well, good. You deserve it, Terence. You haven't missed a beat, and everything is going in the right direction. I know, well, I know all the crap you were dealing with...uh, uh, uh...And I know you were going to stay until you wanted to leave and you handled it just right really. I'm proud of you."

"Well, thanks, and I still get to do the ESPN stuff, the Sunday night show on Channel 2, and all the other stuff. And besides the sports columns for them, I'll do videos for them. Online is where everything is headed."

"That's exactly right, and you know, as much as I grew up with newspapers many years ago, I think I kind of do the same thing. I've got so now that I just turn on my computer and in fact I look at some of the games [on computer]. So that's exactly where it's turning to, and well, with you gone from that paper, I got nothing else to look forward to."

We both laughed.

"I'll tell you what's interesting," I told Hank. "I've only been gone from the paper a few days, and the word is everywhere, and all these people who used to get so upset over what I wrote, I mean, I'm getting all of these people stopping me on the street, and saying, 'Oh man. I want you to come back. The paper is so boring now. Please come back.' And that's the thing. They may not have liked what I wrote, but they read it."

"You know this, and you did this, Terence. You have to be you because you can't please everybody. You write the way you see it and the way you interpret it, and when the White writers do it, they don't have a problem, but you were the problem. Sickening, really, but that's just the way it is. But I still catch you all the time on television, me and my wife, and I'm always pleased with your commentating and the way you handle yourself. Just keep remembering: be honest, keep to your beliefs, and convictions and you'll always find out that things work for the best."

"Well, you've been like that your entire life. No doubt, and I think one of the reasons you and I get along so well is that we've got the same type of personalities when it comes to a lot of things, especially when it comes to dealing with flat-out evil people, always plotting like what I had to deal with for years at that paper.

"Well, just. I'm just so happy and pleased you are getting away from there and that you are spreading out to bigger and better things. And you already know this, but whatever you need from me, I'm here."

SEVENTH INNING

HANK'S DIXIECRATS
ON THE BRAVES

With the CNN folks still waiting for our arrival to the golf club, with
the rain still crashing from the sky, with the driver of the car sent
by the cable channel still rattling on about all things Hank Aaron
through mesmerized eyes, and with the strikingly high distance still
not shrinking from the sidewalk to the floor of the front passenger's
side of the vehicle, I attempted to help the tired and aching man out
of the wheelchair. *One foot at a time*, I thought.

That, and I prayed.

"Listen, can you grab Hank's other arm and let's see if we can do
this without getting somebody hurt?" I told the driver, who nodded
as he tried holding the umbrella he had over us with one hand while
he used his other to do whatever he could do with the tired and
aching man.

The driver couldn't do much, but the prayers worked. Somehow,
despite a few close calls here and there involving the head, the arms,
and the fingers of the tired and aching man as we struggled to get him
seated in one piece, it was done.

Well, that part was over. While my phone kept ringing and buzzing
("Are you here yet?") as I climbed into the back seat, positioning myself
directly behind the tired and aching man, the driver kept talking all
things Hank Aaron, as Hank Aaron tried each time—courtesy of his
contagious laugh, easy smile, and occasional "Why, thank you. Thank

you very much"—to become Hank Aaron for that moment instead of the tired and aching man.

Oh, boy, I thought, as I called the CNN producer to say we were on our way. *If we pull this off, I thought some more, it will rank somewhere on the all-time fantasy scale between the stuff of Mother Goose and those who run baseball saying they're really trying to get more African Americans involved in every aspect of the game while keeping straight faces.*

Jackie always saw through those straight faces.

So did Hank.

Just before Henry Louis Aaron turned 73 on February 5, 2007, he was in a reflective mood during one of our chats at Turner Field. His thoughts involved the good, the bad, and the ugly (and boy, was there ugly) after his post-playing days turned into his ongoing role as an executive with the Atlanta Braves. Time Warner was on the verge of selling the franchise to Liberty Media, and Hank thought about Ted Turner, the cable television maverick who bought the team in the spring of 1976. Turner hired the suddenly-retired Braves icon that fall.

Hank thought about Terry McGuirk, Turner's right-hand man who was much more than that. McGuirk was such the glue for all of Turner's endeavors (TBS, CNN, the Braves, the Atlanta Hawks, and the Atlanta Thrashers) that both Time Warner in 1996 and Liberty Media about a decade later kept McGuirk around when they purchased the Braves. It allowed McGuirk to continue as the final decision-maker for the franchise on just about everything. McGuirk was even more than that. He was Hank's racquetball partner and trusted pal and he ranked among the most decent human beings you'll ever find in corporate America. Hank thought those things as well as about Susan Bailey, his loyal executive assistant.

Then Hank thought about other positives involved with his then 31-year career in the Braves' front office. "Really, the Braves have been very good to me in so much as and as far as what I want to do at this point in my life," Hank said, still conflicted at the time over whether to keep working at his leisure as a Braves official or to retire in his deep senior years with his wife, Billye, by leaving Atlanta for their other home in West Palm Beach, Florida.

Hank leaned toward staying, adding, "You know, Terence, I've been with the ballclub all these many years really and I've never been taken off the payroll. I've never asked them for a raise. Same check I've been getting, and that's fine. The only thing I can say is: they've treated me fairly decent in so much I can go and I have a key to everywhere in the clubhouse, everywhere in that ballpark. I can go to the office and I can do this and I can do whatever I want to do, and they treat me well, and when I say 'they,' I'm referring to Terry McGuirk who invites me to come to spring training, you know?"

Yes, I knew.

I also knew there was the bad stuff for Hank during his three decades in the Braves' front office. Then there was the petty stuff along with the unnecessary stuff, especially given the stature of the man involved.

Henry Louis Aaron played his last major league game as baseball's all-time greatest player on Sunday, October 3, 1976, at Milwaukee County Stadium. At 42 his final swing came in the sixth inning to produce an RBI single between the shortstop and the third baseman for the hometown Brewers against the Detroit Tigers, and then three things happened at once:

- He joined the front office of the same Braves organization (of Milwaukee and then of Atlanta) that featured most of his Baseball Hall of Fame highlights for the opening 21 of his 23 seasons in the major leagues.

- He joined his brother-in-law, Bill Lucas, not only as executives for the Braves under Turner, but as the only African Americans in baseball with such lofty positions in the game.

- He was on the verge of a different type of the hateful things he encountered through death threats and hate mail surrounding his Babe Ruth home run chase of four, three, and two years earlier.

While I was dealing with my Dixiecrats at *The Atlanta Journal-Constitution*, Hank was battling his own (both inside and outside of the Braves organization), and it contributed to our bond. Here's how Hank's Dixiecrats operated: when they thought he functioned as a figurehead in the Braves front office (as a former Black superstar who smiled a lot and kept his mouth shut, especially on racial issues), they hugged him, and that wasn't surprising. Henry Louis Aaron or not, such often is the mind-set for many in White America toward African American males who aren't perceived in the minds of many in White America as threatening in the slightest way.

There were two of those "Everybody Loves Hank" stretches for Aaron with the Braves after his playing career. The first one happened from the late 1970s to the early 1980s. Hank was fresh from the Brewers—with the glow of No. 715 in his recent past and a trip to Cooperstown five years ahead. The public viewed that Hank Aaron as mostly the humble Alabama slugger who mostly kept his head down and who mostly said nothing while facing Ruth-loving racists. The second of those "Everybody Loves Hank" stretches went longer, and it spanned from the time he changed his mind about retiring as a Braves official in early 2007 through his death on January 22, 2021.

Mostly, there was that "Controversial Hank" stretch, and it occurred between those "Everybody Loves Hank" stretches. African Americans often are labeled "controversial" when they give opinions their Dixiecrats don't like, which meant Hank and I regularly compared notes during his middle years as a Braves executive. I was the "controversial" Black columnist for *The Atlanta Journal-Constitution*, and Jackie Robinson was "controversial," too. So, it isn't coincidental Henry Louis Aaron faced external and internal turmoil in the Braves front office during his "Controversial Hank" stretch. He spent that time becoming Jackie often and boldly by speaking on baseball's discriminatory actions toward African Americans and social injustice overall. This was fate wrapped in destiny involving Jackie, Hank, and myself. The way Hank usually distributed his messages as the 21st century Jackie was through me as The Hank Aaron Whisperer, operating either in print with *The AJC* or over the national and local airways. During that "Controversial Hank" stretch, when he kept slamming home runs with his tongue regarding baseball's sorry ways with African Americans, he also kept doing his job (just like the "controversial" Black guy he knew at *The AJC*). Hank was splendid as a major league team executive, by the way. He was too splendid for his Dixiecrats. They tried to portray Henry Louis Aaron, the Major League Baseball team executive, as just another Black guy who was overmatched and incompetent.

Hank's Dixiecrats around the Braves' front office didn't attack with the racist letters and the vicious calls he experienced during his chase of Babe Ruth's record during the early 1970s.

That was the redneck way. Hank's Dixiecrats preferred the necktie way.

I could relate.

That was the redneck way. Hank's Dixiecrats preferred the necktie way. As was the case for my Dixiecrats at *The AJC*, Hank's Dixiecrats around the Braves organization used mind games. He also became a frequent media target over his habit of speaking freely to The Hank Aaron Whisperer on those inequities in baseball and beyond. There were national jabs at Hank here and there. Still, he was ripped the most by supposedly outraged hosts and their callers on news talk radio stations in Atlanta and by *The AJC* opinion writers (sports and otherwise) who weren't The Hank Aaron Whisperer.

Hank also got a blast from the past as a Braves executive when he received hate mail and ugly messages from anonymous cowards. About those mind games hurled at Hank: the in-house ones were crushed whenever possible by Turner and McGuirk, his eternal supporters, always seeking to have his back that was the target for many during that "Controversial Hank" stretch of his post-playing years.

Hank and I discussed the Braves executives as we huddled after one of the yearly events the franchise held in his honor around what the Braves called "Hank Aaron Heritage Weekend," which took place a few years before his death. "I try to keep my distance from most of all these guys," Hank said of the other Braves executives, while shaking his head.

His words took me back to that chat we had in early 2007 at Turner Field, where he said he was appreciative of the slew of personal honors from the Braves, but he added he also was realistic, especially given his Dixiecrats in the organization. "I don't know if I expect anything, whereas I'm treated the way I should be in certain respects, other than Terry McGuirk. I don't bother with too many of the others," Hank said. "The only reason I'm there is simply because the fact that [Liberty Media] wouldn't have the team if it would not have been for them agreeing [in February 2007 with Baseball commissioner Bud Selig, Hank's pal from his Milwaukee Braves days] to all things I was involved in. So, that's the only reason I'm there. The commissioner was not going to give them the team. But anyhow, Terry McGuirk has always treated me with some respect really. I've had a lot of respect from him. In fact, I talk to him right now, and he probably is the only one that I really had any regard for, and that's going back to when I served on the board [of directors for the Braves]. He treated me like I was somebody."

Hank paused with emotion before saying: "But Terence, some of these people just…just…" Hank shook his head without finishing.

"I know. You know I know," I said, as we chuckled in unison over our dealings with enough mind games from our collective Dixiecrats to keep psychiatrists busy through the next millennium.

During the 1990s, when Hank began roaring even louder to me for public distribution about baseball's issues with African Americans, Turner ignored the screaming from Hank's growing critics and he approached Hank about having an office at the owner's massive CNN Center in downtown Atlanta. Hank would keep his nicely structured one at Atlanta-Fulton County Stadium. Turner just thought Henry Louis Aaron deserved another one, something grander. Hank politely declined, but Turner strongly insisted. Then Hank agreed. He spent much of a day adding some of this and a lot of that to his new quarters, which nearly touched the sky on the 14th of the 15 floors at CNN Center. Massive windows dominated the place, and they gave Hank a gorgeous view of the so-called "City in a Forest," featuring Atlanta's combination of skyscrapers, hills, and pines. "Now listen to this, Terence: great big office. I mean, it was huge, man. I had three double windows and everything and I went there the next day, and the office door had my name and Bill Bartholomay's name on it," Aaron said, laughing, referring to the Braves' chairman of the board who bought the Milwaukee version of the franchise in 1962 before he moved it to Atlanta after the 1965 season.

While Hank spent the majority of his time within a short drive to both CNN Center and Atlanta Fulton-County Stadium from his southwest Atlanta home, Bartholomay was only an occasional visitor to Georgia. He mostly traveled between New York and Palm Beach when he wasn't home in Chicago, where he was an accomplished insurance guy. Bartholomay's name on the door made no sense. Well, not unless you understood Hank had his Dixiecrats, but he also had McGuirk, who received a knock on his CNN Center door from his racquetball partner. Hank had a question. "Terry, did you and Ted tell me I was going to have my own office up here? That's what I asked him, and [Terry] said, 'Yeah, it's right down here,'" Hank said, recalling how they walked down the hall to see "Hank Aaron" and then "Bill Bartholomay" in front of them on the door across the way.

With eyes flashing, McGuirk yanked down the Bartholomay sign and then he rushed into the office of the CNN official responsible for the situation. Hank watched nearby as McGuirk shouted, "This is Hank Aaron's office, and it doesn't belong to anybody else." After that, McGuirk flung the Bartholomay sign to the floor and then he stomped on it while telling the CNN official, "When you want to do something, *you come and ask me!*"

Hank laughed with the memory, adding, "I'll never forget that."

I'll never forget my visit with Hank inside of his CNN office during June 1996, when the U.S. postal service kept delivering hate mail not far from the door that finally had only his name near the top.

"You just got another one," Bailey said, yelling from the outer office, where she operated as Hank's personal assistant throughout his post-playing career.

Hank shrugged, looking at me sitting across the way, and then he said without much of an expression, "I'm used to it."

Unfortunately, Hank was.

During Hank's pursuit of Babe Ruth's career home run record, he spent two years during the 1970s battling opposing pitchers and threatening messages from that other group of cowards. Then, after a honeymoon period for Hank of maybe a year as a Braves executive not afraid to speak the truth about racism, he was blasted for more than two decades through those letters, calls, talk shows, and newspaper columnists, particularly over his criticisms of Major League Baseball regarding its dealing with minorities.

There also was Hank's controversy of the moment when I visited him in his CNN office during that 1996 summer day. As part of a CNN documentary on Cuba's love affair with baseball, Hank was shown in widely distributed photos with Turner and his wife, Jane Fonda. That trio became a quartet when Cuba dictator Fidel Castro joined the group, and Hank told me of the memory, "All I know is that I talked to Castro, and they received me very well."

Hank told me something else. With the Summer Olympics prepared to start in Atlanta a few weeks later, he said he would invite the three dozen or so teenagers comprising the Cuban national baseball team to his home for a barbecue. He said his Spanish-speaking daughter, Ceci, would serve as translator for the group seeking to defend its gold medal. "They'll be strangers when they come all the way over here, and I want to make them feel at home," Aaron told me as Bailey shouted in the distance.

"Here's another one," she said.

Aaron shook his head, adding, "We'll have chicken. I'll get some pies. I'll even take a few of them shopping because I know they'll get a kick out of that."

Oh, boy, I thought. I asked Hank if he would try to ease the yells from the yahoos in waiting over this by doing something similar for Team USA baseball players. Hank shrugged, saying, "I don't know the American players. Plus, I'm not into politics when it comes to Cuba or anything else. I just know I got a chance to meet [the Cuban players], and they are great kids."

What about the yahoos?

Hank laughed, saying, "I don't care what people think."

While the Dixiecrats at *The Atlanta Journal-Constitution* put my column detailing everything I just mentioned on Page 5 (at least it wasn't above a tire or lawnmower ad), they reserved a spot at the top of the front page of their sports section for a piece from one of the White columnists on Braves pitcher John Smoltz losing that day to the St. Louis Cardinals.

My column was the talk of the nation. The Smoltz column? Not so much.

As for Hank's Dixiecrats, *The Atlanta Journal-Constitution* columnist Furman Bisher spoke for all of them by writing of Hank in May 1991: "His main service to the Braves has been titular rather than active. In a sense, he has been a pensioned artifact, playing the role of a professional Hank Aaron, Home Run King."

If you go by Bisher's analysis, along with those of others among Hank's Dixiecrats, Henry Louis Aaron was a lousy figurehead. Hank spent his 13 years through 1989 over the Braves' player development office supervising the progress of future baseball All-Stars such as Dale Murphy, Bob Horner, Bruce Benedict, Glenn Hubbard, Rafael Ramirez, Gerald Perry, Jeff Blauser, Ron Gant, David Justice, and Steve Avery. Then there was the pitching duo of Tom Glavine and Smoltz. They evolved under Hank's early watch into All-Stars who became Baseball Hall of Famers.

In addition, Hank was omniscient regarding the hiring of coaches and managers for the Braves organization. Exhibit A: in 1980 after Brian Snitker played four years in the minor leagues for the Braves as a forgettable backup catcher, Hank called Snitker into his tiny yet efficient office in West Palm Beach, Florida. Hank saw something in Snitker that Snitker didn't see in himself, and that was his future as a Major League Baseball manager. But first Hank wondered if Snitker would stop playing the game to begin coaching for the franchise, starting with the Braves' rookies in Bradenton, Florida. Snitker agreed. Before long Snitker spent the next two decades coaching or managing Braves minor league teams in Durham, Danville, Myrtle Beach, Anderson, Sumter, Greenville, Richmond, Gwinnett, and anywhere else from the middle of nowhere.

That was the *CliffNotes* part of the Aaron-Snitker story. "I can't tell you how many times, how many people in the Braves organization wanted me to fire Brian Snitker over the years, saying, 'He can't do this,' and 'He ain't that,' but I wouldn't listen to them, even though they kept saying, 'Why? So why do you keep this guy around?'" Aaron told me, shaking his head before an event in his honor at Atlanta's Truist Park in 2019, when that same Brian Gerald Snitker was in his fourth season as Braves manager. "I always told [the folks who wanted

Aaron to fire Snitker], 'Well, the reason I don't fire him is because he's good. He does a great job.' He knows baseball and he knows how to deal with people the right way. He was loyal to the franchise to the point in which he would do anything you asked him to do, no matter how low somebody else would think it would be. There was just something about him that let me know he was the kind of person the Braves needed. So I didn't pay them any attention really."

Good for Hank, and great for the Braves.

Snitker was Hank's last hire.

With that nudge from Henry Louis Aaron, the former backup catcher who many in the franchise wanted gone, stayed around Hank's system for all of that minor league work. Then Snitker had the first of several highlights of his Braves career by serving as the major league team's third-base coach from 2007 to 2013. Then he was named Braves interim manager in May 2016. Then he got the full-time gig the next season. Then he won baseball's National League Manager of the Year honors in 2018. Then, after a second consecutive award from The Sporting News as National League Manager of the Year, he took the Braves to within two runs of reaching the World Series during the 2020 season. Then, with the Braves dedicating their 2021 season in Hank's memory, Snitker took his team from stumbling through July to jumping with joy in November after wining the World Series.

Through it all, Snitker couldn't stop praising Aaron. That included the emotional speech Snitker gave during a memorial at Truist Park near Hank's statue, following Hank's death on January 22, 2021. "The reason I'm here today is because of Hank Aaron," Snitker said after he paused just shy of forever for the lump to leave his throat.

Hank's homecoming soon followed. On a winter afternoon of warmth and brightness in Georgia, the historic Friendship Baptist Church in downtown Atlanta was sparse on Wednesday, January 27, 2021 due to COVID-19 restrictions. Henry Louis Aaron died five days earlier, and only a handful of family members were allowed to gather inside the sanctuary for his funeral. The few people in attendance beyond Hank's relatives included eulogist Andrew Young, who was among Martin Luther King Jr.'s top lieutenants and long-time pal and neighbor of Aaron; Atlanta Braves CEO Terry McGuirk, who was Hank's old racquetball partner and the person he trusted most around his franchise of nearly 70 years; and Houston Astros manager Dusty Baker, who was Hank's unofficial son when they played for the Braves during the late 1960s and early 1970s.

Among those kept from attending the funeral for pandemic safety reasons were me and other honorary pallbearers. "I can speak to some people to see if there is a way get you into the service," Billye Aaron said, pausing from grieving her recently departed husband to say over the phone she would start by seeking a special exemption for me from Friendship Baptist Church Pastor Richard W. Wills Sr.

Even though I appreciated Billye's offer, I declined. I hadn't a problem watching the exhaustive coverage of Hank's passing on all of the local Atlanta television stations.

I had similar thoughts the previous day, when the Braves held a memorial service for Hank at Truist Park, their home base. With a quick text to McGuirk, who always treated me well through the decades, I knew I could attend that equally pandemic-restricted gathering. Instead, I preferred to commemorate Hank's life and times quietly, which described how the man himself operated more often than not. I said as much on the NBC Nightly News, when Lester Holt called me for an interview about Hank's death. So, after I bundled up for the 40-something degree weather, I cycled the seven miles from my house to Truist Park before the Braves' tribute began. Nobody was around when I rode to the side of the ballpark that allowed you to peek through a set of bars for a glimpse at the majestic Hank Aaron statue located in the Braves museum-like concourse area. All I could do was stare and smile. Even in death, the thought of Henry Louis Aaron triggered joy in my soul.

Before long, I heard sirens. I pedaled in the direction of the Bobby Cox statue, located near one of the main Truist Park gates, and I watched the police motorcycles stop. Billye climbed out of one of the cars. So did Young and other family members. I thought about moving closer to say something or at least to connect eyes with somebody and wave, but I didn't. To me, this was their moment. So was the funeral the following afternoon, and then everything changed over the subsequent days, weeks, and months.

Just like that, the celebration of Henry Louis Aaron extended to the Braves, Atlanta history, Major League Baseball, sports in general, civil rights, and fairy tales.

What happened next was the stuff of Mother Goose.

The Braves dedicated their 2021 season to Hank and they showed as much early and often along the way to concluding with their ultimate tribute to baseball's greatest player ever.

They won the World Series in his honor.

Here was the sequence:

- During that January memorial service for Hank at Truist Park, the Braves announced the formation of The Henry Louis Aaron Fund to continue his crusade for increasing Blacks and other minorities throughout all aspects of Major League Baseball. The Braves donated $1 million to the cause, and Major League Baseball headquarters and the Major League Baseball Players Association each added $500,000.

- To honor April 8, 1974, when Hank slammed his 715th career home run to break Babe Ruth's record, the Braves asked fans in April 2021 to celebrate the 47th anniversary of Hank's iconic blast by donating $7.15 to The Henry Louis Aaron Fund.

- The Braves held Hank Aaron Weekend from July 30 to August 1, and not coincidentally, they played the Milwaukee Brewers, which was Hank's team during his last two seasons in the major leagues. Those attending the Sunday game received a Hank

Aaron bobblehead doll. Before the series opener, I felt a hand on my shoulder while I watched batting practice, and it was McGuirk. "I knew you would be here," he said, smiling and nodding.

• Braves Hall of Famer pitcher Phil Niekro also died before the 2021 baseball season. As a result, the Braves included Niekro's No. 35 with Hank's No. 44 on the back of their caps for the year. Only Hank had his number prominently displayed in center field for the whole season.

I held my own memorial service for Hank at Truist Park and I invited only myself. Hours before the first pitch of the Braves' home opener in early April against the Philadelphia Phillies, I went to his statue. As had been the case since the ballpark opened in 2017, there were the slew of Hank Aaron displays everywhere, and they gave details of his career. There were the 755 bats representing his home runs in Major League Baseball. There also was the continuous video that played high above that part of the concourse to describe Hank's career through film clips, photos alternating between color and black and white, and the voice of a narrator. I had seen it all before and I knew it all in general, but as an audience of one during this solemn occasion, I did it all again. I even took a selfie without much thought of the Hank video playing in the background.

Later, when I got home, I looked at the selfie. I mean, I really looked at it and I noticed it showed Hank on the continuous video smiling his contagious smile over my left shoulder from high above on the big screen—and from High Above period.

It was beautiful.

As for most of the Braves' season, it was brutal.

They lacked their No. 1 starting pitcher all year due to an Achilles injury (Mike Soroka). They lost their cleanup hitter (Marcell Ozuna) after late May following his arrest on domestic violence charges. They spent three months through early August without their starting catcher

(Travis d'Arnaud) due to a damaged thumb. They watched their best player (Ronald Acuna) tear his ACL in mid-July to leave the lineup for the rest of 2021. In addition, the Braves stayed below .500 until the first week of August, but then they used Hank's spirit and six trades around baseball's July 31 trade deadline to spark a miracle.

Somehow, the Braves won the National League East division for a fourth consecutive year, and then a theme developed in the playoffs. The Braves beat the favored Brewers during the National League Division Series. Afterward, with folks still rubbing their eyes from the Brewers upset, the Braves shocked the favored Los Angeles Dodgers for the National League pennant. Finally, the Braves grabbed their first world championship since 1995 after they handled the favored Astros during the best-of-seven World Series in six games.

Before Game Three at Truist Park, Aaron's presence was everywhere. Braves officials held a pregame ceremony featuring a two-minute and 30-second film on the video screen of his career, and that was followed by his widow, Billye, and several of his children walking onto the field to watch Hank Aaron Jr. throw out the ceremonial first pitch. At one point, an emotional Baker left the Astros dugout for the pitcher's mound to greet each of Hank's relatives.

With Hank, Hank, and more Hank dominating the ballpark, the Braves won that night, of course, and they grabbed two of the next three games, including the World Series clincher on the road. Here was the biggest thing: amidst the pixie dust falling on the Braves' road to a world championship, McGuirk kept announcing before television cameras and elsewhere that Hank was High Above guiding the Braves along the way. Most strikingly, when McGuirk stood on the World Series victory stage at Minute Maid Park in Houston, he said through wet eyes that Henry Louis Aaron spent the season operating as their "angel."

McGuirk was correct.

Sometimes, down the stretch of the 2021 season for the Braves, Hank stood at the plate or on the pitcher's mound. Other times, he took the field, ran the bases, or made front office, managerial, and coaching decisions. Then, with Jackie Robinson nodding nearby, Hank retreated to the heavenly shadows, where he laughed his contagious laugh.

With much help from Hank's spirit, the Braves did it.

Snitker did it.

Aside from Snitker himself, Hank got zero to no credit for Snitker's rise, but what else was new? Hank got zero to no credit for those future All-Stars in the organization. What irritated Hank more was how his success as a Braves executive often was given zero to no credit period.

For the longest time, the Braves put this paragraph in the middle of Hank's bio in their media guide before every season: "Following his playing career, Aaron joined the Braves' front office on October 7, 1976, for a 13-year tenure as Vice President and Director of Player Development. In that position he oversaw the development of many players instrumental in the Braves' 1982 National League West Division championship, including Dale Murphy, who won back-to-back National League MVP awards in 1982–83. Among active players, Tom Glavine was signed while Aaron was in charge of baseball operations."

Yeah, okay. What about the rest of the story involving Hank Aaron, the brilliant baseball player turned brilliant baseball executive?

Murphy wasn't the only homegrown Braves player of significance for that 1982 team with Hank connections. On Opening Day in San Diego, where the Braves started their National League record 13-game winning streak against the Padres, right fielder Claudell Washington and first baseman Chris Chambliss were the only players in the Braves' starting lineup who weren't signed, developed, or both by Aaron's farm system.

There was more, and this irritated Aaron as much as anything when he reflected on his Braves' front-office legacy, which was part of his baseball legacy: it was the way his role in the franchise's sprint from the 1991 season to a major league-record 14 consecutive division titles, five National League pennants, and a 1995 World Series title was forgotten, downplayed, and considered irrelevant or nonexistent through the years.

Let's go to the start of the Hank slight. In 1991 the Braves shocked everybody's senses with their worst-to-first trip to the World Series. They lost to a Minnesota Twins team that was their mirror image in the American League after they both swung 180 degrees in the standings from the previous season. Even so, the Braves soared past the Twins and everybody else in baseball history by using that year as the catapult toward their epic streak of postseason appearances. When Baseball Hall of Fame general manager John Schuerholz wasn't getting the bulk of the credit for that Braves' run, the praise went to Baseball Hall of Fame manager Bobby Cox.

What's missing here? Didn't the Braves have a Baseball Hall of Fame player involved with that streak in one way or another?

Schuerholz began his major league career in 1966 with the front office of the dominant Baltimore Orioles of that era. He later was the architect behind a world championship, two American League pennants, and six division titles for the Kansas City Royals before he joined the Braves after the 1990 season. He acquired first baseman Sid Bream and third baseman Terry Pendleton that winter, and they both contributed to the Braves' switch during a year from last place in the National League West to a National League pennant win against the Pittsburgh Pirates of Barry Bonds and Bobby Bonilla. Pendleton even captured 1991 National League Most Valuable Player honors, and Schuerholz added more pieces for the Braves—highlighted in 1993 by his signing of future Baseball Hall of Fame pitcher Greg Maddux and his trading for clutch slugger Fred McGriff.

Cox already was in his second stint with the Braves' organization when Schuerholz arrived. As for Cox's first stint, he managed the team from 1978 through 1981 before Turner said he made one of the worst decisions of his professional life by firing Cox. Five years later Turner pulled Cox away from managing the Toronto Blue Jays to become the Braves' general manager. While Cox served in that capacity, the franchise—which already had Henry Louis Aaron as director of player development for nine years before Cox arrived as GM—acquired Glavine, Smoltz, Avery, Justice, Gant, and Chipper Jones, another future Baseball Hall of Famer.

By the middle of the 1990 season, Cox had enough of the GM thing. With Schuerholz on the way a few months later from Kansas City, Cox named himself the Braves' manager again for a run that lasted through the 2010 season. No question, Cox and Schuerholz deserved accolades for turning the Braves of the 1990s into one of the game's most significant teams ever. Paul Snyder also was recognized on a regular basis as the franchise's nationally revered scouting director for parts of three decades along the way to the Professional Baseball Scouts Hall of Fame.

But what about Henry Louis Aaron? At the start of that Braves' streak, the key contributors were Justice, Gant, Mark Lemke, Blauser, Avery, Glavine, and Smoltz. Some were signed by Cox as general manager, but they all were developed under Hank's supervision as the head of that department.

He got zero to no credit. He had his Dixiecrats. "I had one guy, when he first joined the ballclub [as a Braves executive], he came up to me and said, 'Well, I'm a Marine. I'm used to getting these guys in shape,' and 'I did this,' and 'I did that,' and I said to myself, 'Hell, it's about time for me to get out of here,'" Hank said, shaking his head before a game at Turner Field during the summer of 2008.

Hank recalled how that Braves executive during the early 1990s kept insinuating through mind games that Hank's system, which produced all of those All-Stars and Baseball Hall of Famers, was awful, along with the person who developed and ran that system. Some guy named Henry Louis Aaron. "He and I were always getting into it, and I just said one time, 'Tell me anybody who knows how to fight [as a Marine] and get a damn curveball over the plate or know how to hit a curveball?'" Hank said, growing more irritated by the moment with the decades old memory. "I said, 'We've got some good players in this system and we've got some good people working in this system.' I had already hired a bunch of these coaches that came up, and one of them was [Snitker] who struggled like a son of a gun with a lot of hard work, but he finally got here [as third-base coach]. I said to this guy, 'Man, we spend hours and hours out there,' and I'm telling you, Terence. We used to stay out there from 8:00 in the morning until 8:00 at night training these guys. I'm talking about the likes of Justice, Lemke, Gant, all of these guys. I'm telling you. We used to stay out there hours, then sit down, and debate [with] these guys all the time to see what they learned."

So much for the Dixiecrats questioning Hank's work ethic. They also challenged his competency and his convictions. At one point, when Hank ran the farm system, he said other Braves officials wanted to bury future All-Star Gant deep in the minor leagues and replace the African American player with a rising White prospect. According to Hank, those other Braves officials suggested Gant was a bust at 24 after he struggled as a rookie outfielder for the Braves in 1989. "I said, 'You ain't sending this boy nowhere,'" Hank said, still fuming over the suggestion. "Now I had control of all of that at the time, and I said, 'You ain't sending this boy nowhere. He can outrun mistakes.' What they wanted to do was keep the White player, and they didn't want [Gant] to do anything. Doggone it, I'll tell ya, whew."

Whew, indeed, especially since Gant rebounded for the Braves to become Willie Mays and Barry Bonds for the 1990 and 1991 seasons. At the time, Mays and Bobby and Barry Bonds were the only major league players ever to steal at least 30 bases and rip at least 30 home runs during consecutive seasons. Gant also had productive years at the plate in 1992 (32 stolen bases, 17 homers, and 80 RBIs) and 1993 (26 stolen bases, 36 homers, and 117 RBIs), but he was released by the Braves after he broke his leg in February 1994 riding a dirt bike.

All Hank knew was that Gant had talent. Hank knew talent, for sure, which is why he was as angry as I'd ever heard him when he called me in September 2008. Our conversation involved Jones, Cox, and rewriting history. Our conversation also involved exaggerating or lying. Take your pick. "Something has just been bothering me really," Hank said, sighing, which was enough to let me know in a flash Henry Louis Aaron had an *AJC* column he wanted me to write, and it would be huge. "I don't mind other things, but somehow, some things need to be spelled out correctly. I was listening to something on television where Bobby [Cox] was talking about how, when Chipper came to the team, [Cox] took him aside to tell him what 'we' did to get him here, and I was stunned really."

No, Hank was livid, and I was nervous. In addition to my solid relationship with Hank, I had one with Cox, the Braves manager who was so old school that he still wore spikes before, during, and after games. Even though media folks respected him for his cooperative ways, he had a reputation for ranking only slightly better than Bill Belichick as a quote machine. "Well, he pitched good for me," Cox often responded with a shrug after one of his starters got shelled.

I saw a different Bobby Cox. If he trusted you, he'd tell you many things off the record and sometimes everything.

Cox told me a bunch of things. Contrary to popular belief, Cox hadn't a problem going from ultimate players' manager to crazy man with a red face and he used his tongue to burn the ears of players out of control more than folks knew, but I often knew. Then there was 1992 at the Braves' spring training camp in West Palm Beach, Florida, where Cox confirmed to me what Schuerholz wouldn't admit to anybody with a pen or a camera until 14 years later in a book: the Braves tried to work a trade for Bonds, the Pirates outfielder, nine months before he left as a free agent for the San Francisco Giants. I heard as much through whispers in the Braves clubhouse that spring. Whispers weren't good enough, especially since *The AJC* didn't allow the use of unnamed sources. Standing behind the batting cage, I asked Cox if the Braves were trying to add Bonds to their lineup, he turned to say in a voice meant only for me, "John is trying to get it done." As usual, Cox wanted no part of the sourcing. That left only Schuerholz. Even though he was tight lipped with the media about most things beyond his name, rank, and serial number, I asked him anyway. Nothing. End of scoop, though Cox had tried to help.

Hank might have known what was or wasn't happening with a possible Bonds deal, and the more I thought about it, he probably did. I just didn't think to ask him. Even though Hank hadn't a problem telling me whatever he knew about the Braves organization (or virtually anything else), I leaned toward keeping those types of questions to a minimum during our conversations. I didn't want Hank to believe I wanted *something* whenever he saw my number flash on his phone. If you stick your debit card into an ATM too many times, you'll have insufficient funds. My Hank accounts were never overdrawn.

Now, with that sigh of disgust on the other end of the phone line, Henry Louis Aaron was calling to make a withdrawal from our joint account, and that was fine, but this one involved Jones, Cox, rewriting history, along with either exaggerating or lying. I cringed over the thought of sitting in the middle of a likely nationally elevated feud between a future Cooperstown manager, who always treated me well, and You Know Who on the other end of the phone.

I was The Hank Aaron Whisperer though and I suspected from several of our previous conversations that he and his wife, Billye, never were invited over to the Coxes during the offseason for supper after Sunday services. I didn't know the details of the previous conflict or conflicts, but on this day before we got to Hank's latest issue with Cox, Hank discussed how the Aaron-Cox tension started—or where he thought it started—because he really didn't know for sure.

The way Hank figured it, the whole thing involved Chuck Tanner, his former Milwaukee Braves teammate of three seasons through 1957. Tanner was more noted for his managing than his hitting or fielding as an outfielder for those Braves, and then for the Chicago Cubs, Cleveland Indians, and Los Angeles Angels over eight major league seasons. In contrast Tanner spent 19 years as a manager, and the zenith of his career involved the "We are family" Pirates of Willie Stargell and Dave Parker. They won the 1979 World Series as one of the most charismatic teams in baseball history.

That said, after a 104-loss season in 1985, Pirates officials wanted a divorce from the sometimes ridiculously optimistic Tanner and his refusal to admit it was raining—even when he was drenched. Turner preferred such an approach for his team that spent 1985 on his superstation dropping 96 games. So, the Braves owner hired Tanner as manager. He later decided to bring Cox back to the franchise since he said he erred moments after he fired Cox following the 1981 season. Upon Cox's return to the Braves, only the general manager's job was available. Cox hadn't done anything close to a GM's role before, but he took it for the Braves probably with clenched teeth, Hank suggested. Tanner already was Braves manager. "I guess, I guess, one reason [I had a conflict with Cox is because] Bobby may have always held that against me," Hank said. "When Chuck Tanner was hired and fired, [Cox] thought that I was the one who influenced Ted Turner to hire Chuck Tanner. And, hell, I was not the one who did. It was Paul Snyder who really [got Turner] into hiring Chuck Tanner. It wasn't me. Chuck and I were very good friends, and I certainly said, 'Yes. Give him a chance,' but I was not the one. It was Paul Snyder, and yet, I think Bobby, sometimes, must have held that against me or something.

I'm too old to be explaining anything to anybody. To hell with it. If that's [what he wants to believe], that's too bad."

"I guess Bobby may have come to that conclusion," I said, "just because you guys were teammates. That's what he was going by, maybe?"

"Chuck and I were teammates, but we were very sporadically... Chuck and I never had that much in common really. He knew me as a ballplayer. He respected me for my ability and for what I did, and I appreciate that. But other than that, that was it. But I tell you: the way that I think that Bobby kind of held that, he kind of thought that I was the one that had Ted's left ear and that I could have done something [to make Cox manager over Tanner]."

The September 2008 call from Hank came after he saw a taped interview of Cox talking about his baseball career during a rain delay of a Braves game. Two things caught Hank's attention, and it began with Cox discussing how the franchise used Major League Baseball's No. 1 pick overall of the 1990 Major League Baseball Draft to snatch Chipper Jones. (Cox's story wasn't exactly accurate, according to Hank, who was there.) Cox also told the interviewer he was fortunate after he became the Braves' general manager in 1986 to have an esteemed baseball person in house. "Thank God I had some good guys like Paul Snyder sitting next to me all the time. He helped me out a lot," Cox said, suggesting in Hank's mind he valued Snyder's analysis as a scout on the state of the Braves' players in the organization as opposed to, say, Henry Louis Aaron, the vice president and director of player development.

Cox never mentioned Aaron during the TV show. "I'll get into all of it, but he could have given me some kind of respect, and I guess one of the things that really bothered me is that, here [Cox] is, coming in as a new general manager of this ballclub, doesn't know anything about being a general manager or being a farm director or anything else, and yet he decided to be friends with whoever he decided to be friends with," Hank said. "What bothers me is that when he became general manager, there absolutely was no connection between the two of us. Here I am the farm director, and we have a bad ballclub, and it seems like he would talk to me about the kids we have in the minor leagues. It didn't happen."

Who knows whether Cox avoided Hank during his return to the Braves as a GM after his pitstop in Toronto, but this is for sure: they chatted often enough leading up to that Major League Baseball draft of 1990 to set up a lifetime feud over Larry Wayne "Chipper" Jones Jr. With me in the middle during the fall of 2008, this whole Aaron-Cox thing prepared to explode from private to public.

The old farm director [Aaron] called to say he wanted it known that he was more responsible for the Braves acquiring Jones, a switch-hitting third baseman who reached the Baseball Hall of Fame as the modern-day Mickey Mantle, than the old general manager [Cox] who Hank said was obsessed with Todd Van Poppel, a journeyman pitcher who played for six different teams and retired with a 40–52 record and a 5.58 ERA. "The kid never did anything," Aaron said of Van Poppel, among the all-time flops of major league draft picks. "But every time you listen to Bobby Cox and the rest of them, it's always like, 'Oh, yeah. We always wanted to sign Chipper Jones.' The only reason they didn't take Van Poppel was because of what I told them about what his daddy told me."

Van Poppel's daddy told Hank that his son wouldn't sign with the Braves, and Hank said of the memory, "I told Bobby, I told them all, and I told them, 'Y'all better go and get Chipper Jones.'…Bobby has always been crazy about pitching, and Van Poppel was the No. 1 pitcher out there, but at the same time, Chipper Jones was out there, and I remember when we were so intent with trying to get this pitcher. Like I said, the kid never did anything, never did one damn thing. But Bobby wanted him so bad until we all…hell, I went down there [in Arlington, Texas, where Van Poppel was a high school star], and it seemed like 100 scouts. I looked at him, even though I had just retired as farm director, and here's exactly what his father told me. He said, 'Hank, Todd will never sign with the Atlanta Braves. He won't ever sign with the Braves, and I can tell you that right now: he doesn't want to sign with them and he won't sign with them.' That's when I went back [to Cox and other Braves officials] and said it. I said, 'Y'all better get Chipper Jones.' But now they claim that's who they wanted from the start, and that's so much, well, crap, that it's pitiful. So, I was just listening to this interview, where Bobby said Chipper came down to him somewhere, and Bobby said he took Chipper aside and he told him all the things he needed to do, and I said, 'Oh, hell, Bobby wanted the pitcher.'"

"Now let me ask you this, Hank," I said. "Do you want me to write something about this?"

"Well, yeah. I want to say something about it because I know you'll have all the facts straight. I just think that I need to say something. It's just been bothering me, and I just, well, I've just tried to…It's just been bothering me really and it just needs to be said."

"I can understand why, and I guess I need to make a list here of what I need to check on. And the main thing is: I need to find out exactly what Bobby Cox says he said regarding Chipper Jones and Van Poppel, all that. Before I write something, I'm going have to get with Bobby and see what he says."

"Yeah, and I think, if you want to, I mean, if you want to because you do a great job and I don't want to tell you how to go about it, but I would think you would ask Bobby, 'Well, when you guys were deciding who to draft, well, Hank said the father told him his kid wasn't going to sign with the Braves,'" Hank said, raising his voice, getting angrier by the millisecond. "The first player Bobby wanted was Van Poppel really in all fairness, and he did. And the reason he didn't sign him was simply because it's a known fact that if I had not told them [what the father said], they would have gone ahead and drafted this kid, and they would have lost a draft pick."

"I'm going to flat-out ask him all of these questions, and is it okay to tell him I've been talking to you?"

"Yeah, yeah. Whatever, really."

"You've said a lot of stuff here. I'll tell you what: after I talk to Bobby, I'll tell you what he says, and I'll see how you want to handle everything after that. How's that?"

"That's fine, Terence. You can let me know. I'm just saying what needs to be said and what I want to say."

It was time to for Cox's side. Oh, boy.

The secret to getting Bobby Cox to speak beyond his normal mantra ("He pitched good for me") on the Braves began with Cox's outer office at Turner Field. He preferred that one for candid talk (involving those he believed wouldn't violate his trust) over his fancier one down the hall from the home clubhouse. Actually, Cox's outer office wasn't even an office. It barely was a room. It was slightly smaller than your average walk-in closet and it was tucked away near the stairs that led up to the home dugout. It officially was the weather room, where the Braves' head groundskeeper and his crew went to check the ever-present radar map on the TV screen for rain, sleet, snow, or whatever else appeared for the viewer in various shades of yellow, green, and red.

When Cox was at Turner Field, he spent most of his life in that room fully dressed in his Braves uniform, usually leaning back in a chair with his spikes on the ledge before him while smoking a cigar. He watched the radar map for hours—but only if a NASCAR race wasn't happening. If you entered Cox's outer office, if he trusted you, and if you talked Dale Earnhardt (senior or junior) between mentioning a Doppler-related something here and there, you were good with Cox.

If another coach was present, he'd be okay. If it was one on one, hallelujah.

For this Hank situation, this was hallelujah. I caught Cox, puffing away, studying a few green spots forming above him on the screen. Instead of mentioning the Earnhardts, I got straight to the point:

*Bobby, I talked to Hank, and he said...*Basically, I told Cox essentially what Hank told me: that Bobby wanted Todd Van Poppel from the start during the 1990 Major League Baseball June draft as the No. 1 overall pick, that Hank informed Cox and other Braves officials about Van Poppel's father saying his son wouldn't sign with the Braves, that Hank said Cox was overstating his desire to pick Jones, that Hank thought Cox was full of resin bags regarding Jones, along with the way Cox reacted to Hank's authority when Cox re-joined the Braves as general manager with Hank as farm director.

Cox took a couple of more puffs, whirled his spikes off the ledge in front of him, and then leaned forward in his seat toward me. "Was he serious?" Cox said, softly before he added a few words not found in Matthew, Mark, Luke, or John.

"Yes sir," I said before telling Cox I needed a response. I told him Hank wanted me to use everything he said, which was potent. Then Cox took a few more puffs, and I expected him to do what he usually did after he told me exactly what he thought, which was to add, "Don't write that," or "That's between us," or "Keep this off the record," but he didn't say any of that.

Cox answered the questions. Every one of them.

"What do you recall thinking leading up to that 1990 Major League Draft with both Todd Van Poppel and Chipper Jones out there?"

"Well, we had a lot of people see [Van Poppel], and they liked him. Some other [Braves scouts] went to see Chipper, and they liked him a lot," Cox said, before squinting between more puffs. "I can't remember if I had Hank talk to Van Poppel's father or not, but [Van Poppel] was unsignable. And we needed to know that beforehand. So that's why it really was an easy decision to take Chipper. He wanted to sign. He wasn't playing games with the college thing. It was simple. I mean, Chipper was the guy."

"Hank said you didn't talk with him much or at all when you took over as Braves general manager in 1986? Is that true? If so, why?"

"I like Henry," Cox said. "I thought he did everything great. We tried to include him in everything."

That was it. That was all Bobby wanted to say. After I wrote both sides of the Chipper Jones/Braves draft story for my column in *The Atlanta Journal-Constitution*, I ended by saying of Hank and Bobby: "Here's my suggestion: How about Jones joining Aaron and Cox in the same room this winter for a group hug?"

EIGHTH INNING

BARRY BONDS

The windshield wipers were working overtime. *Will it ever stop raining?* That's what I kept thinking in the back seat of the huge SUV, when I wasn't saying to myself, regarding the driver, *Will he ever stop talking?* His conversation was all about Hank Aaron, which was good. This wasn't good: instead of Henry Louis Aaron, this was mostly the tired and aching man in the front passenger seat, trying and succeeding to remain polite with a smile or with a "thank you" or even with one of those Hank laughs, as the driver discussed the time he remembered "Mr. Aaron" doing that, heard about "Mr. Aaron" doing this, or why the driver was filled with joy to have the opportunity to talk (and talk and talk) to the greatest baseball player who ever lived.

I hung up my cell phone after I told the CNN folks we were pulling into the driveway of the golf club and were at the entrance. As I sat behind the tired and aching man inside that huge SUV with the rain still pounding, I said to myself, *I just hope he doesn't slip when I'm helping him from way up there in this vehicle to way down there into his wheelchair and with nobody helping me.*

Hank is and Hank was the Home Run King, no matter what happened on August 7, 2007.

On that night Barry Bonds spent an evening in San Francisco for his Giants ripping his 756th career homer into the right-center-field bleachers at what was then AT&T Park. In doing so, Barry Lamar Bonds surpassed Henry Louis Aaron's previous career record by one, but Hank wasn't there.

He didn't even watch on television. He was home. Asleep. On purpose.

Six years before Barry snatched Hank's crown...ahem...with a little help, I discovered emphatically what I already knew, and that was the relationship between Henry Louis Aaron and Barry Lamar Bonds wasn't complicated. It was non-existent. Just the way Hank wanted it. "They asked me to do a commercial," Hank told me, shaking his head while sighing during the fall of 2001. His reference was to folks from Charles Schwab, the financial company whose marketing staff had an idea for an advertisement during the upcoming Super Bowl that January, but Henry Louis Aaron wasn't into it. Not since the other guy was involved with the project.

Even when the controversy surrounding Bonds and performance-enhancing drugs in baseball kept growing as much as Barry's ever-expanding body, Hank wasn't against Barry Bonds, the ballplayer. Hank wasn't a fan of Barry Bonds, the person, which made sense. If you wished to find the most extreme of personalities involving two of the all-time greatest athletes inside a given sport, this was it. This was Hank as the Pacific and Barry as the Atlantic—with the entire solar system in between.

More specifically, this was Hank and his contagious laugh always seconds away compared to Barry, who could use his brilliant smile to brighten up a room when he wanted to, but he often didn't want to. This was Hank who preferred privacy but who nevertheless made strangers feel warm and special compared to Barry, who preferred privacy and let people know it—and sometimes rudely. This was Hank causing those around him wanting to get closer compared to Barry causing those around him wanting to stay as far away from the guy as possible.

Hank and Barry had cultural differences, too. Gigantic ones. Hank grew up as a proud Eagle Scout on the poor side of segregated Mobile, Alabama, during the 1930s and 1940s, when Southern Whites still shrugged over the Emancipation Proclamation, and his family home lacked the basics, ranging from electricity to inside plumbing. Barry was born and raised three decades later in California, where his father was Major League Baseball star Bobby Bonds, his godfather was Willie Mays, and his household was so upper middle class south of San Francisco in San Carlos that he jumped in his Trans Am to study criminology (oh, and to play baseball) for Arizona State.

While you never heard a negative syllable hurled at Hank by a teammate, here's all you need to know about this particular Aaron-Bonds comparison and contrast: Barry's peers for the Arizona State Sun Devils disliked him so much they voted to kick him off the team.

So, during the autumn of 2001, with Barry racing toward finishing the year for the Giants with 73 homers to break Mark McGwire's three-year-old record for a season by three, the Charles Schwab folks called Hank to join Barry in some kind of commercial, and Hank called to tell me, "I'm not doing it. Terence. I have no desire to get involved with that really."

Barry. It was all because of Barry.

Hank never said it this way, but he didn't wish to tarnish his lifetime brand as a public figure—classy, friendly accommodating, merciful, polite, giving, loyal, understanding, compassionate—by associating with somebody who wasn't close to any of those things in the minds of most.

Then, a few days later, Hank called me again. He said he was doing the commercial. "Why the change of heart?" I asked.

He laughed, saying, "They told me I could do my part without having to deal with him. We don't even have to be in the same room."

The commercial was a classic. It lasted 30 seconds and it ran twice (at a cost to Charles Schwab of $1.9 million each time) on February 3, 2002, when the New England Patriots slid past the St. Louis Rams for a 20–17 victory in New Orleans during Super Bowl XXXXVI. First, the commercial appeared after the coin toss with former U.S. president

George H. W. Bush and Pro Football Hall of Famer Roger Staubach. Then the commercial surfaced again in the fourth quarter, when Kurt Warner tried and failed to rally his Greatest Show on Turf group past Tom Brady, who earned the first of his seven Super Bowl rings.

With *Field of Dreams* type music playing in the background, the commercial opened with Barry in an empty stadium, ripping shots from a pitching machine toward the heavens. Suddenly, out of nowhere, you heard Hank's voice whispering as if he was coming from the stars of those heavens: "Barry Bonds, it's time."

Barry looked around for the sound and then he kept hitting.

"It's time to walk into retirement."

Confused, Barry glanced toward the top of the stadium. Then he returned to his typical spot from the left-handed batter's side of the plate and he delivered a weak dribbler down the first-base line with Hank whispering afterward, "Why hang around just to hit the all-time home run record?"

With more irritation on Barry's face, he whirled around, looked high up toward the upper deck with the music stopping, and said, "Hank, will you cut it out already?"

The next scene showed Hank alone in the stadium press box, sitting behind the microphone for the public-address system. There's a moment of silence with only crickets chirping in the background, and Hank's eyes darted around in search of possible witnesses before he said through another whisper into the microphone, "Hank? Hank who?"

The commercial ended with a professional-sounding ad guy saying, "Want retirement advice from somebody you can trust? At Charles Schwab you'll get expert advice that is objective, uncomplicated, and not driven by commission. To discuss your retirement plan, call 1-8884-SCHWAB."

The only thing more intriguing than the commercial itself was everything leading up to making it happen. During early fall of 2001, the Charles Schwab folks wanted a 2002 Super Bowl ad to equal or surpass their one of the previous year. That Super Bowl 2001 commercial featured Sarah Ferguson spoofing her divorce from Prince Andrews while speaking to a young actress playing her daughter. ("Someday when you grow up, your knight will come, and he'll take you off to a beautiful castle, and he'll marry you, and give you everything your heart desires forever and ever…Of course, if it doesn't work out, you'll need to understand the difference between a PE ratio and a dividend yield.")

The theme of that Ferguson commercial? Instead of getting your retirement advice from a biased person, get it from the right people, as in those at Charles Schwab, as in the reason the company's advertising folks thought of a follow-up script involving Home Run King Hank Aaron and Barry Bonds, who was still six years away from overtaking the throne but charging fast…ahem…with a little help. Nevertheless, this was when "Barry Bonds" and "performance-enhancing drugs" weren't mentioned in nearly every other sentence about the Giants left fielder.

While Barry said yes to the commercial, Hank said no.

That was until the Charles Schwab people guaranteed Henry Louis Aaron that the two stars of the commercials could remain hemispheres, if not light years, apart when they arrived weeks later in Arlington, Texas. This was soon after the Arizona Diamondbacks spent that November interrupting the last dynasty for the New York Yankees by winning the 2001 World Series.

The filming took an entire day at The Ballpark in Arlington, the former home of the Texas Rangers. Jack Calhoun chuckled with the memory when we chatted over the phone in May 2021. For the Bonds-Aaron commercial, Calhoun was the executive vice president of advertising and brand management at Schwab and he also was in charge of making sure Mr. Aaron and Mr. Bonds weren't close enough to lock eyes during the filming. "There was definitely [a problem]," Calhoun said, chuckling some more during our conversation, reliving his referee's role involving Hank and Barry. "They weren't really physically together on the shoot, and I remember [production staff members], saying, 'Yeah, they don't really like each other. Hank doesn't really like Barry Bonds that much.' And if you think about it, Hank was really way up there in the press box. They weren't in a room together, physically standing with each other, and I remember they weren't physically much together and I think it was partly because [Hank requested it]. I'm not the biggest baseball fan, but I remember one of the [production crew members] saying, 'Yeah, it's probably best that they keep their distance. They agreed to do [the commercial], so let's just go with that.'

"It was so long ago. I don't remember all the details, but I definitely remember walking away, saying to myself, 'Barry Bonds is not the nicest guy.' But Hank was so nice and so generous and so pleasant during the whole shoot, and I felt like how can Barry Bonds not like him? Again, I'm not the biggest sports fan, so I didn't understand any of the rivalry stuff. But I was like, oh my God. How can you not like Hank Aaron?"

Hank and Barry. Barry and Hank.

That combination was about to become as much of my life as Jackie and Hank but only because Barry kept slamming home runs. He topped McGwire's single-season record in 2001, just weeks before the great Charles Schwab commercial that almost didn't happen. Three years later, Barry hit No. 700 on September 17. Then he passed Babe Ruth at No. 715 on May 28, 2006. Then, with the Aaron tiebreaker for Bonds slightly more than a year away by the end of 2006 and with Hank dropping more into the shadows regarding media folks not named Terence Moore, here's what I knew: I was about to go from The Hank Aaron Whisperer to The Hank Aaron Spokesperson.

I also suspected I'd have to become Hank Aaron In Spirit on more than a few occasions in print and before cameras. That's exactly what happened.

Once the ball dropped in New York's Times Square on Sunday, December 31, 2006, I was destined to spend 2007 receiving voice messages, texts, and emails along these lines:

"Hey, Terence. Hope all is well. I'm [fill in the blank] and I was wondering if you can help me get in contact with Hank Aaron."

"Hey, Terence. Hope all is well. I'm [fill in the blank] and I was wondering if you can answer a few questions about Hank Aaron."

Hank wasn't talking, and his self-imposed seclusion from the public in 2007 was built for Susan Bailey, his pleasantly uncooperative personal assistant of just about forever. Even before the stretch drive of Barry chasing Hank's home run record, she was always available for a "no" to reporters seeking an audience with Hank because Hank wanted as much. Now with Hank wishing nothing to do with this Barry Bonds thing, Bailey's "no" became "NO."

Among Hank's best laughs ever came whenever I'd huddle with him in 2007 to mention yet another national or local reporter contacting me to determine how to reach "Mr. Aaron" beyond Bailey (basically to see if I would call Hank on their behalf) or to discuss my thoughts as The Hank Aaron Whisperer on Hank's thoughts regarding Barry Bonds.

Hank wasn't talking. To anybody but to me.

There were two reasons Hank became invisible during Barry's record-breaking year for lifetime homers. One: every time Hank discussed Barry on the verge of owning more home runs than anybody in baseball history, it returned Hank to the awfulness he experienced during the early 1970s, when he battled major league pitchers as well as racist comments and death threats while chasing Babe Ruth's old record mark of 714 homers. Two: Hank wasn't fond of Barry Bonds, the person (see that Charles Schwab commercial), and even if Hank was, he knew Barry's chase of No. 756 was just a wrong word from Hank creating a media circus he didn't need in his orderly life.

As for Barry Bonds, the player, Hank defended that Barry Bonds more often than not. He even did so after Barry's steroid allegations exploded with the March 2006 book called *Game of Shadows: Barry Bonds, BALCO, and the Steroids Scandal that Rocked Professional Sports.* Among other things, the book's authors gave a detailed report of why they believed Barry began using steroids through jealousy over McGwire breaking Roger Maris' single-season home run record of 61 with his 62nd blast in 1998 along the way to 70.

During the spring of 2006, I called Hank to discuss Bonds, steroids, and *Game of Shadows*, which claimed Barry had been playing and juicing for years.

"My take on this whole thing is—and I still say—there has been no guilt of admission from anybody, you know?" Hank said. "Until you're proven guilty, you're innocent, and I know that may sound kind of [naïve] because these people have gone out and done this, done that. But I just don't, being who I am and living in this country for so long and [having seen] injustice prevail the way it has in numerous occasions, I just prefer waiting until the final verdict is in, and the final verdict is that you've got to put Mr. Bonds somewhere on the stand and say, 'Hey, didn't you or did you or did you or didn't you?'

"That's my take on the thing. I've stayed out of it because I, hell, I don't know the answer. I just don't know the answer. I don't think anybody else does. I think we all sit here. We try to pretend. I read the papers and people say, 'Well, you know, he don't deserve [going for the home run record].' I don't know how you can do that. I wish somebody could tell me how you can, the man's got 700-something odd home runs, and [because of suspicion of steroid use], you're going to take 500 away from him, 100 home runs away from him."

"Right," I said.

"I just don't know, I really don't know in all fairness to everybody."

"Uh huh. Do you feel sorry for Barry in a way?"

"I...I do feel sorry for anybody who's gotten himself in this position. I don't—as I've said before and I've told this to you many times—I don't know Barry. I knew Barry's father [Bobby, who played in the major leagues from 1968 to 1981, primarily with the San Francisco Giants]. I knew his father was someone that I always admired his ability to play the game. And I just met Barry, well, I've been knowing him for about seven or eight years but not being in his company. I'm not a buddy and pal, you know."

"Right, right."

"But I do feel sorry for him. I feel sorry for him and I guess I feel even sorrier for his family. His father is no longer with us, but I know what kind of person he was, and [for Barry], I'm not saying guilt or no guilt. It doesn't really make any difference to me right now. It's just, to me [Bobby Bonds] is dead, and he needs to be resting peacefully."

"Let's say if he goes forth this year, and it looks like he's going to break Babe Ruth's record pretty quickly. With all the shadows and with all the rumors and allegations that are out there, if he goes forth and breaks your record, do you think that puts a cloud over his accomplishment?"

"I don't know. As I said before, Terence, I can't answer that. I think the only person who can answer that question would be Barry, and whether he answers it or not, I don't know. I can't answer it. His home runs were hit the same way with a baseball bat and by somebody throwing 90 mph fastball—same as mine. I don't know what else he used as far as to juice him up or whatever. I don't know. That is something…he has to live with himself. So, I really can't answer that and be fair."

"And I guess along those same lines, you've said this many times before that, when that time comes with Barry or Ken Griffey or whoever, it's not one of those type of things where it doesn't bother you one way or the other."

"No. I'm not. Even when I broke Babe Ruth's record, when I went through so much crap, records are made to be broken. That's just the end of it. You make records, and people try to break them. You make records, and somebody can come along and break that record. No matter whether it's Barry, McGwire, or anybody else. Records are going to be broken."

"And it doesn't matter or not to you if it's done in a tainted way?"

"See, I have no, I can't…to me…to be honest with you, I can't sit here and say anything about being tainted. I don't know enough about it. I can't say that is tainted because Barry hasn't said anything other than what people have accused him off."

"Yeah, that's a very good point."

"Yeah, so I don't know and I'm not going to be the one to sit back here and be the one to point a finger at anybody to say, 'You done this or you done that.' I think I'd be as wrong as hell to do that really. I just got to let Barry do his own thing. If he did anything wrong, he's the one who is going to have to pay for it. Whatever. I'm out of it."

"Which I think is the appropriate way to proceed."

"I just can't. No matter what happens, whether or not Barry hits 756 home runs, 757, 800, 900, whatever it is, mine, 755 is going to be there next year and the year after that," he said, causing us both to laugh. "It ain't going no further. I'm not going to hit another home run. My home run days are over with."

Later, during that same conversation in March 2006, Hank foreshadowed his hermit ways to come the following year, when half the world turned toward Barry getting close to baseball's all-time home run record, and the other half searched for a reaction from Henry Louis Aaron. "I was telling somebody today that it has gotten so now that they don't even want me to come to court to even to participate in trials anymore. You get to be a certain age, and they say, 'See ya later,'" Hank said, laughing, tying the end of his jury selection days to Barry's chase, which reminded him of his own chase, which was the worst time of his life. "So, I don't worry about any of that [regarding Bonds]. I'm happy. My life is really good. I'm happy with it and I don't have to go through that anymore. I went through chasing Babe Ruth's record for…it was enough for me for two-and-a-half years, and God knows I had my fill of it. I really had a lot…of good things and I had a lot of bad things."

That meant Hank wanted nothing to do with Barry Bonds things in 2007, which made me quite popular. I was everywhere: CNN, CBS, NBC, MSNBC, ABC, PBS. In addition, any Atlanta station owning a TV camera asked for my Hank comments, along with national and local radio. Most prominently, I talked Hank Aaron often during my gig as a regular panelist on *Rome Is Burning*, Jim Rome's ESPN show, and I'd frequently appear as The Hank Aaron Whisperer somewhere on one of ESPN's slew of other entities two or more times per day.

As the baseball gods would have it, the Giants of Barry Bonds played hosts to the 2007 All-Star Game on July 10 in San Francisco, and the day after the American League's 5–4 victory, I was the only non-ESPN employee or non-Major League Baseball player used for the cable network's lengthy feature on Aaron's legacy while Bonds streaked through the first half of the season toward breaking Hank's career home run record. "Hank Aaron is not going to be diminished," I said, during one of the several times I was used in the piece. "He is going to be as big as he was before, even bigger, simply because people are going to see him against a very controversial figure, whereas Hank Aaron was a very beloved figure, and in a way, it's going to strengthen his legacy even more."

A few days later, I was on ESPN's *Outside the Lines*, and host Jeremy Schaap asked me, "As well as you know Aaron, Terence, what do you think of his decision not to be there when his record is broken by Barry Bonds?"

"I'll tell you. I think this is absolutely perfect," I said. "If he had a long-standing relationship with Barry Bonds, which he does not, if they were very close, which they are not, then you could say he should be there. Willie Mays is his godfather. It makes perfect sense for Willie Mays to be there, and it does not make perfect sense for Hank Aaron to be there except that people are making this to be a bigger deal than it should be."

Besides my TV and radio stints as The Hank Aaron Whisperer, I also was everywhere through the written word. Whenever I searched "Hank Aaron" and "Terence Moore" during much of 2007, I found something from one of my columns for *The Atlanta Journal-Constitution* (often the whole piece) or from one of my television interviews. Those searches produced that Aaron-Moore combination, stretching from *The New York Times* to the London papers (both in England and Ohio) and even to the *South Bend Tribune*, which pleased all of my aunts, uncles, and cousins who dominated that small Indiana city of my birth and youth.

Sports Illustrated was the pinnacle of sports print media at that time, and the magazine displayed that Moore-Aaron combination. In late July 2007, I got a call from *SI* staff writer Tom Verducci who did the magazine's cover story called "The People's King." It read: "Henry Aaron is about to be displaced from his spot atop the all-time home run list, but 755 will endure as one of baseball's magic numbers, a lasting monument to an underappreciated star and to the courage and integrity with which the Hammer attained his crown."

Hank wouldn't talk to *Sports Illustrated* because Hank would only talk to me. So, Verducci used me as The Hank Aaron Whisperer, The Hank Spokesperson, and Hank Aaron in Spirit as a substitute. Verducci's article included this passage: "'Hank is genuinely a soft-spoken, private guy, and he truly doesn't want to relive 1972, '73, and '74,'" says Terence Moore, a columnist for *The Atlanta Journal-Constitution* and an Aaron confidant. [Aaron has declined all interview requests, including several from *SI*, on the subject of the home run chase.] 'Those are bad memories for him. With Barry Bonds going through the chase, it's like it's putting him back in that era. And he doesn't want to go back there.'"

Through it all—my endless Henry Louis Aaron-related appearances on national and local television shows; my interviews with radio stations, newspapers, and magazines, including the one for *Sports Illustrated*—Hank and I kept in touch with phone calls coming and going both ways.

He loved it. "I see you, Terence," Hank often said, chuckling on the other end. "You're doing a great job really. I don't want anything to do with any of it, but if you need something from me, I'm here." Hank kept his promise to me, and I appreciated it. But never once did I take for granted that Henry Louis Aaron designated me as the only media person on the planet to know what he was thinking at all times, while Barry slugged and sulked his way toward the home run crown. Sometimes, I wanted to call Hank about something I contemplated writing for *The AJC* about Barry's home run chase, but I would move away from the phone, even though I knew Hank wouldn't mind whatever it was. I only dialed Hank for the big stuff involving Barry or I waited for Hank to call me about his thoughts of the moment, which happened often in 2007.

The whole Barry thing was bizarre. It was this bizarre: after Barry did the inevitable by breaking Hank's career home run mark with No. 756 in San Francisco on August 7, 2007, he slowly became a national afterthought. He was 43, but he finished the 2007 season with good numbers for the average baseball player. He hit 28 home runs. He batted .276 with 66 RBIs and he led the major leagues in walks with 132. He also retained the ability to rip pitches beyond the farthest fence…ahem…with a little help, which was part of the problem.

Even so, despite Barry's 762 homers overall and seven National League Most Valuable Player awards, his career was done. Nobody wanted to sign the new home run champion after the 2007 season— not the Giants, not anybody. Not since he was tagged as the guy who had more than a little help at the plate through performance-enhancing drugs and he also owned the reputation for alienating folks.

In one of life's great ironies, I could have been The Barry Bonds Whisperer under different circumstances. I was The Hank Aaron Whisperer though. That reality, along with what could have made me The Barry Bonds Whisperer, created an interesting situation on Thursday, April 6, 2006, inside the Giants home clubhouse at AT&T

Park in San Francisco. Across the way, there were members of the always sizeable Giants media contingent watching in amazement (including the Giants beat writer who once called me the N-word) as Barry waved me over to his famously private corner. He wanted a one-on-one chat and he wanted to make sure no other ears were listening. This wasn't unusual. Barry and I had long and deep talks from the time he made his Major League Baseball debut with the Pittsburgh Pirates in 1986 through his only season in 2016 as a batting coach for the Miami Marlins. As for the latter, that's when he confessed to me for a Sportsonearth.com column that went viral. No, he didn't come clean about steroids but about his personality. In a lengthy session from the visitor's clubhouse at Sun Trust Park in Atlanta, he said he spent much of his baseball career fluctuating between a "jerk" and a "dumbass." He said he wanted to apologize and he said he wished to spread the message through me, which sounded like what I had been doing for decades with the guy with 755 home runs to his 762.

I got along as well with Barry Lamar Bonds as any reporter in history—and probably better than that. Except for Sunday, April 13, 1997.

The truth is this burst of Barry pettiness was his fault in the short run, but it was mine for making it a medium-run thing. Back then Major League Baseball prepared to celebrate the 50th anniversary of Jackie Robinson breaking the game's color barrier in a huge way on Tuesday, April 15 in New York City. Perfect. The Los Angeles Dodgers were coming to town. That was Jackie's old franchise when it resided in Brooklyn, located maybe a 45-minute subway ride from Shea Stadium, where the modern-day Dodgers would meet the New York Mets. Before a huge group of dignitaries led by president Bill Clinton and Rachel Robinson, Jackie's widow, baseball used the occasion to retire Jackie's No. 42 forever.

I flew to New York a couple of days early on purpose. The Giants were around that weekend to play the Mets. I figured I could spend time before Sunday's game talking Jackie Robinson with two of my favorite African Americans in the game for insight: Giants manager Dusty Baker, a former teammate of Hank's on the Braves and one of the game's all-time renaissance men, and Bonds, who always gave me thoughtful answers on everything and anything. I often defended Barry before others, saying the truth: once you got to know Barry, he was quite cerebral.

My plan worked perfectly.

Well, at least the Baker portion in the visiting manager's office at Shea Stadium, where he was his typically superb self. He told personal stories regarding Jackie's legacy, especially since Baker spent the prime of his playing career as a Dodgers outfielder for eight seasons through 1983. Then I was off to seek Barry in the visiting clubhouse, which was ridiculously small and cramped, and Barry's locker was on the far wall as soon as you walked through the door. As I entered, I began moving toward Barry, and when he looked up from the distance while sitting at his locker, he didn't do what he usually had done for nearly the decade of our interactions.

He didn't flash his brilliant smile.

He frowned instead and he went further. As I continued to walk his way—with teammates, Giants officials, other clubhouse folks, and fellow reporters squeezed into the tight quarters—Barry rose from his seat to shout obscenities around his dominant message of the moment: "Okay, I don't want to talk about Jackie Robinson! Don't come over here talking to me about Jackie Robinson! I'm tired of talking about Jackie Robinson!"

The closer I got to Barry, the more he repeated his mantra (*"I don't want to talk about Jackie Robinson"*) but only in softer terms. By the time I reached him, he gave me another "I'm not talking about Jackie Robinson" before he said just above a whisper, "T, we can talk about anything else, but I'm tired of talking about Jackie Robinson."

Whatever, dude.

At that point with Barry's mostly contrived tirade threatening to place the both of us on the back pages of the New York tabloids, I was fuming. I told him in a slightly loud voice, "Thanks, sir," as I turned and left the clubhouse. I didn't need Barry Lamar Bonds or anybody else that badly.

He never apologized, but during Baseball All-Star Game events and his trips to Atlanta with the Giants, he tried to ease the tension over the next couple of seasons. I wasn't having it. I finally came to the conclusion that I might as well drop my anger over SheaGate because it was what it was and it was Barry being Barry.

It was just the first (and only) time it happened to me.

That brings me back to Thursday, April 6, 2006, when Barry and I were nearly back to our normal relationship. I traveled to San Francisco to write columns for *The Atlanta Journal-Constitution* on the Braves' West Coast road trip at the start of that season. I entered the Giants home clubhouse at AT&T Park, which was famous (or maybe infamous) for Barry's World in a far corner. Barry Lamar Bonds had four adjoining lockers, including the largest one in the room, and with the help of a huge TV set and a vibrating reclining chair, he was able to control who entered Barry's World.

Visitors to Barry's World almost never included reporters—among his least favorite people on Earth. Still, as was the case on this day, that typically large core of media covering the Giants always gathered before games in the middle of the AT&T home clubhouse. The reporters waited for the player or the coach they needed for an interview at that moment or they wondered if Bonds would do the improbable by inviting them into Barry's World for a chat.

Barry did the improbable on Thursday, April 6, 2006, but it didn't involve anybody covering the Giants. As soon as he glanced up from his recliner to see me walking into the Giants clubhouse, he said, "Hey, T" and then he waved me through the invisible attack dogs. He flashed his brilliant smile, both of us exchanged pleasantries, and I could sense the Giants press corps joined everybody else around the room in wondering, *Why isn't Barry being Barry, and he's being kind to a reporter?* I *knew* Barry Lamar Bonds, the whole one.

Even though Barry could become King of the Jerks within seconds, which was something he tried to address during my 2016 interview with him, he was extremely sensitive. He cared more about his public image than you would think. As I once wrote for *The Atlanta Journal-Constitution*, "You probably don't know that the rugged exterior that Bonds often shows is a fraud…Bonds just wants to be loved. He really does."

So, this wasn't surprising: about a couple of minutes into our conversation in the middle of Barry's World, Barry's brilliant smile left, and the dominant thing on his face were sad eyes. Then he said, "I've followed what you've been writing about me and I see you on television all the time. As a Black man to another Black man, if I were on the other side of things, I would be more supportive of you than you have been of me."

Barry stared at me in silence with those sad eyes. Instead of thinking about his slow start at the plate that season, he was recalling how I was spending the middle part of his chase of Hank's home run record saying—through print, cyberspace, or the airways—that Barry Lamar Bonds wasn't Henry Louis Aaron in character. I told Barry I had issues with the reports connecting his power surge to performance-enhancing drugs, but Barry never responded to my response. He just kept those sad eyes and he moved to another topic.

Actually, it was the same one but in a different way. "Let me ask you this: why doesn't Hank ever call me and why won't he even try to get in touch with me?" Barry said, knowing that I was The Hank Aaron Whisperer. He added, raising his arms in despair, "I never hear from Hank. So when is he going to give me a call?"

I asked Barry why Hank needed to contact him? "You just think he would," Barry said before I mentioned Henry Louis Aaron had zero obligation to call Barry Lamar Bonds or anybody else.

Then I added, "If you want to talk to Hank, you should call him. If you need his telephone number, I'll give it to you."

Barry nodded with those sad eyes, but he never asked for Hank's number, and the conversation jumped to something else.

When I told Hank about my Barry conversation, he laughed, but he didn't want to respond to Barry's comments. Not then. Hank did give his thoughts almost a year later to the day, and they came in early April 2007 when Barry was just four months shy of the career home run record. Hank called me to say he'd just gotten off the phone with Bud Selig, the baseball commissioner and Hank's old pal from his Milwaukee Braves days. Barry was asking Selig and others why Hank wasn't corresponding with him. *Sound familiar?*

Hank had enough. He wanted me to put his response to Barry's plea for Henry Louis Aaron in newsprint because Hank knew it would spin around the globe and right into Barry's ears, which it did.

Here's what Hank said and what I wrote for *The AJC*: "I'm sorry Barry feels that way and I don't have any resentment toward him whatsoever, but I have no intention of trying to get in contact with him or doing anything with him in regard to his chasing the record. Nothing. Why should I? It's really not a big concern of mine. I don't know why I should have to do anything. I might send a telegram, and that would be the extent of it. The commissioner told me that [Bonds] has asked him several times about why I haven't contacted him. I don't talk to anybody really and I've never talked to Barry outside of that commercial we did together a few years ago and a few other short times. I'm 72 years old and I'm not hopping on a plane and flying all the way to San Francisco for anybody."

"Would you like to be around when Barry breaks the record, you know, if you just happened to be in the vicinity," I asked Hank.

"Uh-uh. No, no. I'm not going to be around. I'd probably fly to West Palm Beach to play golf. Again, it has nothing to do with anybody, other than I had enough of it. I don't want to be around that sort of thing anymore. I just want to be at peace with myself. I don't want to answer questions. It's going to be a no-win situation for me anyway. If I go, people are going to say, 'Well, he went because of this.' If I don't go, they'll say whatever. I'll just let them make their own minds up."

Then came Tuesday, August 7, 2007, in San Francisco. None of the 43,154 folks packed inside AT&T Park was named Bud Selig or Hank Aaron, but the atmosphere remained electric. In the fifth inning of what would become an 8–6 loss for the Giants against the Washington Nationals, Barry ripped a 3–2 pitch from Mike Bacsik before Barry raised his hands with joy during the typically cool northern California night as the ball sailed into the bleachers beyond the wall in right-center field. Only the screaming throughout the stands was louder than the fireworks around the ballpark.

The grandest moment of this moment was coming.

No, it wasn't the way Barry pointed to the sky with both arms as a salute to Bobby Bonds, his father who died just shy of four years earlier on August 23, 2003. No, it wasn't all of those relatives who joined Barry on the field to show the gentler side of a guy who rarely displayed compassion in public. No, it wasn't Willie Mays, his 76-year-old godfather and the eternal baseball icon, joining Barry and the others throughout the 10-minute celebration. It was the AT&T Park public-address announcer telling the crowd to view the jumbo screen beyond the bleachers.

Suddenly, as the hushes throughout the ballpark became gasps and then cheers and then roars, there was Henry Louis Aaron, bigger than life, preparing to deliver a message to Barry though a pre-recorded video. For some perspective, Hank told me Bud Selig talked him into doing it. "He figured that this would be the best way to handle the

Barry Bonds thing, and I agreed," Hank said. "Just make one statement and then be done with it."

Here was the statement: "I would like to offer my congratulations to Barry Bonds on becoming baseball's career home run leader. It is a great accomplishment, which required skill, longevity, and determination. Throughout the past century, the home run has held a special place in baseball, and I have been privileged to hold this record for 33 of those years. I move over now and offer my best wishes to Barry and his family on this historical achievement. My hope today, as it was on that April evening in 1974, is that the achievement of this record will inspire others to chase their own dreams."

Through misty eyes Barry pointed at the image of Hank on screen in appreciation, and Barry Lamar Bonds told reporters later of the tribute from Henry Louis Aaron: "It meant everything. It meant absolutely everything. We all have a lot of respect for him—from everyone in the game. Right now, everything's just hitting me so fast. I'm lost for words again. It was absolutely the best, absolutely the best."

While all of that was happening in San Francisco, Hank was back in his southwest Atlanta home, looking at nothing but the back of his eyelids with a fluffy pillow holding his famous head. "Well, first of all, I was asleep. It was 1:00 in the morning," Aaron said, laughing a few days later, giving me his first public comments about Barry as baseball's new home run king. "Heck, I'm not going to sit up and watch a baseball game. It's just like I wasn't going to be able to travel all over the world to watch [Bonds trying to break the record]. It wasn't being disrespectful or anything. It's just a matter of, hey, the body needed to go to sleep."

I had a final question for the moment about the other guy. I asked Hank if he ever would call or meet with Barry for whatever reason. "Eventually, if I happen to see him somewhere, I'd probably say something to him," Hank said. "To be honest, I'm as happy for him as anybody really."

THE HATERS

The rain couldn't care less that we had arrived at the main entrance of the golf club, but that was fine. Even though the driver kept talking Henry Louis Aaron, he stopped long enough to grab the wheelchair from the rear of the SUV and race around to the side of the vehicle with his massive umbrella as I helped Hank from the passenger's seat.

The waiting crowd of CNN folks and those associated with the golf club watched with wide eyes above open mouths. I read the expression on their faces: *Hank Aaron!* Not... *The tired and aching man in a wheelchair!*

Even though I knew time was of the essence (I mean, that CNN camera crew had to hop that plane to Afghanistan), I had a flashback. Five, eight, maybe 10 years before this moment, I was heading for a flight at the Atlanta airport and I saw Hank in the distance. He was moving with his quick yet graceful steps during the post-playing prime of his life and he was heading somewhere. I just wanted to watch. I kept following him, falling back far enough to remain anonymous to the scene, and saw two reactions during the many times he was recognized along the way. There was the joy of those encountering Henry Louis Aaron, mostly for the first time, and then there was the patience of Hank's response—complete with his easy smile and maybe one of his "Why, thank you" replies before he excused himself to take care of his business of finding his gate.

The flashback was nice, but I had the present to handle. I needed to get the tired and aching man in the wheelchair to the golf course's ballroom disguised as a CNN remote studio. The problem was Hank's partially rain-soaked admirers were huddled near the front entrance of the place, and they kept talking to Henry Louis Aaron almost as much as the driver.

Finally, I had enough. "Where's the back way? Is there a back way? I really need to get Hank to where we need to go," I said, almost shouting to the head of the golf club, and he nodded, asking me to follow him down a few hallways and then through a kitchen, but it didn't matter.

"Oh, wow! Hank Aaron?"

"How's it going, Mr. Aaron?"

"You're still the home run champion to me."

"Why thank you," said the tired and aching man in the wheelchair as I tried to stay quick without hurrying after we rolled into the make-shift studio.

Who are all of these people? I thought, recognizing only a handful of them while not having a clue about the others. To me, the half of CNN that wasn't greeting us at the golf club's front entrance was lounging around this room. Some carried baseballs and other items for Aaron to autograph. No, no, NO, I said, transforming from The Hank Aaron Whisperer to The Hank Aaron Enforcer, thinking whatever energy the tired and aching man had left shouldn't involve him scribbling his name across souvenirs.

At least they weren't haters.

About the haters.

Beyond our Dixiecrats, Hank and I had a slew of haters, and we shared our stories since they were similar in nature. Our haters were the kind that attacked African Americans with strong convictions, especially when those strong convictions involved racial issues, social injustice, or a combination of both. Our haters reacted out of jealousy or ignorance, and the majority of our haters were oblivious to their flawed logic for becoming our haters.

Our haters were various colors. We had the obvious ones exemplified by our Dixiecrats, mostly consisting of Whites who executed racism through mind games instead of billy clubs or large crosses on front lawns. Then we had the least obvious ones, and they were African American haters who had issues with our strong convictions when our strong convictions turned into an equal opportunity reaction from us. Simply put, if Hank and I didn't totally hug an African American sports personality who didn't deserve hugging, our African American haters viewed us as worse than Uncle Toms.

In their minds, we were Uncle Hank and Uncle Terry—and not in a good way to that segment of the Black community.

The overwhelming majority of the African Americans that Hank and I encountered were highly supportive. They were our Earth angels. Either publicly or privately, they did whatever they could to help us survive our Dixiecrats. Even so, there was our small yet significant group of African American haters, and they were persistent in their attacks. The most striking example of their existence for Hank and me occurred in the same year: 2007. While Barry Bonds was closing fast on Hank's career home run record of 755, Atlanta Falcons quarterback Michael Vick was in the midst of a dogfighting drama.

The two stories were similar. As a result, they both were enough to do what I previously thought was impossible: they strengthened the relationship even more between Hank and myself. They both were stories involving two of the most prominent sports figures in history. They both were stories covered daily, hourly, and then moment by moment throughout local, national, and international media. They both were stories leading to controversies for the ages. They both were stories featuring African Americans as central figures. They both were stories with much of Black America supporting those African Americans in the middle of those controversies, which meant they both were stories that caused some among Black America to look at Hank and me as traitors.

Maybe worse.

Fantasy trumped reality for our African American haters, and here was reality regarding Hank and Barry: throughout Barry's pursuit of surpassing Hank with a record-breaking 756th homer for his career— marred by allegations that he continued as a steroid user after he reportedly began juicing slightly less than a decade before—Henry Louis Aaron never said anything negative about Barry Lamar Bonds in public.

I know. As The Hank Aaron Whisperer, I was the only one delivering Hank's words to the planet throughout the year leading up to Barry surpassing Hank's old home run mark on August 7, 2007. Afterward, with Barry as the new King of Swat in front of his hometown Giants crowd in San Francisco, Hank delivered a 50-second taped video tribute to Barry that received a standing ovation from the sellout crowd at AT&T Park. In addition, Hank's message got universal praise, including from Barry, who was so emotional watching Hank speak that he pointed toward the screen with misty eyes.

None of that mattered to Hank's African American haters. To hear them tell it, Hank was the hater. Specifically, they thought Hank was the Barry Bonds hater because they said Hank didn't spend months or even years saying positive things about Barry and because they also said Hank didn't volunteer to serve as mentor to the significantly younger Black slugger who was attacked by so many people, especially White ones.

Hank's African American haters often mentioned this: even though Barry kept swinging and begging in the shadows for Hank to say something through the summer of 2007, Hank said nothing on purpose. He had nothing to say, which was fine. He didn't dislike Bonds, but he wasn't a fan of what was his polar opposite in personality. Mostly, Henry Louis Aaron was permanently scarred by the racist messages and death threats he experienced during the two years of his pursuit of Babe Ruth's home run record. He finally surpassed The Designated White Saint of Baseball on April 8, 1974, and in Hank's mind, that meant he was forever finished talking about chasing milestones of magnitude. "Things were pretty normal for me at one point after going through what I did [with the Ruth situation]. Then, all of a sudden, it crops up again with all these questions, and to be honest, I still don't know how I managed to get thrown into this Bonds thing," Hank told me in November 2007, three months after Barry grabbed the home run crown.

At that point, Henry Louis Aaron was 73. He was more interested in fulfilling his role on a limited basis as a Braves executive than finding ways to make Barry Bonds feel good about himself. Hank also served as a vocal and financial supporter of disadvantaged youth and he remained the overseer of his many business endeavors across Georgia and into Wisconsin, his old stomping grounds with the Milwaukee Braves before he finished his major league playing career years later with the Milwaukee Brewers. Hank laughed, adding, "I try to work out every day and I have this trainer here to help me try to keep this old body in shape. Oh, I feel tremendously relieved. I'm so glad [Bonds' home run chase] is done with and now I can just go my own way."

It didn't happen.

Many haters still surrounded Hank even after Barry officially owned the record, and those African American haters were creeping into his daily existence. That's when Hank did some thinking. He analyzed the conversations he had with those inside of his inner circle—from the start of Barry's chase through the end—and then he confided in me that November night in 2007 that he determined many of his "friends" were only acquaintances, associates, or haters. "It really got to the point where a lot of people started wanting to give you advice about what you should do, and they didn't know what the hell the situation was," Hank said, as visibly irritated as I'd ever seen him. "I mean, these were people that you had been knowing for a long time, but they couldn't figure out why I wasn't getting involved in this thing. Then they would come forward and say like, 'Well, you need to do this. You need to do that.' They wanted to give you all of this advice and they didn't know what was all involved in it really. That's the thing that really bothers you. Friends that you've had a long time are all of a sudden coming forth and telling you things like, 'Well, I don't understand why you aren't making comments or why aren't you doing blah, blah, blah?' Well, you know what? You're not supposed to understand any of it because you're not in it."

I could relate, and Hank knew it.

We flipped back and forth in our discussions from Hank's trials and tribulations with his African American haters involving Barry Bonds, steroids, and home run records to the arrows slung my way by African Americans during the Michael Vick saga, regarding the fighting, the drowning, the strangulation, the burying, and the execution of dogs. Whenever I wasn't on national or local television throughout 2007 as the Hank Aaron Whisperer regarding Barry, I was on the airways discussing Vick, Vick, and more Vick. I still wrote columns for *The Atlanta Journal-Constitution* about Hank, Barry, Michael, and everything else, but I also was ESPN's primary go-to person in Georgia on the Vick situation. So, with Hank, Barry, and Michael spending most of 2007 in the daily headlines, I often did three or four hits per day for various combinations of ESPN channels.

My Vick-related appearances began that spring after the first rumors surfaced about the Falcons' Pro Bowl quarterback and dogfighting. Then my ESPN role grew in April 2007, when Surry, Virginia, cops served a warrant to discover 66 dogs (including 55 of them as pit bulls) inside a series of dark-colored buildings in the woods of a house owned by Vick. Afterward, I dominated ESPN channels discussing Vick and dogfighting through December 2007, when a federal judge in Richmond, Virginia, sentenced Vick to 23 months in prison for running a "cruel and inhumane" dogfighting ring and lying about it. I was among the few in the tiny Richmond courtroom, where the judge chastised Vick, who looked surrealistic in his black-and-white striped prison outfit. I later was part of an ESPN town-hall meeting in Atlanta during prime time that fall and I became a constant target for audience members airing their media-related grievances over the Vick mess.

Hank watched. "Yeah, I saw how they were getting all over you," Hank, said laughing, "but I like the way you handled yourself," he said before laughing some more. "Boy, Terence. You have some thick skin, buddy."

So did Henry Louis Aaron and Jack Roosevelt Robinson.

Throughout the 2007 Vick saga—from when I ripped Falcons officials that May in *The Atlanta Journal-Constitution* for years of coddling their undisciplined superstar (unpaid parking tickets, stiffing U.S. Congressmen in Washington, flipping off a hometown fan, etc.) to when Vick became the guest of the state of Kansas as inmate No. 33765-183 in Leavenworth—I kept writing and saying what I knew: Vick was guilty and he needed to come clean.

My African American haters kept responding to my honesty by saying I was nothing but an Uncle Terry.

Uncle Hank could relate. "Once I found out 'who was who' and 'what was what' and what they were all about, I just went about my business really," Hank told me during one of our note-comparing sessions. On this day he referred mostly to the African American haters from his inner circle who thought he was nothing but an Uncle Hank for doing the right thing by keeping "Barry Bonds" off his tongue for public consumption down the stretch of 2006 and for all of 2007. "It's hard to ignore [the haters], but you have to do the best you can and you just have to try to stay away from them."

That was difficult for both of us. When it came to the Bonds thing and the Vick thing, our African American haters were everywhere, and they were weaved into the fabric of our lives. During much of 2007, the majority of my trips to the barber shop or to the supermarket featured confrontations with African American haters telling me (and loudly) that I was "picking on Vick," and that he wasn't guilty of anything, and that even if he were involved in this media-hyped dogfighting controversy somehow, it was only dogfighting.

Several of my worst experiences came at church.

Yes, church…a predominately Black church, where I had a bull's-eye on my back whenever I walked through the doors: "I saw what you wrote…And you call yourself a Christian. Uh."

"Brother Moore, we need to talk…That ain't right what you're saying about Michael Vick. Why so much hate? What did that young man ever do to you?"

I always wanted to counter with the truth, but I didn't. The truth was these folks were more members of The Latter-day Church of Michael Vick than they were of the church they claimed they joined. They only worshipped the Falcons quarterback because he thrilled them with his ability to perform miracles on the football field with his legs and his left arm. If he were just ordinary, I wouldn't have heard a syllable from my African American haters, but it would have been useless for me to tell them as much. When it came to Vick, their ears were closed, along with their eyes and their minds. The opposite of John 8:32 was happening in their hearts. To paraphrase: ye shall know the truth about Michael Vick and dogfighting, and the truth won't make you free because you're too busy bowing to somebody who is as guilty as an African American sports columnist at *The AJC* and on ESPN keeps saying he is.

The Latter-day Church of Michael Vick wasn't buying it. I walked into the sanctuary to help lead praise and worship service, and a middle-aged Black woman rushed toward me while screaming, "Leave him alone. *Leave him alone!*" She lunged at me with eyes bulging, as one of the ministers pulled her away, but she kept screaming, "I saw what you said about me. Delusional. *I'm not delusional.*"

It took me awhile to determine what she meant, but the best I could figure, she was talking about *The Atlanta Journal-Constitution* column during the previous week in which I wrote, "If you think Michael Vick is innocent regarding this dogfighting situation, you're delusional."

By the end of 2007, I was bitter regarding my African American haters over the Vick thing, especially given my two decades at that point of battling the Dixiecrats at *The AJC* to honor the spirit of Dr. Martin Luther King Jr. and to help future African Americans in the media. African American haters toward anybody within the Black community also bring glee to the Dixiecrats. As for pure anger, I felt it, but I knew I couldn't go there. I thought about my parents overcoming so much to get so far by using brain over brawn. I thought about Hank's classiness while dealing with his African American haters despite wanting to explode. Then I remembered Page 178 of Jackie Robinson's autobiography. That's where Jackie shared a letter he received from Malcolm X, among his African American haters.

Jackie Robinson? African American haters?

In 1973, which was the first of the many times I read Jackie's book, I couldn't fathom Jack Roosevelt Robinson having African American haters after April 15, 1947, followed by the massive work he did (and continued to do) in the African American community.

Suddenly, in 2007, I could fathom it all. After the rise of those African American haters around Hank and me over the Bonds thing and the Vick thing, I even could fathom Jackie's African American hater named Malcolm X, the Nation of Islam leader. Here's partly what Malcolm X wrote to Jackie as was shared in Jackie's autobiography: "You became a great baseball player after your white boss [Mr. Rickey] lifted you to the major leagues. You proved that your white boss had chosen the 'right' Negro by getting plenty of hits, stealing plenty of bases, winning many games and bringing much money through the gates and into the pockets of your white boss…You stay as far away from the Negro community as you can get, and you never take an interest in anything in the Negro community until the white man himself takes an interest in it. You, yourself, would never shake my hand until you saw some of your white friends shaking it."

In his autobiography Jackie responded to Malcolm X's letter. In part, Jackie said, "I replied to Malcolm, saying I would cherish his reply and that I was honored to be placed in the distinguished company of [Ralph Bunche, a Black Nobel Peace Prize winner who marched with Dr. King] whom he had also attacked."

Jackie took the higher than high road.

So did Hank. His closest "friends" heard the same things from Henry Louis Aaron that I did regarding his reasons for staying mostly silent during Bonds' pursuit of his home run record. Several of those "friends" still didn't get it. They preferred their feelings over the facts.

We both could relate.

As for the facts: while Hank praised Barry, the player, even when the steroids allegations went from whispers to shouts, I tried to help Vick five years earlier. I spent a summer day at the Falcons' 2002 training camp in Greenville, South Carolina, where Andrew Young waved me across the field for a three-person huddle.

Young was one of Dr. King's right-hand men before he became a U.S. Congressman, the United States ambassador to the United Nations, and Atlanta mayor. He also served on the Falcons' board of directors and he ranked among Hank's "true" friends. He wanted me to join him during an impromptu mentoring session with Vick in his second NFL season. Young thought No. 7 needed guidance beyond reading defenses. When practice finished the three of us talked for 45 minutes about the pitfalls of a young athlete in Atlanta, and then Young told Vick, while pointing to me, "You need to get his telephone number. He can give you advice on dealing with the media and other matters."

Vick asked for the address to my church. "I'll call you when I'm coming," Vick said, but he never dialed my number. Still, despite the nonstop drama I experienced from The Latter-day Church of Michael Vick throughout 2007, I had zero issues with the man himself before, during, or after his dogfighting controversy.

None of that mattered. To my African American haters, I remained the problem. To them, I could have done *something* through softer words to keep their guy out of the slammer to produce more thrills for his "delusional" followers. To Hank's African American haters, Henry Louis Aaron could have done *something* through any words to keep Barry Lamar Bonds from making 2007 his last year in Major League Baseball. As for the Bonds thing, we're back to facts, and the facts were: nobody wanted a 43-year-old slugger who had respectful numbers during what would be his final season (.276 batting average, 28 home runs, 66 RBIs) but saw his performance-enhancing drugs controversy grow instead of shrink and didn't exactly own Hank's personality for congeniality.

The bulk of Hank's haters were White, though. He had the blatantly racist ones during his youth in segregated Mobile, Alabama. Then he encountered more of the same as one of the first African American players in the South Atlantic League after he spent the 1953 season playing for the Milwaukee Braves' Class A team in Jacksonville, Florida. While his White Jacksonville teammates stayed together at hotels and restaurants, Hank had to make his own arrangements for both of those things around the land of separate but unequal. He later experienced the Babe Ruth home run chase, which was ruined in the early and mid-1970s by those death threats and racists messages.

All of that was tangible racism.

Down the stretch of the 20th century and into the new one—when Henry Louis Aaron became Jack Roosevelt Robinson by spending his post-playing career speaking frequently about racial issues and social injustice (usually to The Hank Aaron Whisperer)—he faced a different type of racism from Whites, and I've got my hand raised with other African Americans.

The mind games.

In July of 2000, I continued to do what I did several times over the years. I introduced Henry Louis Aaron during a ceremony or a banquet. This one involved a charity event at the Ritz-Carlton in downtown Atlanta, and Hank was Hank for the diverse crowd packed inside the hotel's largest ballroom. In addition to Hank's riveting tales from his playing days, he spoke with passion about the ills of society (in general) and of his sport (in particular) regarding African Americans. Those present were glued to his deep and distinctive voice. They laughed at his quick wit. They applauded when they thought it was appropriate. They stood with cheers during his trip to the podium for his speech and they did so again as he returned to his seat.

They cherished Henry Louis Aaron...or did they?

As hundreds of folks mingled near the close of Hank's speech, a White man in his 50s pulled me away from the crowd. He spoke for himself and for others—not only in the room but elsewhere—and it was about *this* Henry Louis Aaron. That was opposed to the other Henry Louis Aaron of whom my visitor of the moment and his peers perceived as the humble Henry Louis Aaron, the one who slammed home runs while keeping his mouth shut, particularly on topics that made people (you know, White people) feel uncomfortable. "Hey, Terence, loved your intro. I'm from a small town in Mississippi and I picked cotton as a White man," the guy said, pausing before a long sigh, while looking at the floor. Then he looked up to say, "I like Hank. I always have, but I take offense to his obsession with talking about racial problems, always Black and White with him now. Why does he always have to go down that road? I saw a damn good player out there when he played. I didn't see color. Why stir up old stuff? I just want you to tell him that he doesn't have to hate White people. He needs to move on and stop alienating [White] people."

After I smiled at the guy, I pointed across the way, and I said, "Why don't you tell Hank yourself? He's right there." The guy responded by talking and walking in a direction away from Hank, "Yeah, but I'm telling you. I know you guys like to keep things, well, to stir things up, so I'm just asking you to pass it along." Such was the attitude of many Whites toward Hank after their honeymoon with the slugger led to a separation. That honeymoon began upon his retirement as a player in October 1976, but it ended when he leapt into high gear as a frequent spokesperson against social injustice during the early 1980s as an Atlanta Braves executive. Just like that, Henry Louis Aaron was the disgruntled home run king to his White haters. They moaned he still harped over what happened to him while chasing Babe Ruth's record. They groaned he did so despite his entry into the Baseball Hall of Fame on a near-record 97.8 percent of the ballots, despite Braves owner Ted Turner giving him a bunch of money to become that executive for the franchise after his retirement, and despite his ability around Georgia to drink out of the same water fountains as Whites.

To Hank's White haters, he turned into The Bad Jackie, and that Jack Roosevelt Robinson had his own set of haters. See if this sounds familiar: Jackie's White haters surfaced in droves after his Baseball Hall of Fame playing days evolved into his opportunity to fight for African American equality throughout society even in the major leagues. To Jackie's White haters, he was ungrateful for saying racial stuff whenever he saw a microphone or a camara. To them, The Good Jackie was so pleasantly docile in his early days with the Brooklyn Dodgers—when death threats and hate messages dominated his world—that he could have starred in something like that scene from *Animal House*, when a willing pledge accepted paddling and humiliation during the initiation process for a White fraternity. ("Thank you, sir. May I have another?")

Mostly, to Hank's White haters, Henry Louis Aaron spent that stretch—ranging from the early 1980s through seven years after that

White guy from Mississippi approached me about The Bad Hank in 2000 inside that hotel ballroom—refusing to move on. They couldn't understand why he kept alienating White people by telling the truth that the death of racism had been greatly exaggerated, particularly in The South.

Then the change came.

It was slight for Hank, but it was drastic for revisionist history because his White haters began evolving into his White supporters. Not coincidentally, the transformation began during the 2007 season, when Henry Louis Aaron became less visible as Barry Lamar Bonds edged closer to his home run record, and something else happened. Hank started the early stages of his two-year plan to drift farther into the shadows in his executive role on the Braves.

The combination triggered the Muhammad Ali thing. That Ali thing started for Hank before he became an octogenarian. He suffered during his 70s from enough aching joints to need a cart or a cane to maneuver during his ceremonial appearances at ballparks around the country and other events in his honor. That Ali thing soared to its apex for Hank from the time of his hip replacement surgery in February 2014 through the end of his life on Friday, January 22, 2021, and afterward.

About that Muhammad Ali thing: if you're an African American with strong convictions, your haters eventually get amnesia. I cherished Muhammad Ali. By the time he died on June 3, 2016, I kept shaking my head after seeing, reading, and listening to the slew of tributes about the three-time heavyweight boxing champion who was more important to humanity than he was to athletics. Those tributes were glowing—sometimes over the top—with words meant for deity. They came from everywhere, including from his former haters (both Black and White) who praised his outspokenness, who boasted about his courage, and who celebrated his convictions.

Those tributes made me sick.

I was old enough to remember the 1960s and 1970s, which featured Muhammad Ali haters (both Black and White) everywhere you turned. They viewed the boxer formerly known as Cassius Clay as That Vietnam War Draft Dodger and they insisted he was "The Greatest" but only in his own mind. During the hype before The Fight of the Century on March 8, 1971, between Joe Frazier and Ali at Madison Square Garden in New York City, my freshman year at a Cincinnati high school was a microcosm of society. As a Black person, you had to choose and then you had to defend. Were you for Joe Frazier, which made you an Uncle Tom even if you liked his bulldozing style along the way to an Olympic gold medal and a 26–0 record, or were you for Muhammad Ali, which made you down with the Black Panthers, Malcolm X, and anything darker than daylight even if you thought Frazier would win, which Frazier did?

Inside and outside my Cincinnati high school, most people in White America (and many in Black America) were for Frazier because if Ali won in their minds, the sky would crash to Earth.

Then the change came.

Unlike Hank, this one was drastic for Ali, and that's because Ali's haters (Black and White) saw his drastic change in health. Three years after he lost on December 11, 1981 in Nassau, Bahamas, to the forgettable Trevor Berbick during a 10-round decision, he was diagnosed at 42 with Parkinson's disease, a degenerative disorder of the central nervous system that leads to everything from walking problems to tremors throughout your body.

I was a firsthand witness to Ali's early physical issues. In June of 1986, I had a one-on-one interview with the recently retired boxer in his downtown Atlanta hotel room, and that was two years after his Parkinson's diagnosis. I asked Ali to sign a poster I had that was slightly younger than my Hank Aaron one. My Ali poster was from January 28, 1974, when he captured his rematch against Joe Frazier at Madison Square Garden. Before we got to the Ali poster, the man of the moment did a magic trick in the room, and despite his balance-challenged legs, he levitated (or so it appeared) off the floor in front of me. Then, with Ali's hand shaking, along with other parts of his body, he signed the poster, "To Terry. Love, Muhammad Ali. June 18, 1986." Ali needed almost an eternity to sign it.

After the interview I watched Ali's handlers help him move through gatherings around various parts of Atlanta, and the scenes resembled those of everywhere else Ali traveled in the world. Folks of all nationalities, religions, colors, and creed hugged him—literally and figuratively. Between their poses with fake jabs to Ali's famous chin, they shouted "You're the Greatest," "We love you, Muhammad," or "The champ is here!" There were smiles when there weren't tears. In so many ways, this Muhammad Ali lovefest around Atlanta foreshadowed what happened a decade later in the same city, where a trembling Ali was the highlight of the 1996 Summer Games, when he stood as a singular figure atop a tower over the stadium to light the Olympic cauldron with the brightest and thickest of flames.

Yeah, but I was old enough to remember the 1960s and the 1970s, and all of that embracing of Ali in the 1980s and 1990s by everybody was such a contrast. Former heavyweight boxing champion George Foreman recalled 1967, when Ali faced five years in prison for avoiding the U.S. military draft before his conviction was overturned by the Supreme Court in 1971. "Everyone turned on him. I mean literally everyone," Forman told CNN the day after Ali's death in June 2016 at 74. "I hadn't even gone into boxing yet. No one wanted to be in his presence. No one wanted to be his friend, and he was dropped."

Even so, with Muhammad Ali holding that Olympic flame in his trembling hand and with his famously active tongue unable to utter more than a syllable or three in public, he officially was anointed "The Greatest" in the minds of everybody. At the very least, he was considered The Good Ali from that moment through his death and beyond, which brings us back to the Muhammad Ali thing, Hank Aaron, and amnesia.

Ali became lovable to his haters, but only when they viewed him as harmless, gentle, safe, pitiful, and unable to pound their ears with the truth, the hard truth, and nothing but that kind of truth.

The same thing happened to Henry Louis Aaron.

Except Hank fooled them.

Even during the ninth inning of Hank's life, when he could have coasted to his final out by keeping his Jackie Robinson-shaped convictions to himself and away from another generation, Henry Louis Aaron still told the truth, the hard truth, and nothing but that kind of truth.

I know. I was The Hank Aaron Whisperer.

EXTRA INNINGS

His Sense of Humor, Business Savvy, and More

Despite those frantic phone calls and urgent messages from CNN folks ("Are you and Mr. Aaron on the way?"... "What's your ETA?"... "Hey, don't forget that camera crew has to get out of here for the airport"), several of those CNN folks were among the many surrounding the tired and aching man in a wheelchair after I pushed him into the ballroom. They wanted Hank to sign things, but they mostly wanted to see him for maybe the first time ever. While they did so, they shared their appreciation to Henry Louis Aaron for his past and present, and several of those CNN staffers weren't even involved with the filming. They tagged along from the cable station's national headquarters in downtown Atlanta to see baseball's all-time greatest player-turned-American-treasure.

Nevertheless, after maybe seven minutes of watching just about everybody present in Baseball History Wonderland, I became The Hank Aaron Enforcer again. Since I fretted over the welfare of the tired and aching man in the wheelchair, I pushed him away from the growing crowd toward his designated spot for filming in the middle of the room. Along the way, I tried and failed not to sound irritated by saying to the epidemic of frowners I was leaving behind, "Why don't we wait to do all of that after the taping?"

Everybody nodded, especially those cameramen with Afghanistan dancing in the back of their minds.

• • •

The morning after Tuesday, November 4, 2008, when Barack Obama was elected the 44ᵗʰ president of the United States, I thought of Hank. I called him, but he wasn't home. We finally connected three days later. Since Henry Louis Aaron was an African American trailblazer and since he was the biggest admirer ever of Jack Roosevelt Robinson, the first Black player in Major League Baseball, I figured he might feel a kindship with the man who just became the country's first African American commander-in-chief.

I was correct. Boy, was I.

"First of all," I asked, "where were you when you first found out that Barack officially had become—not Candidate Obama anymore but President-Elect Obama—and just kind of describe your emotions?"

"I was here [at home]," Aaron said. "I was scheduled to go to two or three outdoor or some parties or something. Not parties, but just some viewings, and I, things like that, I like to keep to myself because you hear a lot of noise and you want to hear everything, you know?"

"Right, right."

"I had two televisions going and I had them on everything but FOX. I was not going to let them tear my emotions up," he said laughing. "Yeah, I had on everything but FOX. That was No. 1, and I can tell you that and I was here at the house. My wife and I, we both were here, you know. I just told her, the two of us, we were just going to stay here and view it here. So I was here in Atlanta, right here, and I tell you: I was the happiest person I guess in the world. I was really ecstatic really because I had two things that had happened to me that same week. I had been to Mobile and I had seen my house being moved from where I was born and was moved to [Hank Aaron Stadium], and that was emotional to have my home moved to the ballpark. Then I came here, and Barack gets to be elected for president of the United States of America, the highest office in the world. So, I had a very good week."

"Wow."

"I'll tell you. It was—I don't know," Aaron said, sounding emotional. "It's just hard to zero in on something like that because it's just, uh, well, the average White person couldn't understand the thoughts of how you feel. You've been in this country all this time and all you've talked about for years are the White candidates and all of that. Then you look back and say, 'I don't think we've got no more than three Black senators.' Do we? As a matter of fact, I was thinking about that earlier today. Is there anybody besides Barack? Barack is the only one. Yeah, and you know, he came up and he just has demonstrated, just came up through the ranks and files as rapidly as he could, and I'll tell you. It's just...Terence, I'm still on Cloud Nine," he said, leading us both to laugh. "I got all the papers and all of that and I tell a lot of people, 'We may not have gotten a mule.' And what else they were supposed to give us? The 40 acres or whatever they call that? But we got 50 states."

"That's pretty good," I said, laughing.

"Yeah, we got all 50 states, but anyhow, it's just, it was a happy moment for me. I know given what I've been through and a lot of Black people in this country, what they've also been through and seen, and I was not going to let a station like FOX deflate my emotions."

"Did you have any tears when you were watching it?"

"I did so. I did. I did. I really did. All that night I was on edge, and when I was watching CNN and when they officially declared him as the president-elect, I got...I got full. I just got teary eyed really. I was ecstatic."

"That's an amazing thing, and the thing is: are you like me and other Blacks? I mean, here we are [a few days after the presidential election], and it still feels like it really hasn't sunken in."

"It hasn't and it's going to get even more so the day he's standing on that platform to be sworn in, in January. That's going to really be another emotional day for a lot of Blacks in this country. I mean, when he stands up there and gets sworn in [by the Supreme Court chief justice], that's going to be very emotional for me. For him to stand there and for him to have two little Black girls behind him and his wife, it's just, it's just, it's just indescribable really. You can't describe what it's all about. You try not to let a thing like this get to the point where it's an ego trip, but for a Black person in this country, you have to be emotional. You can't help it. You think about all the things we've been through, all of the things we've been through. You can talk about Little Rock, the bombing, the hanging, and all of these things and stuff. We're not talking about 50 and 60 years ago. We're talking about things that are happening recently. So, here he is coming up, and my wife, she told me that he has to be a messiah. God had to touch him and say, 'Hey, I'm putting somebody out there. He's the one.' I don't know whether he's that or not, but I do know he's going to do fine. I think he's going to be a helluva president really."

"How much did you think about the struggles that you went through over the years when you watched him actually getting over the top? Did you think back to your baseball career at all?"

"I thought about a lot of things—not only about mine. I thought about John Lewis. I thought about all of the things with the civil rights movement. I thought about Dr. King and all of his speeches. I know he's Up There, looking down, smiling, and saying, 'I knew we would overcome.' Yes, I thought about all of the things, all those things you think about. I, playing baseball, I think about when we couldn't dress in the same clubhouse with White players, and that was not long ago. And the night I clinched the pennant for the Braves [on September 23, 1957 at Milwaukee County Stadium against the St. Louis Cardinals], that was the night [Arkansas governor Orval Faubus] wouldn't let [nine African American students] in Little Rock integrate a high school. It was that same day, and here I was piggyback, riding on the shoulders of White guys into the clubhouse, and [those African American students] had to be marched into the school [by federal troops]. Now we're looking at the first Black president in this country, and I just hope he can transcend all of this and let people know that as long as the playing field is even, that's all we're asking for."

• • •

Hank was hilarious, and his humor seemed to come out of nowhere. Even if I heard Hank say something before, he would do so in a way to make it fresh every time. This was one of my favorites: on several occasions through the decades, when I asked Hank about this major league executive, manager, coach, or scout…or that one, he'd say with a straight face: "The only thing he knows about baseball is that it's hard to hit."

> "What city are you in, by the way?" I asked.
>
> "I'm in West Palm Beach, Florida."
>
> "Oh, that's a good place to be."
>
> "Having breakfast with some friends of mine, getting ready to go back to the house, and about 4:00, I'm going to play some golf."
>
> "You can't beat that now," I laughed.
>
> "But, whew. It is hot. It is *hot.*"
>
> "I just saw in *Sports Illustrated.* I didn't know this, but they've got a street named for you in West Palm Beach."
>
> "Hell, it ain't much of a street. I was just talking about it yesterday. Ain't no houses on it," he said, causing us both to laugh.
>
> "Yeah, ain't no houses on it, and excuse my French: you can piss farther than it is long. Aaahhh, yeah, there's nothing on it really. It's just part of something. It really isn't much of a street. But, but, hey, you know, it didn't cost me anything," he said, causing more laughter from us.

Except for one person (me), Hank wasn't a fan of *The Atlanta Journal-Constitution.* That was particularly true of Furman Bisher, mostly a columnist and partly a sports editor in town for nearly 60 years. From the time the Braves left Milwaukee for Atlanta after the 1966 season through Bisher's retirement from the paper in October 2009, Hank fumed over the subtle or blatant digs at Henry Louis Aaron that often appeared in Furman's columns.

After I arrived at *The Atlanta Journal-Constitution* in January 1985, the Hank-related rips by Bisher nearly always followed something I wrote involving Hank discussing race or social injustice. Here are several examples of Bisher countering Hank/me. In 1989 he wrote: "Al Campanis [fired as a Los Angeles Dodgers executive for uttering bigoted remarks on live national television] didn't get Bill White this job [as a Black man named as National League president], Bill White did. It even brought Henry Aaron off his soapbox but for the wrong reason. Aaron is still campaigning for the free lunch."

In 1991 he wrote: "The truth is: Aaron never practiced what he preaches when he was a celebrated player. Perhaps he didn't feel comfortable with it, felt no urge to, happily accepted what came his way and rolled with it. The fact is, he didn't. He might reflect on his own peace with himself as a player when he casts aspersions on Michael Jordan [for not speaking out more on social issues]."

Later that same year, he wrote: "It strikes me as passing strange that one of the loudest voices protesting [Cincinnati Reds owner Marge Schott, who was suspended for a year and fined $25,000 by Major League Baseball for racial slurs] was that of a former home run slugger no longer connected with baseball. Henry Aaron is now a vice president of Turner Broadcasting System, majoring in selling cable news channels to airport terminals. Aaron was protesting not the severity, but the lightness of the penalty. 'A pat on the hand,' he said. I think he meant a slap on the wrist. He was very disappointed, he said. Did he want her burned at the stake? Put to sea in a lifeboat with a week's supply of water?"

In the 1990s he wrote: "Of all the solutions proposed to pitcher [John Rocker, nationally blasted for his racist viewpoints when he wasn't serving as closer for the Atlanta Braves], one that fascinated me most is that he should 'resign from baseball.' How do you resign from baseball? It's a process that defies logic. I am reminded that the man who made the proposal, Henry Aaron, once smashed a sportswriter in the face with a basket of fresh strawberries, not for something the writer had written, but because his boss had written something Aaron disliked. While no sociological matters were involved in his act, it was rather untoward. No penalty followed. There was no public outrage."

In 2004 he wrote: "You think Henry Aaron wasn't relaxed after he arrived in the major leagues? He became known as 'the all-time sleeping champion of the Braves' in Milwaukee."

Hank held up a copy of the paper with a Furman Bisher column on the front page and while shaking his head, he said, "The stuff he writes don't go no farther than the toilet."

I laughed, and Hank shook his head some more.

On the opposite end of the spectrum, Susan Bailey, his executive assistant throughout Hank's post-baseball playing days with the Atlanta Braves, was one of his favorite people. If you weren't a close family member, one of the few people he called a dear friend, or The Hank Aaron Whisperer, the only way you would come within a hemisphere of Henry Louis Aaron was through this gatekeeper of gatekeepers.

Susan's job wasn't to determine if a caller should interview with Hank and then search after an approval to find a date and a time convenient for both parties. Susan's job was to tell that person Hank wasn't available. To hear Susan tell it, Hank wouldn't be available within the next few days, several weeks, or upcoming months.

Hank never would be available. Period. Sorry.

Susan did all of that in a nice way. Not that it ever happened to me as The Hank Aaron Whisperer, but I heard the stories. Hank did, too, and he was appreciative of Susan's responses to those seeking either a large or a small moment with Henry Louis Aaron, and here's why: if he spoke to somebody outside of his inner circle, that was fine. If he didn't, that was even better. He preferred privacy over everything else, and Susan understood as much.

Hank and Susan were a splendid pair, even though Hank probably wouldn't have invited Susan to join his wife, Billye, and himself on that Tuesday night of November 4, 2008, when the Aarons sat around their southwest Atlanta home challenging the all-time record for joy.

Barack Obama had just won the first of his two elections for president of the United States.

"I'll tell you what. Susan and I have been together for a long time, and sometimes she drives my car," Aaron said, laughing. "I'll send her out to do little things and I leave my radio on—shoot, whatever that number is—the Black radio station."

"Oh, okay," I said.

"Every time I get in there, she comes back, and [the station] is on—what's that guy's name?"

"Rush Limbaugh," I said, causing us both to laugh.

"Yeah, she's got it on Rush Limbaugh. I'm like, ohhhhhhh."

"She forgets to switch it back?"

"Yeah, she forgets, and it's like, ohhhhh."

I regularly had these moments of reflection while in the presence of Henry Louis Aaron. Such was the case during the summer of 2015, when we sat in a room near the home clubhouse at Turner Field, and I told Hank how I enjoyed watching from the distance as he moved around Atlanta. Folks rushed up to greet him with smiles or they remained several feet away, saying openly or subconsciously through wide eyes, "There he is. That's Hank Aaron."

"How does that make you feel?" I asked Hank.

He responded with one of his baritone chuckles and then he said, "It makes you feel good. They don't know I can hear them, but some people will say, 'Is that really Hank Aaron? I thought he was dead.'"

We both roared with laughter.

Showing that humorous side that many didn't know he had, Hank even appeared on the *Late Show with David Letterman*.

"Hey, it's Terence," I said.

"Hey, Terence, buddy. How ya doing?" Hank asked.

"Oh, great on this end."

"Anyhow, I've just been hanging around."

"Oh, I can tell. As a matter of fact, one of the things I was going to tell you: you did a tremendous job on David Letterman. That was a very, very good show."

"Oh, thank you. Thank you. Thank you."

"That was superb. I heard a lot of other people say the same thing. You know, he can be a little tricky in there, and I kept watching and saying to myself, *Oh, man. I hope he doesn't do anything crazy,*" I said, causing Hank to laugh. "But he was on pretty good behavior."

"He was. He was. I've been in his company before, and he's always treated me with a lot of respect. So, I kind of like that, you know. I was on his show many, many, many, many years ago. So, I know him, but he's [advanced in show business] so much and he's done so many things until he just, you're right, he can be tricky," he said, causing us both to laugh.

● ● ●

Stan Williams spent the opening five of his 14 major league seasons with the Los Angeles Dodgers and then he played with five other teams through 1972. For a pitcher of his era, he was gigantic. He stood 6'5"and 230 pounds and he wasn't afraid to use all of his scary dimensions to convert baseballs into rockets with his right arm. Sometimes, his pitches headed for the plate, and other times they drilled various parts of the hitter's body. It didn't matter who you were. Even if your name was Henry Louis Aaron.

"There was no protection for a hitter," Hank Aaron said during a phone call in the spring of 2020, discussing his playing days in the 1950s and 1960s. "They would throw inside and knock you down, and the umpire would just say, 'Ball one, ball two,'" he said, laughing. "You gotta get up. Nowadays, you come close to a guy, and the first thing you know, you've got a whole two teams out there fighting with each other."

"That's a very good point, and that's one of the biggest ways the game has changed, and I don't think the average fan really realizes how much back then that could affect hitters if you weren't tough-minded," I said.

"Oh, no question about it…And I tell this story, and it's a true story. The guy who used to be with the Dodgers. Great, big guy. Mean. Very mean."

"Don Drysdale?"

"Naw, it wasn't Drysdale. It was…um…it will come to me in a few minutes. But anyhow, I had had a pretty good series against the Dodgers. Oh, Stan Williams. Stan Williams. I had had a pretty good series against them, and he was coming into pitch, and [Dodgers catcher John] Roseboro said, 'Be careful now. You know what I mean. Be careful.' This is a true story, and sure enough: three balls and no strikes, and he was a great, big guy. And, boy, the 3-0 pitch, he hits me dead in the head with a fastball. It wasn't no Stu Miller fastball," he said, laughing. "It was a fastball. It brought me to my knees, and then Fred Haney, I think, was managing [the Milwaukee Braves] at that time. They all came out there and they're giving me some smelling salts and all that, and I had enough sense to realize that I said, 'I better stay in this game because if I get out of this game, news is gonna get around that all you have to do is hit him, and he's out of the game.' I said, 'I better stay in this game,' so I stayed in the game. So, sure enough, I get to first base and then I get my lead off first base, and the first [thing Williams does] is try to pick me off first base, and he hits me right in the knee."

"Oh, man."

"And [Dodgers first baseman] Gil Hodges, God rest his soul, he says to me, 'Why don't you go out there and pinch his goddamn head off, big boy?'"

We both laughed.

"That's the truth," Aaron said. "And I said, 'Well, my mama didn't raise no fool, you know.' So, then, the next time up, I think the next day, I don't think I went to bat any more times that night, but I think the next day, I hit a home run."

The more I think about it, the most emotional I ever saw Henry Louis Aaron before a crowd was on Friday, January 19, 2001. It also was emotional for me.

For the second time in eight months, I was given the honor to introduce Hank to a packed ballroom during an event. At a five-star Buckhead hotel in downtown Atlanta, Hank received a lifetime achievement award from the Boy Scouts of America.

Hank might have challenged the world's record for getting honored locally, nationally, and internationally. Less than a day before the Boy Scouts affair, he was at the White House with the likes of Muhammad Ali and Elizabeth Taylor, receiving the Presidential Citizens Medal from Bill Clinton. He told me and his Buckhead audience that his Boy Scouts award was bigger than his presidential one and he said as much while battling misty eyes throughout his speech. "There weren't too many thrills growing up in Mobile, Alabama," Hank said, chuckling, along with everybody else in the room. His reference was to the joy he received as a Boy Scout stopping traffic during the 1940s for the safe passage of other youngsters in the middle of a Mobile intersection. "I wore these short pants while standing out there on the street because my dad couldn't afford the long ones. Do the Boy Scouts still make those short pants?"

There was nodding and laughing.

"If it had not been for scouting, I wouldn't have hit my first home run," Hank said, trying but failing to hold back tears as I watched near the podium to notice wet eyes everywhere from others. "What scouting taught me was discipline, having respect for others, and the Golden Rule."

Then Hank held up the massive ceramic eagle he received from the Boy Scouts for his longtime commitment to the organization and he said, "Believe me: this means a lot to me, and I'll find a special place for this at my house."

He did. As soon as he got home.

• • •

If Hank Aaron was in Atlanta and if he wasn't at home or at the ballpark, I knew I would find him at his other place.

"Good afternoon, Hank Aaron BMW."

"Hey, good afternoon," I said. "This is Terence Moore. Can you connect me to Hank's office?"

"Please hold."

Then I would hear that familiar recording while waiting on the other end of the phone, and it began with a woman's voice saying: "Hank Aaron has put together the ultimate team of Atlanta's All-Star BMW sales and service veterans. Hank Aaron. What a career: 6,856 total bases and an unbelievable 755 home runs."

Then I would hear a recording of Hank saying: "Wait a minute. You better meet my All-Star team of veterans at new Hank Aaron BMW. It's my latest home run."

Then the woman's voice would return: "It's the ultimate team of Atlanta's BMW veterans. Hank Aaron's BMW: the signature of experience."

Finally, after maybe another loop of the same recording, the operator would return to say, "Hello, Terence, let me transfer you."

A half of a ring later on the average, I'd hear Hank's typical greeting to me: "Hey, Terence, how you doing, buddy?"

Hank Aaron, The Business Man, was more profitable than Hank Aaron, the Home Run King, by a bunch. Yes, down the stretch of his sprint toward a record 715th career blast on April 8, 1974, he already was wheeling and dealing with a five-year contract worth $1 million from Magnavox. Yes, he promoted Lifebuoy soap. Yes, he starred in one of my favorite commercials as a teenager, and it involved a candy bar that wasn't named after him but was called "O Henry" nonetheless. Yes, music executive Clarence Avant lived up to his nickname as "The Black Godfather" for his work with politicians, entertainers, and athletes such as Jim Brown and Muhammad Ali by brokering a financial relationship between Hank and Atlanta-based Coca-Cola.

Consider this, though: the average salary for a Major League Baseball player entering the 2021 season hit $4.17 million. That fell just shy of twice as much as what Henry Louis Aaron made ($2.14 million) through Major League Baseball contracts during his entire 23 seasons with the Braves of Milwaukee and Atlanta and the Milwaukee Brewers.

Now consider this: on January 22, 2021, when Hank died, his estimated net worth was $25 million. That was 12 times more than his take while becoming the greatest baseball player ever. His salaries (the most he ever made on the field was $240,000 per year during his last two seasons with the Brewers) were nice for his era, which mostly existed before free agency triggered a financial boom among players, but given Hank's stature, those endorsement deals near the end of his playing career were just okay.

None of that mattered for Hank in the long run. After he shed his major league uniform for the last time in October 1976, he proved he could excel beyond hitting, fielding, and running. For one he wasted no time earning the "nice paycheck," as Hank called it, from CNN founder and Braves owner Ted Turner, who promptly brought the franchise's legendary player into its front office upon his retirement.

Hank used his role as Braves director of player development for 13 years to hire, train, and supervise the employees who contributed to solid enough rosters for the franchise to capture the National League West in 1982 and then to go from 1991 and beyond triggering a record 14 consecutive division titles, five National League pennants, and a Word Series championship.

Through it all, The Home Run King morphed into The Business King, and he continued as The Front Office King.

Hank ran a family-owned company called (what else?) 755 Restaurant Corporation with as many as 27 Popeyes Louisiana Kitchen restaurants as well as a couple of Krispy Kreme Doughnut places. That was before he was huge into Arby's franchises, Church's Chicken, and whatever else was enjoyable for consumers and profitable for Hank. In addition to those food entities, he had The Hank Aaron Automotive Group. He owned car dealerships throughout Georgia that sold Land Rovers, Toyotas, Hyundais, Hondas, and of course, BMWs, including the dealership in which I found him often. It was located in Union City, Georgia, near Atlanta. If you bought one of those BMWs in Union City, you got an autographed ball from Hank, The Home Run King, The Front Office King, and The Business King.

The Business King thing didn't just happen for Hank. Something caused it to happen.

Hank told me as much in March 2006, when *The Atlanta Journal-Constitution* asked me to do what it was requesting other staff writers to do regarding prominent local figures of those times: prepare a pre-obituary just in case the paper needed to publish something right on deadline. (It happened regarding Hank, who died on a Friday morning, and *The AJC* was able to get my Hank obituary on its Internet site within minutes.) "To be honest with you, I had all of this planned out because I knew it was going to be hard for me after 23 years of playing baseball to just get into something else," Aaron told me for that pre-obituary. "I started out in real estate when I first started working for the Braves and I ended up with the biggest crook in the world, losing about $1 million. I lost everything I had through my insurance and some other things. *Whew!* And back then $1 million was $1 million. But having said that, I wasn't going to let that keep me from doing well. I did have some money that I had saved through the years and some deferred money. And the reason I was such a great ballplayer and did some great things is because a lot of people said that I couldn't do certain things. When I got out of baseball, for instance, I read what somebody wrote in the paper after I got my first dealership: 'Don't put too much stock in this because he's going to fail.' I remember that and

I said, 'If I have to crawl at night, I won't fail.' I said, 'I'm going to make all of these people eat their words.' I'll do anything not to fail, and that's why I kept pushing."

• • •

In September of 2018, I jogged along one of those tree-filled, winding roads of beauty in Oxford, Ohio, where I served as a visiting professor of journalism at Miami University, my alma mater, and the phone beeped through the music on my AirPods. With about a mile to go, I wasn't going to answer, but then I saw those two words flashing across the screen: Hank Aaron.

I answered. I always answered for him.

This time Hank asked if I would rush into cyberspace his anger over Serena Williams receiving a $17,000 fine over three code violations the previous day in Flushing Meadows, New York, from a chair umpire during her loss to Naomi Osaka in the finals of the U.S. Open.

Here's what happened: with Williams searching to tie Margaret Court's tennis record of 24 major championships, she was penalized a point and then that game after chair umpire Carlos Ramos said she was getting signals from her coach, which is "technically" against the rules during grand slam play. Then Serena broke her racket after she banged it against the ground in disgust while calling Ramos "a liar" and "a thief." "It takes me right back to what I had to deal with when I was chasing Babe Ruth's home run record because I think the whole thing with Serena is so rude and so cruel," Hank said before I replied I'd get more from him after another mile on my end, along with a shower and a pad and a pen in front of me to make sure I captured his every word.

When those things happened, Hank recalled watching Serena's punishment from the couch in his Atlanta family room, and Hank said, "I spent 23 years in baseball. And then before I knew it, I was getting all of this hostile mail and all of that during my last couple of years and with Serena I started thinking about those things again. I saw how Serena was being treated and then I thought about coming back to my locker one day as a player, and there was [a reporter] in my chair. I said something to get him out, and he wrote a letter to [baseball commissioner Bowie Kuhn], and the commissioner wrote me back saying, 'If you do it again, I'm going to suspend you from baseball.'"

Hank told me Kuhn's threat of a suspension hadn't been mentioned before in public. Then he said, "I thought about those things, watching Serena, and I said, 'This kid has been playing all of these years, and I don't think she's ever been accused of cheating before it happened on Saturday.' And [tennis coaches,] they all cheat, no matter how you look at it. They're sitting up there in the stands saying, 'Go this way. Do that.' Watching tennis for as long as I've watched it, I've seen players get angry, break rackets, and curse the umpires. So, for an umpire in this case to take a game away from somebody like Serena is uncalled for."

Just about 900 miles away, all of that drama from Serena produced a shrug of agreement on the couch from Hank, a self-proclaimed "tennis buff" who was overjoyed when baseball commissioner and old Milwaukee pal Bud Selig helped to have a court built on his Atlanta property. "When I first came out of baseball, I started playing a little golf and I was fooling myself that I was a golfer and then I started fooling myself that I was a tennis player," Aaron said, chuckling. "But I got to be pretty good at tennis, even though I wasn't a top player or anything like that. I used to have all of the guys over to the house every Sunday after church to play tennis, and we would get into little matches. You had everybody thinking they were better than what they were, including me, but I love tennis."

Hank and his wife, Billye, took several trips through the years to the U.S. Open, and during one of them, they met Serena, along with her sister, Venus, and father, Richard. "I met them all. Not that they would remember that time, but they probably know who I am," Hank said, downplaying his fame. "But the thing that bothers me is that I looked at Serena during that match, and I said, 'This young lady has just had a baby and has come all the way up and has played very well and has gotten to the finals.' I'm not saying she would have beaten this 20-year-old [Osaka], who would have won anyway, but I'm saying, 'Don't take the game from Serena like this.' Let her play and now you have the other umpires saying they're mad [over the treatment of Ramos] and talking about boycotting. It just doesn't make any sense to me really. I was going to write a letter to [World Tennis Association] officials to let them know how I feel about the whole thing."

He did. Through The Hank Aaron Whisperer.

• • •

It was the wild, wild west (east, north, and south) in baseball regarding the use of performance-enhancing drugs during the late 1990s and the early 2000s. So while searching for a column for *The Atlanta Journal-Constituiton* in May 2001, I asked Hank Aaron his opinion on the Steroid Era, and he stunned me a little.

Well, Hank stunned me a lot.

Not only did Henry Louis Aaron say he understood why a massive number of players were juicing, he added, "If I knew back then that steroids and all of these other things would have enhanced me and helped me hit more home runs and do all of these things, would I have wanted to do that, personally? You know, it's hard to say. It's really hard to say. Just being honest with myself and everybody else, I don't know whether I would have done it or not."

Hank eventually concluded over the years he would have taken the Nancy Reagan approach to performance-enhancing drugs: just say no. Then came that night of May 7, 2015, when Hank had completed his 180-degree turn on the Steroid Era by chastising everybody involved with such a blatant assault on Major League Baseball's integrity. He called me after Alex Rodriguez ripped his 661st career home run over the left-center-field wall at Yankee Stadium against the Baltimore Orioles. With a little...ahem...help, Rodriguez passed Willie Mays for fourth place on the all-time list behind Barry Bonds at 762, Hank Aaron at 755, and Babe Ruth at 714.

Hank was upset after he flipped to enough TV channels to hear folks rank A-Rod ahead of the "Say Hey Kid" as a hitter. This was the same Rodriguez who confessed the year before to the Drug Enforcement Administration that he used performance-enhancing drugs. "This bothers me to the point that it's [fictitious] to say this makes Rodriguez better than Willie Mays because there is absolutely no truth to it," Hank said. "I played against Willie for many, many, many years and I know what kind of ballplayer he was, and there is absolutely no comparison between what he did and what A-Rod did. I mean, history will tell what's what really. Here's the thing about A-Rod: he didn't need to use drugs. I saw him when he first came up as a young kid and he had all of the ability to do everything and anything he wanted to do. But now you've got people deciding they can go out and play baseball by shooting themselves up and hitting 50 or 60 home runs every year. That shouldn't be the case."

Hank didn't use performance-enhancing drugs while playing. Instead, he worked hard on his conditioning. Just as Hank was obsessed with staying in shape during his major league career, he kept that same attitude after his retirement from playing. He was a regular in workout rooms (usually involving the Atlanta Braves) right up to the moment he slipped on his ice-filled driveway in February 2014 to break his hip, which led to more rehabbing than exercising the rest of his life.

During those post-playing workout years, the routine rarely varied for Henry Louis Aaron at Atlanta Fulton-County Stadium, the Braves' home ballpark and the location of his office as the team's director of player personnel. Then the routine switched to Turner Field, which replaced the old place after the new stadium hosted events for the 1996 Summer Olympics. Here was his routine:

- Arrive at the ballpark between 5:00 AM and 6:00 AM
- Warm up with light cardio
- Go through range-of-motion exercises
- Cool down period

In addition:

- Mondays: legs and shoulders
- Tuesdays: chest and biceps
- Wednesdays: back and triceps
- Thursdays: balance work
- Fridays: a combination of the week's work and hydro pool, where he worked on resistance training with the whirling jets.

For a couple of decades, Hank exercised mostly on his own, but that changed during a spring morning in 2000, when he interrupted his BMW dealership duties in Union City, Georgia, for breakfast at a local Shoney's restaurant. As Hank was arriving, a solidly built Black man of average height in his early 30s named Mykell Vital was leaving with his young daughter. That was until Mykell realized The Home Run King stood across the way. Mykell returned to his seat with his daughter to mill around a little bit, just long enough for Hank to finish his last bite, and then Mykell rose to start a conversation.

Hank discovered Mykell was a trainer. Soon, the two strangers were clicking like Hank Aaron and Eddie Mathews, and Mykell received Susan Bailey's number from Hank to have her set up his schedule for a series of workouts. The Aaron-Vital combination lasted for the next 14 years. "Hank liked to get in and out of there because on game days everybody had a lot of questions for him," Mykell said, laughing, referring to Braves players and coaches, always mesmerized when baseball's all-time greatest player was in their presence. "Hank didn't like attention that much, so he wanted to get in there before a lot of activity began and then he would get out of there and go on with his day. Typically, it was just Hank and me. He was a hard worker. He did pretty good. Actually, he did very well. I was able to take him, not to the max, but to take him out of his comfort zone, where he would have to put forth a little more effort than he normally would by himself. He was very resilient and he was able for me to push him a little bit. But, yeah, he worked hard and we had conversations over the years as things developed in baseball. That was part of the beauty of the relationship because at that level not only was it business, he was very personable." Mykell paused before he added with emotion, "Like a lot of people, I looked up to him like a father figure."

Speaking of father figures, one of the reasons Hank and I got along so well is that he easily could have been a member of my family. Easily.

Henry Louis Aaron sounded at times like a combination of my Uncle Holmes, Uncle Edgar, Uncle Ed Lee, Great Uncle Herbert, and Cousin LeRoy, all sons of the South (mostly Mississippi) during about the same time Hank grew up with his family in segregated Mobile, Alabama. Oh, and I have to toss in Samuel Moore, my father, originally from Dell, Arkansas, before he joined his family in moving to South Bend, Indiana, during the early 1940s, when he was an adolescent. "Yeah, come to think of it, your dad and Hank Aaron do have mannerisms that are similar. I can see that," my mother said, and I passed her remarks onto Hank several years before his death.

Hank's eyes sparkled. Then after he eased into a smile, he said, "Why, thank you, Terence. Thank you very much."

• • •

Hank Aaron was the ultimate sports fan. In the fall of 1982, when Dominique Wilkins was mostly that former star basketball player for the University of Georgia in his adopted state after growing up in rural North Carolina, Ted Turner owned much of Atlanta, at least when it came to media and sports. He had CNN, along with the Atlanta Braves and the Atlanta Hawks, and among his most trusted advisors was Henry Louis Aaron. Officially, Hank was the director of player development for the Braves and he was on the board of directors of the Hawks.

Unofficially, Hank functioned as The Ted Turner Whisperer, which was on full display that September afternoon in 1982, when Hank joined a bunch of others sitting around a large table in a Hawks meeting room. Turner couldn't decide whether to let his management folks for the franchise trade John Drew, Freeman Williams, and cash to the Utah Jazz for the recently-drafted Wilkins. Then, with Turner preparing to end the meeting by saying no to the deal, he decided to give Hank the last word. "What do you think?" Turner said.

During separate interviews I had through the years with both Turner and Aaron on that Wilkins brainstorming session, their recollections were exactly the same regarding Hank's response. "If you have the chance to get Dominique Wilkins, *get him*," Hank said.

The Hawks got him, and the man who became known as "The Human Highlight Film" helped make slamming basketballs fashionable throughout the NBA. He reached the James Naismith Basketball Hall of Fame and he is so entrenched in Hawks lore that he is the only player in the franchise's history with a statue outside of its home arena.

Then there was the NFL. Henry Louis Aaron lived in Atlanta for 55 years, and when he first arrived with his Braves from Milwaukee in 1966, the Falcons prepared for their maiden NFL season inside of the city limits. Hank spent years on the Falcons' board of directors, but his heart always was with the Dawg Pound—and not the one 72 miles away from Atlanta in nearby Athens, where the University of Georgia Bulldogs reigned as local darlings with Uga, their live canine mascot.

Hank's Dawg Pound belonged to the old Cleveland Browns. He was obsessed with them. He became a Baltimore Ravens disciple after those Browns bolted northern Ohio, following the 1995 season, for

Maryland. Cleveland eventually got an NFL expansion team in 1998, and it was named the Browns, but Hank kept his loyalties to the new Browns (the Ravens) in Baltimore.

With energy and knowledge, Hank could discuss the old Browns/ Ravens for as much time as you had. It was like he read every media guide in the history of the franchise right down to every stat.

This was typical: our conversation at the end of the 2008 NFL season involved Matt Ryan for the Falcons, but Hank pivoted to Joe Flacco of the Ravens before either of us could exhale for the first time. Both players were the first NFL rookie quarterbacks ever to start all 16 games for their teams along the way to the postseason. *Who was better?* "Oh, Flacco. He's got a better arm than what Ryan has really," Hank said of Flacco, the University of Delaware graduate who took the Ravens to the AFC Championship Game during his first season before losing to the Pittsburgh Steelers. "He's done excellent. He's just like a veteran really. What [the Ravens have done], which is smart, is they've surrounded him with good running backs. It takes the pressure off the quarterback. He's a very smart kid. He's starting to learn more of the playbook and he's done well for himself."

Hank was rolling, saying of the Ravens' running game without taking much of a breath, "They've got this kid Ray Rice from Rutgers. You may have seen him, and they've got Willis McGahee. Oh, and they've got that big, old guy they drafted last year from Alabama [Le'Ron McClain, a 6'0", 260-pound fullback]." Then Hank sort of chuckled, before adding of McClain, "All he does is run up the middle and gains two or three yards."

On Baltimore coach John Harbaugh he said: "I'm impressed with his progress. He has surrounded himself with young men [as assistant coaches] who know what they're doing, like the one from Miami. What's his name? Cam Cameron? Yeah, I mean, he turned that whole franchise around."

On Baltimore general manager Ozzie Newsome: "I don't think he has really gotten the credit that he deserves. He has lost [longtime NFL executive Phil] Savage who is going over to Cleveland now and [Newsome] has always drafted players that you don't hear anything about beforehand, and they do well. [Newsome] goes out and gets guys, and everybody says, 'So what's he drafting?' But he also went out and got that big, old guy from Auburn, [310-pound offensive guard Ben] Grubbs. They put him out there and they run right behind him."

Hank went on and on.

Then there was golf. Hank dialed my number often to discuss Eldrick Tont Woods, especially whenever he did something amazing, which was often. That was before back and knee injuries turned Tiger into a mortal.

On Thursday, August 29, 1996, in Glendale, Wisconsin, Tiger made his pro debut at the Greater Milwaukee Open. Among those in the gallery that afternoon, following the new guy around various parts of the course, was Henry Louis Aaron. On the 14th hole during the final round, Tiger swung his 6 iron from 202 yards into a hole in one, and Hank was there for what ranked as the only highlight for a PGA Tour rookie who finished tied for 60th place.

Eight months after Milwaukee, Tiger crushed his competitors for the first of his five green jackets at The Masters and he caused Augusta National to start an epidemic of places seeking to Tiger-proof their courses. It didn't work. Prior to Hank's death on January 22, 2021, Tiger owned 15 major golf titles and 82 victories overall on the PGA Tour to match Sam Snead for the all-time record. When Tiger had *just* 12 major championships and *only* 63 PGA Tour victories, Hank called me with something incredible. He said Tiger wasn't the most dominating golfer ever.

He said Tiger was the most dominating athlete ever. "I don't know of anybody who would be better," Hank said, ignoring a couple of obvious choices. There was Henry Louis Aaron, of course, reigning as the greatest baseball player ever. If Hank's modesty kept him from choosing himself, remember he was the world's biggest fan of the old Cleveland Browns/Baltimore Ravens, which means there was Jim Brown, the Pro Football Hall of Fame running back who led the NFL in rushing eight of his nine seasons to produce three Most Valuable Player awards. Brown also held the distinction by *The Sporting News* as the greatest professional football player ever. "As great as Jim Brown was, and as great as Michael Jordan was, and as great as anybody you'd want to keep mentioning, I don't know of anybody who was as great at his sport as this man is now," Aaron said. "I mean, he's totally incredible. He's phenomenal. Sometimes, I hear people say, 'He's lucky.' Well, you can throw that talk out. You can be lucky and good, but he is absolutely good. Even when he's way ahead, he wants to make every putt and every golf shot as perfect as possible. I don't know of anybody who has ever played any sport who was able to concentrate as much on perfection at all times as Tiger Woods."

• • •

Loyalty might be the word that best described Hank Aaron when it came to the devotion he gave to his relatives, closest friends, acquaintances, and associates, along with to the causes he cherished to the hilt. About those causes: nothing surpassed Henry Louis Aaron's Chasing the Dream Foundation, and its formation was inspired by his life. After he grew up in the segregated South as a part of a financially poor Black family, he became The Home Run King, The Front Office King, and The Business King. He also was the most prominent person keeping Jackie Robinson's legacy alive as a high-profile champion of social justice through words and deeds.

Hank wanted younger folks to do their version of those Hank things. As a result in 1994, he and his wife, Billye, established the Chasing the Dream Foundation for youth without financial means. Over the years recipients of grants from his foundation entered fields, ranging from veterinary medicine and engineering to marine biology and aviation.

There also was Atlanta's Friendship Baptist Church, which once held services in a railroad boxcar years after it was founded in 1862. The Aarons became Friendship Baptist regulars as a couple at Billye's church after they married during the early 1970s. When a new sanctuary opened in August 2017, they helped pay for the pipes of the Casavant organ. They also contributed to Friendship Baptist in other ways. Dr. Richard W. Willis Sr., the church's pastor, told me during the summer of 2021, "It really was absolutely a privilege and an honor to have gotten to know Hank Aaron, and his generosity of spirit and his philanthropy were just second to none."

Hank was a habitual giver and not just at Friendship Baptist. Some of the many times he became an African American Santa Claus were known, but most weren't, and that's what he preferred. Near the end of the following phone conversation, Hank turned into Old Saint Aaron again but only without fanfare. This was several years before his death, when he battled the aches and pains of what was then an 80-something man who regularly needed a wheelchair and a cane due to his age and his hip replacement after that 2014 slip on an ice patch in his driveway.

"During a course of a month or a week, how many speaking requests do you get and how many do you actually do?" I asked him.

"I don't do that many because," Aaron said, laughing, "I guess I have turned down a lot of things I used to be involved with because I want to enjoy myself a little bit more really. Yeah, but I turn down quite a few. Next year, I'm going to be honored at two or three universities, but most of them, I've turned down really. I do a lot of work for the Boys & Girls Club, and [Billye] does a lot of work with them, which I'm very proud of, and I do a lot for my own foundation. But other than that, I don't do that much at all. I just kind of stay between here and West Palm Beach."

"That's right. You all still have that home in West Palm Beach."

"Yeah, yeah…I'm getting ready to do something in West Palm Beach of which I'm very happy to be a part of. It's Coleman Park,

which is an area where a lot of Black kids stay in. It's a lot of crime.
It's a high crime area. The mayor and I are getting ready to do
something. First of all, we're going to put on a golf tournament
and then we're going to try to build a lot of homes in that area,
in Coleman Park, which is going to be great, because it is really...
it's just pathetic when you see so many young people being killed.
That's what we're going to do. The mayor and I are going to put
on this fund-raiser to try to get Coleman Park put back together,
where kids can go out in the evening at 7:00 or 8:00 when it gets
dark and enjoy themselves rather than worrying about some drug
dealer coming through, shooting them up, or making them shoot
themselves up with drugs, you know?"

I know that was Hank being Hank regarding his Coleman Park
project, when he preferred to ease into a steady diet of relaxation.
Several weeks after that conversation, I called Hank to follow up on
something he told me the year before. He said he was going to retire
for good. He said he planned to leave the Braves, leave baseball, leave
the spotlight to move from Atlanta to West Palm Beach on a full-time
basis. He said he wanted to take his wife, Billye, on a series of cruises.
"She deserves it, and I promised her we would do it," Hank told me
the previous year, asking me to call back at that same time the next
year, so he could give me the exclusive story for the world.

So, I asked Hank a year later if he was ready to make that
announcement.

Hank paused over the phone, then he said, "Let's hold off on that,
Terence, okay? I just found out, well, if I hang in here a little longer, it
will help Susan [Bailey] with her retirement situation."

That was Henry Louis Aaron.

So was this: Hank's chat during the late 1990s with Darrell Moore,
the youngest brother of The Hank Aaron Whisperer. Darrell was
among the guests of one of the organizers involved with The Hank
Aaron Celebrity Golf Tournament at Bristlecone Pines Golf Course
in Hartland, Wisconsin, and between holes Darrell left his cart for a

brief trip to the one ahead carrying Hank. "After I introduced myself as Terence Moore's little brother, Hank Aaron got this big smile on his face, and he said, 'Oh, yeah, yeah, yeah, Terence is a good friend of mine,'" Darrell said, chuckling before he described something more telling that occurred during the tournament-ending banquet.

Darrell stood from his table with former Major League Baseball standouts Tony Oliva and George Foster, and from a distance, Darrell saw Hank, who waved Darrell over to his table. Hank pointed at his wife, Billye, saying with a wide smile, "Hey, this is Terence Moore's brother."

A light conversation followed, and Darrell said, "All eyes were on me talking to Hank, and then I just had to say, 'Mr. Aaron. I hate to ask you this. But do you think it might be possible for you to sign a baseball for me?'"

Hank nodded and he scribbled his name. Darrell was set for a lifetime, but this part of his lifetime lasted about 20 minutes. As a die-hard baseball fan, he was in a room dominated by NFL notables such as Jim Brown, Ray Nitschke, Paul Hornung, and Richard "Night Train" Lane. Then Darrell saw Baseball Hall of Famer Reggie Jackson.

Even though Darrell knew the media described Mr. October as sometimes accommodating but other times not, Darrell approached the former slugger of sluggers anyway to sign a ball. Jackson stared at Darrell for a few seconds, and then Jackson grabbed the ball, along with a pen from Darrell's hand, and Jackson said, "Whatever Mr. Aaron does, Mr. Jackson will do the same."

EPILOGUE

As I moved the tired and aching man away from his latest admirers of the moment at the golf club and toward his spot in the middle of the room for the CNN filming, I had several thoughts in rapid fashion.

First, somehow we made it. That was despite everything:

- The phone call I received out of nowhere earlier that morning from Hank Aaron, saying he was ready to do the CNN interview, but he said he only felt good enough to do it right then.

- The need to search my home in a rush for stuff that might fit Henry Louis Aaron, especially after he said he had nothing to wear due to his lengthy stay in mostly a bed away from home.

- The horror to discover upon my arrival at the "rehabilitation center" that it really was a nursing home.

- The sight of the tired and aching man sitting on the edge of a bed in the body of Henry Louis Aaron.

- The messages I kept getting from CNN folks—*Hurry!*—as I tried to maneuver the tired and aching man down the hallway in John Wooden style. (*Be quick, but don't hurry.*)

- The rain, the endless rain.

- The struggle to move the tired and aching man out of the wheelchair and into the front passenger seat of the massive SUV.

- The starstruck SUV driver (or rather, the Henry Louis Aaron-struck SUV driver) who wouldn't stop talking.

• The need to maneuver through the hidden areas of the golf club with the tired and aching man in a wheelchair as further proof that Hank Aaron fans were everywhere.

That other thing also sprinted into my mind: from the time Hank called me a couple of hours earlier to right then, I hadn't spent a millisecond preparing questions for baseball's greatest player ever for a one-on-one interview I was about to do on national television.

I told the producer I needed 10 minutes. He said I had about five. Afghanistan was waiting, you know.

While the makeup woman dusted the shine from my face, I scribbled a few key points into my reporter's notebook and then I prayed. It was a simple one because I hadn't a choice: *Lord, help me, please!* Then, after the producer urged me to hustle into one of the two chairs facing each other in the middle of the room—with the bright lights glaring, and with the cameras preparing to roll, and with more people in the room than was needed for such a thing, I noticed something.

Across the way, I didn't see the tired and aching man. The wheelchair was nowhere in sight. It was vintage Henry Louis Aaron, looking fresh and vibrant even beyond what the makeup woman did with her spraying, rubbing, and patting around his 80-year-old face of fame. He sat in a chair, a regular chair, the kind that was perfect for the setting. Imagine a large family room complete with classy pictures, crown molding, a fireplace in the corner, and the kind of furniture your Aunt Flossie would purchase to make everything cozy.

Then there was Hank, smiling his smile, donning mostly his clothes and some of the ones I brought. Casual was the theme. We both wore sports jackets, jeans, and sneakers. He was so relaxed. By the time the producer said the cameras were rolling for this interview that was "live-to-tape" (meaning no do-overs, not with Afghanistan always waiting in the background), it felt familiar. It felt like nobody else was

there. It felt like all of those other times Hank and I spoke privately about everything you could name.

It felt spiritual.

I had those points of emphasis, sitting on my lap inside of that reporter's notebook, but I didn't refer to them. It wasn't necessary. With Hank right there, replacing the tired and aching man, this was the kind, eloquent, wise, humble, funny, reflective, charitable, enjoyable man—who just happened to be the greatest baseball player ever as well as one of the biggest civil rights icons in American history—right there. This was the man I spent more than 30 years huddling with at that point either on the phone or in person.

I spoke to Hank Aaron during that CNN interview the way I normally spoke to Hank Aaron, and he did the same with me. Hank provided more insight than he ever had before regarding both his kinship with Jackie Robinson and everything surrounding April 8, 1974, when he surpassed Babe Ruth's record of 714 career home runs in Atlanta. Afterward, things got personal during the interview as I provided just one of the many reasons I was born to become The Hank Aaron Whisperer.

"I can remember clearly that Monday, the night you hit the home run. The parents, the two brothers, and I gathered around the television set," I said. "It was very similar—it had to be—to where, back when you and others back on April 15, 1947, gathered around the radio for Jackie Robinson. I mean, you were our Jackie Robinson. Did you get the sensation of how important you were to the Black community in what you were doing, in what you were going through?"

"Yes, I did," Hank said. "In some ways, I felt the importance of what I was doing was really sending a signal to the world, was telling people that, 'Hey, yeah, all we wanted to do was have the playing field level. Just give me an opportunity.' Yes. I felt that way. I felt that way that not only did I have the world on my shoulders as far as baseball was concerned, but I also had the world on my shoulder to demonstrate that, hey, just give me the opportunity. But at that same time, if you think about it, Dr. King was marching, and civil rights was at its peak, and we were just telling people to just give us a chance to drink water out of a fountain," he said, laughing, "or to go to the bathroom or to go anywhere really. And [trying to improve] all those things had something to do with what I was doing as far as playing baseball."

"Then came that moment…when you were running around the bases. I'll never forget this because you could hear this *bang, bang!* There were fireworks, but were you thinking about something else?"

"No, not really. I wasn't thinking about much of anything. But speaking of that, a very good friend of mine, he was on the [Atlanta] police department at that time. I don't know if you or anybody would notice, but any picture you would see of him, you would see he would have a little briefcase, just a little thing around his neck. And on the inside of that little thing was a snub nose .32. He told me, 'Hank, I didn't know what to do when you started running around those bases [after hitting No. 715]. Then you had those guys running behind you [as fans from the stands].' I told him, 'I'm glad you didn't shoot because those two guys were having nothing but fun.'"

Hank could rejoice as well because the chase was over.

We continued to talk as the cameras rolled and then we talked some more. We talked about Hank's calling in October 1972 to take the place of the late Jackie Robinson as an outspoken former sports star on social injustice and we talked about how the likes of Willie Mays and Ernie Banks wanted no part of it. We talked about the plunging number of African Americans involved with baseball. We talked about Barry Lamar Bonds.

"Barry Bonds—to me—is not the legitimate home run king. You are the legitimate home run king," I told Hank.

"Why, thank you," he said.

"Yes, and for various reasons. But throughout that entire run, you never said anything negative about Barry Bonds, and that's something a lot of people couldn't do during that stretch. You were able to hold it in."

"Well...and it wasn't trying to hold anything in. That's just the way I am. I felt like I had been through an awful lot, chasing Babe Ruth's record. I know exactly...Some guy wrote me a letter, and he asked me and he said, 'Hank, if you can—without calling his name—if you can come and follow Barry for the next four or five days before he hits the [record-breaking] home run, we'll give you $300,000 for each game.' You know, for each game."

"I think I would take that," I said, laughing.

"I told him, 'I don't think I want it. I don't need it.' I don't want it because I didn't want to get involved in it. This was Barry's time to shine. It was his time for people to look at him being who he was, and I was not going to take anything away from him and I said, no. So, I decided I wasn't going to take it. But no, I refused to get involved with that and for a lot of reasons really and for one reason I just mentioned. And for another reason: I know that Barry—and not only Barry—some of the other players were involved in doing some shady things [referring to steroids], but I had no concrete evidence about it and I wasn't going to get involved in it. I was waiting for [other] people to make that judgement."

A few Hank stories later, the interview ended.

There were "wows" around the room, along with a few wet eyes from members of the CNN production crew. They were moved by Hank's distinctive voice delivering captivating thoughts for nearly an hour. They all said the same: *it was as if Hank Aaron was sitting in your living room, just chatting in private about all sorts of things with somebody he knew for decades*, which was the case since I was The Hank Aaron Whisperer.

As the camera folks scrambled in the background to stuff pieces of this and that into various containers for their Afghanistan dash to the airport, others in the room gathered around Henry Louis Aaron for an autograph or for a handshake or for a personal message of thanks not only for Hank doing the interview, but also for Hank being Hank over the years.

I gave the CNN folks and others time for some of that. Then I had to become The Hank Aaron Enforcer again. Even though I still saw Henry Louis Aaron in the chair across the way with the vintage smile and the "Why, thank you" responses, I suspected it was a combination of adrenaline and his eternal graciousness toward others. The makeup woman rubbed the powder from his face, and I rushed to the other side of the room to grab the wheelchair. Some members from the CNN crew helped me slide Hank from his interview chair into the one that had become his home away from home over the previous weeks.

I thanked everybody on my way through the door while pushing the wheelchair with John Wooden in my head again. *Be quick but don't hurry.* I knew Henry Louis Aaron was on the verge of evolving back into the tired and aching man, which he did. He tried to hide it, but as I moved through the back hallways of the golf club, I could tell he was exhausted. "Hey, we'll get you back to the place in no time," I said, as he looked up and gave me a smile and a nod.

I kept thinking to myself, *Please, stop raining.* And if we get the same SUV driver CNN sent before, *I hope he has run out of stories and questions for Henry Louis Aaron.*

It was still raining and it was the same driver.

He had even more stories and questions.

Even so, while the driver juggled his large umbrella in one hand to battle the pounding rain, he did do a better job this time of using his other hand to help me raise Hank out of the wheelchair and into the top of the skyscraper, which described the distance from the sidewalk of the golf club to the floor of the gigantic vehicle on the front passenger's side.

The ride back seemed quicker probably because my phone wasn't buzzing anymore about ETAs and Afghanistan. There also was this: the closer we got to the nursing home disguised as a rehabilitation center, the more I saw the return of the tired and aching man. In my mind he was sitting there, dreaming of replacing his hodgepodge collection of clothes with a soft pair of pajamas.

After we arrived the driver performed his circus act again. He maneuvered his umbrella against the raindrops and he used his other hand in conjunction with both of mine to proceed with caution as we transferred the tired and aching man from the front passenger's seat into his wheelchair while keeping him dry. I thanked the driver, but Hank thanked him more because that was Henry Louis Aaron being Henry Louis Aaron. Then I rolled the tired and aching man back into the facility right by many of the same faces who greeted us on the way to the golf club, and the messages were similar.

"Hey, Hank."

"How you doin,' Mr. Aaron?"

"I see ya, I see ya."

"There goes Hammer."

Just like before, the tired and aching man acknowledged every one of them in his easygoing way. Sometimes he motioned for me to pause, so he could deliver an extra sentence or three to those speaking either across the way from their beds or from nearby in wheelchairs of their own. We finally arrived at his room filled with quiet, and as I steered the tired and aching man over to his bed, it hit me again: *I'm pushing the greatest baseball player of all time around a nursing home in a wheelchair!*

I wanted to cry...again.

I probably did but only on the inside.

Outwardly, I remained upbeat for the tired and the aching man who had done so much for me. There was the present, when he called me that day to do a CNN interview he probably shouldn't have done. He helped me survive my Dixiecrats for nearly 25 years at *The Atlanta Journal-Constitution* while we compared notes about his. He gave me an even deeper appreciation for Jack Roosevelt Robinson since he was the same guy in spirit. He made me laugh and he mostly wasn't trying. He reminded me so much of uncles, of cousins, of neighbors, and of Samuel Moore, my father who was nearly the same age. He was a pretty good baseball player, too. I still had my Hank Aaron poster—the one I bought at 12 years old, the huge one, matted and signed by the man himself, inside of a glass frame, and hanging prominently in my home.

"Anything else you need?" I asked after I thanked the tired and aching man for everything as he sat on the edge of his bed.

"No, Terence, thank you," he said before he turned into Henry Louis Aaron with one of those smiles that hinted something else was coming. "I'll tell you what I need. I need some sleep."

We laughed, as I headed for the door.

I looked back, then I looked back again. I thought that might be the last time I would see Henry Louis Aaron, but as Hank would say, "the Good Lord" gave me, along with everybody else, another seven years. Hallelujah.

ACKNOWLEDGMENTS

Since I was a sophomore at a Milwaukee high school in March 1972, I knew I wanted to become a nationally known sports journalist.

Talk about bizarre.

Outside of wishing to become president of the United States, that was an ambitious (maybe ridiculous) goal back then for a Black teenager regarding an overwhelmingly White profession.

I reached that goal, though.

Not only that, but with much help from my parents, my love for Jackie Robinson and his autobiography *I Never Had It Made*, and a slew of other folks, I soared way behind that goal.

Regarding those "other folks," I give special thanks...

To Clara Flores, Oren Miller Sr., Phillip Pluister, Mary Griesbach, and James Stabenaw, my favorite teachers and/or coaches through the years.

To all of those friends, acquaintances, and associates who answered the phone whenever I needed to vent about my racial horrors as the first Black sports columnist in the history of the Deep South.

To my colleagues during the mid-to-late 1970s at *The Miami Student* newspaper at Miami (Ohio) University, where we got on-the-job training as journalists while functioning as an unofficial fraternity.

To great-grandfather Charles H. Graham, who died when I was 10 at the age of 111, and whose stories about functioning as a water boy during the Civil War and other memories of segregated Mississippi helped turn me into a lover forever of storytelling and history.